THE FUNDAMENTALS

OF PRODUCTION

PLANNING AND

CONTROL

ONE WEEK LOAN

KT-568-156

St

PEARSON

Prentice Hall

Upper Saddle River, New Jersey 07458

Library of Congress Cataloging-in-Publication Data

Chapman, Stephen N.
  The fundamentals of production planning and control / Stephen N. Chapman.
    p. cm.
  ISBN 0-13-017615-X
 1. Production planning—Automation. 2. Production control—Automation. 3. Computer integrated
manufacturing systems. I. Title.

TS176.C454 2006
658.5--dc22

2005000191

Editorial Director: Jeff Shelstad
Senior Sponsoring Editor: Alana Bradley
Executive Marketing Manager: Debbie Clare
Managing Editor: John Roberts
Production Manager: Arnold Vila
Manufacturing Buyer: Indira Gutierrez
Cover Design: Bruce Kenselaar
Composition/Full-Service Project Management: Pine Tree Composition, Inc.
Printer/Binder: Courier-Stoughton

Credits and acknowledgments borrowed from other sources and reproduced, with permission, in this textbook appear on the appropriate page within text.

Pearson Prentice Hall™ is a trademark of Pearson Education, Inc.
Pearson ® is a registered trademark of Pearson plc
Pearson Hall® is a registered trademark of Pearson Education, Inc.

Pearson Education LTD.
Pearson Education Australia PTY, Limited
Pearson Education Singapore, Pte, Ltd
Pearson Education North Asia Ltd
Pearson Education, Canada, Ltd
Pearson Educación de Mexico, S.A. de C.V.
Pearson Education—Japan
Pearson Education Malaysia, Pte. Ltd

10 9 8 7 6 5 4 3 2 1
ISBN 0-13-017615-X

Brief Contents

Contents

Preface

Many years ago I began my first industry job in planning and control armed only with enthusiasm, energy, a strong desire to be successful, and absolutely no real knowledge of the area. My formal education had virtually nothing to do with industry or business. I can only guess that my employer saw the energy and enthusiasm and figured the knowledge would come. Well it did come, but not easily. I learned from some university courses I took in the evenings, I learned a lot from APICS (American Productions and Inventory Control Society) material, and, unfortunately, I also learned a lot by making many mistakes.

As I went through those agonizing years, I frequently recall myself thinking, "There must be an easier way to get a fundamental understanding of these concepts and how they relate to each other and to business without going through all I went through." Those thoughts lingered as I advanced in my career—first in industry management in planning and control, followed by many years of consulting. I finally got the formal education as well, completing a PhD in Operations at the somewhat advanced age of 40. As I entered academics, I continued to be very actively involved with industry, both in consulting and research. I would continually encounter young people (both in the university and in industry) that reminded me of myself at the start of my career—greatly in need of a fundamental understanding of planning and control.

I was very aware of the extent of the great sources of information that were available. My position as an academic and as a member of the Curriculum and Certification Council of APICS made it critical for me to keep up with publications in the field. My perception of much of this material is that it is very well done and extensive in its coverage. There is also a great deal of it, and much of it is often too detailed for the needs of someone like myself at the beginning of my career.

That recognition brought about my plan for this book. The focus is a fundamental knowledge approach. There are many very good general operations management books that bring the reader a much farther breadth of knowledge than just planning and control. There are also a few extremely good books focused more on just planning and control, but the depth of coverage can often overwhelm someone relatively new to the field. Since I noticed a lack of a focused approach that covered primarily fundamental principles, it made sense to fill this void. In addition to fundamental principles dealing with the focused area of planning and control, it also seemed important to explain how these principles and approaches interact within the context of the business environment for which they are providing support. That is also a primary focus for this book.

This book is, therefore, focused for use by those interested in planning and control, but are early enough in their learning to possibly be overwhelmed by the depth of detail in other sources. The book provides some references to some of those sources, but not extensively. It represents some of the knowledge I have gained over many years from many sources and many personal successes and failures. Rather than being written in a typical academic style, I attempted to present the material in logical form that while not academically exhaustive, hopefully will provide the understanding and integrative focus that took my many years to accumulate.

ACKNOWLEDGMENTS

Since this book represents many years of accumulated knowledge and experience, there are far too many people involved to recognize them all. Some, however, come to mind as being significant sources of learning for me, and therefore their influence on me is reflected favorably in this book. I would like to recognize some of them: Ronald Pannesi, University of North Carolina; Philip Carter, Arizona State University; Steve Melnyk, Michigan State University; William Berry, Ohio State University; David Denzler, San Jose State University; David Dilts, Vanderbilt University; and the many colleagues I have served with on APICS Certification Committees over the years. I would also like to thank Cecil Bozarth (NC State University) for contributing several end of chapter exercises.

In addition, I would like to thank the following reviewers whose kind comments helped to shape this manuscript: Antonio Arreola-Risa, Texas A&M University; Lisa Betts, Kent State University; Geza Paul Bottlik, University of Michigan—Ann Arbor; Carol L. Davis, Ross Video; Michael R. Godfrey, University of Wisconsin—Oshkosh; Vijay R. Kannan, Utah State University; Moutaz Khouja, University of North Carolina—Charlotte; William Kime, University of New Mexico; R. Lawrence LaForge, Clemson University; Frank Montabon, Iowa State University; Michael Pangburn, Penn State University; Nicholas C. Petruzzi, University of Illinois at Urbana—Champaign; Srinivas Talluri, Michigan State University; Ping Wang, James Madison University; and Fredrik P. Williams, University of North Texas.

Finally, I must acknowledge the most important person in both my learning and in the completion of this book: my wife, Jeannine. Her support and encouragement during my career and while writing this book provided a major role.

Stephen N. Chapman, PhD, CFPIM
North Carolina State University

CHAPTER 1

Overview of Planning and Control

Chapter Outline

Introduction—This chapter introduces the nature of planning and control as it has evolved and is in use in many organizations today, and also discusses the use and implementation of the fundamental principles of planning and control systems. Virtually every organization—large, small, manufacturing, service, for profit or not for profit—has as its central function the production of some defined output from its processes. In order for that organization to be effective and efficient in serving its customers, the managers of the organization must understand and apply certain fundamental principles of planning for the production of the output and also controlling the process producing the output as it is being produced. The subject of this book is to identify and explain those fundamental principles. While the planning and control approaches discussed in this book are most commonly used in manufacturing companies, many are used or have been adapted for use in service companies. Those differences in operations leading to different uses are discussed, as are several of the environmental issues that heavily influence the design and use of the approaches to planning and control that are selected.

1.1   MANUFACTURING VERSUS SERVICE OPERATIONS

While the major focus for the book is manufacturing, the same principles also apply (in many cases) to service organizations. Service organizations are, of course, those organizations whose primary outputs are not manufactured goods, but instead services to individuals. Legal services, accounting services, banking, insurance, and haircutting are all examples of "production" outputs that are services. There are clearly some major differences between a service and manufacturing environment, and these differences do impact the formality and approach taken in the application of these principles, but often the principles do still apply. This book approaches the explanation of the principles in their most formal and structured application, which tend to reflect the manufacturing environment. Where applications can be applied in service settings, an attempt is made to describe those applications as well. To that extent, this book applies to both manufacturing and service operations. It is interesting to note in this discussion that as service organizations become larger and have many "branches," such as banks, that some services (particularly the "home offices" of banks, insurance companies, etc.) have been able to organize to take advantage of some of the efficiencies of a typical manufacturing environment. These cases are sometimes called "quasimanufacturing" organizations.

To some extent the service organization's approach to planning and control is more difficult to manage, for at least four major reasons. It is these four issues that generally provide the major influence on the way that planning and control approaches are designed for service organizations:

Timing.   In service organizations there is often little time between the recognition of demand and the expected delivery of the process output. Customers enter some service establishments and expect almost instantaneous delivery of the output. Service organizations often attempt to control this to some extent, especially if the capacity to deliver the service is relatively fixed and/or very costly. Appointments and reservations in some service establishments are examples of how they attempt to control the demand for process output.

Customer Contact.   Related to the issue of timing is the fact that the customer in a service environment is often much more involved in the design of the "product" or output of the experience. In addition, the contact point is often the person who will be delivering the service. In that respect the service worker can be thought of as both a sales person and an operations worker.

Quality.   A key dimension of quality in service organizations is that much of the quality may be intangible, making it much more difficult to effectively measure.

Inventory.   "Pure" service organizations (those that have virtually no physical goods involved in their output) often do not have the luxury of inventorying their output. It is impossible, for example, to inventory a haircut. Many people in manufacturing may be taken aback by the image of inventory as a luxury, given that they are often pressed for inventory reduction, but in fact inventory in the perspective of manufacturing planning can be thought of as "stored capacity." Essentially, inventory (especially finished goods) can be viewed as the application of the organization's capacity prior to the actual demand for that output. It will, in this context, allow the firm to provide a somewhat smoother application of the output processes, thereby making them more efficient and often more effective.

1.2   CUSTOMER INFLUENCE IN DESIGN: PRODUCTION ENVIRONMENTAL CHOICES

The design of the planning and control system will be impacted by several factors in addition to the points mentioned above. Among the most critical of these factors are the volume and variety of the expected output, and those issues in turn tend to be largely driven by the amount of influence the customer has in the design of the product or service delivered to them from the organization's processes. In some cases the issue of customer design influence is a part of the firm's basic strategy, but in some cases it is a reaction to market drivers. Many automobiles, for example, are purchased as finished goods from a dealer's lot primarily because the customers do not wish to wait for an automobile that is ordered with the exact options they want. That extent of customer influence tends to be described by the following categories, listed here in the order of influence, from less to more:

Make-to-Stock (MTS).   As the name implies, these are products that are completely made into their final form and stocked as finished goods. The collective customer base may have some influence on the overall design in the early product design phase, but an individual customer has essentially only one decision to make once the product is made—to purchase or not to purchase. Again, these purchase patterns can influence overall product design changes, but not usually in the case of an individual customer. Examples of these products are very common, as found in virtually all retail stores such as hardware, clothing, office supplies, and so on.

Assemble-to-Order (ATO).   In this case the customer has some more influence on the design, in that they can often select various options from predesigned subassemblies. The producer will then assemble these options into the final product for the customer. As in the case of the MTS, the collective customer base can influence the overall design of the options and final products, but the individual customer can only select from the specified options. Automobiles and personal computers are good examples of these types of products. If a customer orders an automobile from a dealer, for example, they can often choose from a variety of colors, body styles, engines, transmissions, and other "pure" options, such as cruise control. In some industries this approach is sometimes called **Package-to-Order,** in that it is the packaging that is customer specified. In products such as breakfast cereals or baking products (flour, baking soda, etc.), the product does not change, but can be placed in several different sizes and types of packages according to customer need. A service example of ATO may be in some restaurants, where the customer can specify their choice of side dishes for their meal. They may have little option as to how those side dishes are prepared, but do have some say in which ones they select.

Make-to-Order (MTO). This environment allows the customer to specify the exact design of the final product or service, as long as they use standard raw materials and components. An example might be a specialty furniture maker or a bakery. In the bakery, for example, a customer may specify a special cake be produced for an occasion such as a birthday or anniversary. They have many design options for the cake and its decorations, although they may be limited to certain sizes of cake pans, cake flavorings, and so on.

Engineer-to Order (ETO). In this case the customer has almost complete say in the design of the product or service. They are often not even limited to the use of standard components or raw material, but can have the producer deliver something designed "from scratch."

1.3   PROCESS CATEGORIES

The nature of the customer influence issue described above not only impacts the design of the product or service, but also has a profound impact on the design of the process used to deliver the product or service. There are essentially five categories given to describe the process used in production, although in practice there are several combinations of these basic types. The five categories typically given are:

Project. A project-based process typically assumes a one-of-a-kind production output, such as building a new building or developing a new software application. Projects are typically large in scope and will often be managed by teams of individuals brought together for this one-time activity based on their particular skills. The planning and control approaches to managing a project are so specialized they are not covered in this book. The reader is referred to one of the many good references specifically focused on the management of projects, such as "5-Phase Project Management" by Weiss and Wysocki.

Job Process.   Job processes (job shop processes) are typically designed for flexibility. The equipment is often general purpose, meaning it can be used for many different production requirements. The skill in delivering the production as specified by the customer is generally focused on the workers, who tend to be highly skilled in a job process. This environment is generally focused for production of a large variety of special production requirements, as may be found in an ETO or MTO design environment. The high variety of design requires the flexible processes and higher skills of the workforce. Work in these environments will often move in a very "jumbled" fashion because of the high variability in designs for each job. Again because of the variability in design and work requirements, information linkages tend to be informal and loose. An example is a general-purpose machine shop or a specialty bakery or caterer.

Batch or Intermittent Processing.   Many of the production facilities in the world today fall into this "middle of the road" category. The equipment tends to be more specialized than the equipment in job shops, but still flexible enough to produce some variety in design. As more of the "skill" to produce the product rests in the more specialized equipment, the workers do not usually need to be quite as skilled as the workers in the job shops. Often these organizations are organized with homogeneous groupings of worker skills and machines, forcing the work to move from area to area as it is being processed. The category is often called batch since products are often made in discrete batches. For example, a batch process may make several hundred of one model of product, taking many hours before they switch the setup to produce another batch of a slightly different model. Some batch processes can produce MTO and some MTS, but this environment is usually well suited to the ATO environment. There are many examples of products built in this environment, including clothing, bicycles, furniture, and so on.

Repetitive or Flow Processing.   As the name implies, this type of process facility tends to be used for a very large volume of a very narrow range of designs. The equipment tends to be highly specialized and expensive, requiring little labor, and the labor that is used tends to be unskilled. The expense of the special equipment is placed into the overhead cost category, allowing the relatively fixed cost to be spread over a large volume. This makes the cost per item lower, making it price competitive. Repetitive processing is typically used for make-to-stock (MTS) designs, such as refrigerators and other appliances.

Continuous.   As with project processing, this type of process is at the far extreme of the processing types, again making it focused on highly specialized applications. The equipment is very specialized, and little labor tends to be needed. High volume chemical processes and petroleum refining

TABLE 1.1   Summary of Process Categories

	Job process	*Batch*	*Repetitive*
Equipment	General purpose	Semi-specialized	Highly specialized
Labor skills	Highly skilled	Semi-skilled	Low skills
Managerial approach	Technical problem solver	Team leadership	Efficiency—keep the process moving
Volume output per design	Low	Medium	High
Variety of designs produced	High	Medium	Low
Design environment	ETO, MTO	MTO, ATO, MTS	ATO, MTS
Flow of work	Variable, jumbled	More defined	Highly defined and fixed

will fall into this category. This book will cover some, but few of the fairly specialized planning and control issues in this category.

While these are the common types, it should be noted that some products are produced in "hybrid" operations, which can be thought of as combinations of these common types. For example, some chemicals might be produced in a continuous process, but then packaged in a batch environment. Table 1.1 summarizes some of the key points and differences between the middle three types of processes: job process, batch, and repetitive.

In addition, there are several implications for planning and control that will need to be highly specialized and different across these types of processing environments. Virtually all aspects of planning and control will be impacted depending on the type of production environment.

An easy way to illustrate the differences in volume and variety relating to the various process types was developed several years ago by Robert Hayes and Steven Wheelwright, often called the Hayes-Wheelwright Product/Process Matrix. As can be seen in an example of the matrix in Figure 1.1, the horizontal axis shows the range of products from high variety of designs with low volumes (MTO) to those with little variety in design and high volumes (MTS). The vertical axis shows the range of processes, from those with general-purpose machines with variable flow to those with fixed flow. The diagonal shows the optimal type of processing that is usually used for each type of product.

It should be noted that producing a product or service off the diagonal is not impossible, just often not wise from a business perspective. It is not that one *cannot* produce off the diagonal, but more that one *should* not. An example may illustrate. Take the example of a quarter-pound hamburger produced in a fast-food restaurant. That would fall into the lower right-hand quadrant of

FIGURE 1.1   The Hayes-Wheelwright Matrix

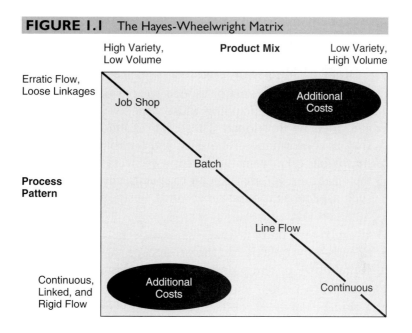

the matrix, in that it is a low-variety, high-volume product typically produced in a fairly rigid, repetitive process in a fast-food restaurant. Now the question could be asked if a fancy, gourmet restaurant could also produce such a hamburger. Clearly they would have both the equipment and skills to produce such a product—but to do so would place them in the upper right-hand quadrant. The additional cost in this case is represented by the highly skilled and expensive labor in such a restaurant, which represents an opportunity cost (such skilled labor would be better utilized to produce a meal with higher profit margins). In this case, they could produce the product, but could not compete well in the price-sensitive market that typifies such a standard high-volume product.

To explain the other "off-diagonal" (lower left-hand part of the matrix), we could ask the question "Can a typical fast-food restaurant produce a fancy prime rib dinner?" The answer is possibly yes, but to do so would clearly take an investment in equipment and training for the employees. Therefore, it may be possible, but not without extensive extra costs.

1.4   ORDER WINNERS AND QUALIFIERS

Another aspect of the business environment that will impact the design and management of the planning and control system is the market drivers for the product or service. To start this discussion, it first must be recognized that there are several dimensions by which customers in the market may evaluate the desirability of buying a certain product or service from a given producer. Some of the more important dimensions of competition include:

1. Price. Usually related to cost of product or service. There are two primary types of price categories:
   a. Standard price, such as a catalog price
   b. Custom pricing, usually negotiated
2. Quality. There are two major aspects to consider.
   a. Tangible quality, including those aspects for which specific measures can often be developed. These can include standard quality measures such as conformance, reliability, and durability.
   b. Intangible quality, including those aspects that may prove of value to the customer, yet are difficult to specifically measure. They may include such aspects as reputation (brand), aesthetics, responsiveness, and customer service.
3. Delivery. Again, there are two major aspects:
   a. Speed—how quickly can the product or service be delivered?
   b. Reliability—once a promise for delivery is made, is it kept?
4. Flexibility. Two major issues must be considered:
   a. Volume—can the producer easily produce a wide range of product volumes?
   b. Variety—can the producer easily produce a wide range of product designs and/or options?

It should be noted that these four major dimensions on this list are major issues for the production function within the organization. There are issues that tend to be heavily shared by nonproduction functional areas of responsibility, such as marketing and engineering. A prime example is the issue of intangible quality, many aspects of which are often the responsibility of functions other than direct production.

It also should be noted that it is virtually impossible for any one producer to be the "best" in the market for all these dimensions of competition at the same time. As part of the development of the operations strategy of the firm, the producer must determine which of these dimensions represent order winners and which are order qualifiers for their market as defined by the corporate strategy.

Order qualifiers.   order qualifiers represent the dimension by which a potential customer determines which suppliers of a product or service meet certain criteria to be considered for receiving the final order from the customer. Qualifiers only allow consideration, and meeting the order-qualifying criteria does not necessarily mean the supplier will be successful winning the order. Not meeting the criteria, on the other hand, will almost ensure the order will not be won.

Order winners.   once potential suppliers have been evaluated as to their order-qualifying criteria, the final successful supplier for the product or service is selected based on the order-winning criteria in the mind of the customer.

As an example, suppose a person is in the market for a basic color television. They may first check out producers that have a reputation for quality and reliability (order qualifiers). They may then look at sample pictures and products from the producers that qualify on the quality and reliability perspective, and further reduce the possible products based on the features and basic look of the television (another qualifier). Finally, they may actually purchase the television from the possible qualifying products based on price (the order winner).

1.5   BUSINESS ENVIRONMENT ISSUES

A major message from the discussion above is that it is critical for a producer to understand their market(s) and design their systems to at least meet the minimum level of criteria for the order qualifiers in their market, but at the same time strive to be the best in those dimensions that represent order winners. While that may appear on the surface to be a fairly basic and simple approach, there are a number of complicating issues. They include:

- *Customer "learning."* Competitors often attempt to approach the market in the same way (emphasizing the same competitive dimensions) as each other, but from time to time a competitor may attempt to gain market share by emphasizing they are the "best" at it. As this happens, the customer expectation may also change. For example, if delivery speed is an order winner, as producers change their system to improve delivery speed, the customers may come to expect an ever-shrinking delivery time, continually "raising the bar" for all companies in the market.

- *Competitor moves.* Some competitor moves may disqualify order winners, turning them into qualifiers, and thereby establishing new order winners. For example, suppose an order winner in a market has been price. The competitors have been working hard to cut costs, thereby allowing lower prices to be charged. Suppose all the competitors have developed cost controls to now charge almost equal prices—to the point where customers perceive very little difference. In such a market, they may become sensitive to another order winner, such as delivery speed. If all competitors have roughly the same price, but one has a much faster delivery, then the order winner may now become delivery speed, leaving price as a qualifier. Effective marketing and advertising plans can also sometimes change customer perceptions as to what is important as an order-winning dimension.

- *Multiple markets.* It is likely that most companies have numerous products or services serving numerous markets. In such cases, there may be many different order qualifiers in many different markets—and all may be subjected to the changes described in the first two points. The effective producer needs to be aware of and continually monitor all the markets, and the company planning and control systems need to effectively support all.

- ***Product design changes.***   New products and changes in product design, especially as technology impacts customer expectations, will also often change order winners and qualifiers. A good example of this is how Internet technology has altered customer perception of how to purchase many goods and services.

As the discussion in further chapters progresses, there will be several references to different approaches to designing and managing the planning and control of an operation that will be impacted by several of these issues. For example, the approach to inventory and capacity may be very different for a company competing on price as opposed to a company competing on delivery speed. Companies competing on price may want to have very little extra capacity or inventory because of the cost involved, but a lean approach to capacity and inventory may have a negative impact on delivery speed. In contrast, a company competing on delivery may be willing to accept the extra cost of extra buffer inventory or capacity to ensure they are able to meet the customer expectation of delivery speed.

1.6   PROCESS ANALYSIS AND INFORMATION FLOWS

In the previous discussion we see how the business environment (the external environment) can impact the design of planning and control approaches. There are also several issues that must be determined with respect to the analysis of the internal processes used to deliver goods and services to the customer. The first of these issues is one of *process analysis and improvement*. There are several aspects to process analysis and improvement, including:

- ***Control and reporting points.***   These are points in the process where the activities of production are captured. They often require formal, structured process transactions, and many times also represent points where formal scheduling of production activity is required. Some systems, such as Material Requirements Planning, may require many of these points while others, such as Just-in-Time, may require very few. These will become clearer as the explanation of those and other systems become better developed.
- ***Process analysis and improvement.***   As production and production processes change in response to the business conditions mentioned above, the change in processes needs to be improved systematically to ensure it matches the needs of the business in the best manner possible. Some of these approaches include:
  1. ***Process mapping.***   Process mapping involves developing a detailed flow of information and activities used to produce some defined activ-

ity. It will often indicate times for those activities and assign responsibilities. Development and analysis of these process maps may be used to determine

- *completeness*—are all critical activities and transactions being captured?
- *efficiency*—are there activities or transactions that are not needed and therefore adding cost without adding value?
- *redundancy*—are there multiple activities essentially accomplishing the same task or collecting data more than once?
- *effectiveness*—are all activities and transactions done in the best manner?

2. ***Process improvement.***   there are several methods for evaluating and improving processes that have been developed over the past several years. Some of them have been developed into an approach known as **Kaizen,** a Japanese word generally meaning "continuous improvement." The general issue here is one of incremental, as opposed to radical, process improvement.

3. ***Process reengineering.*** If there are substantial problems with a process, it may need to be completely redesigned. Using only the definition of the inputs and required outputs of the process, a new process can be developed to most effectively use the inputs to meet the demands of the process output. Unlike Kaizen, process reengineering generally implies a radical change in the process.

4. ***Value stream mapping.***   This process analysis and improvement approach is generally considered to be associated with Lean Production, but could be effectively used in almost any environment. The analysis starts with the customer, and generally includes *Takt time,* or sometimes called the "heartbeat of the customer." It is found by taking the average customer demand for a given time period (a day, for example), and dividing that number by the amount of time available for production during that day. The result gives the average amount of product required to be produced per unit of time in order to meet customer demand. In addition, the value stream map includes inventory level and queue times for material throughout the process, and compares that to value-added time. That comparison provides a very good estimation of the opportunity to improve. Finally, the value stream map provides information flows that are not often part of a regular process map. Once the current state value stream map is completed, the opportunity exists to make appropriate improvements in the process.

It is important to note that all improvement and mapping activities need to be accomplished in the context of a vision based on a company strategy, and that all measures for improved processes be linked to the strategic imperatives of the company.

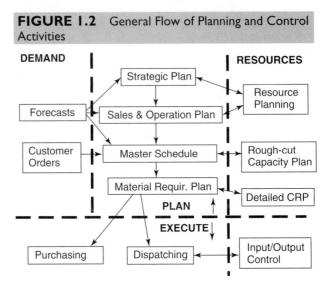

FIGURE 1.2   General Flow of Planning and Control Activities

1.7   GENERAL INFORMATION FLOWS

The diagram in Figure 1.2 illustrates the general flow of information for planning and control for many manufacturing firms.

All these activities will be explained in some detail in subsequent chapters, but in general, as the diagram flows from top to bottom, the level of detail increases and the time horizons tend to decrease. The center part are the major planning activities, while the sides show supply (resources) and demand flows. Note that many of the arrows are double-headed, meaning that information flows back and forth in what is sometimes called "closed loop" planning. The very bottom of the chart indicates execution activities, meaning these activities control the actual activities after the planning is complete and production has actually started.

This figure shows primarily the internal activities and flows of information. As more companies adopt the concepts of supply chain management, however, some of the information will flow between, not just within, organizations. Often the purchasing information will be directly linked to suppliers and customer order information will flow directly from the customers.

1.8   BOOK STRUCTURE

In general, the approach to developing the discussion of the fundamentals of planning and control proceeds in the order in which the actual analysis is done in many firms. It moves from the long-range, more general approaches to the very detailed and short-term decision tools. Specifically, the next chapter discusses the approaches to forecasting product and service demand while Chapter 3 presents some approaches to high-level planning. Chapter 4 discusses the approaches to master scheduling, which often represents the first time that specific customer orders interface with the operation (although that may somewhat depend on the specific software being used). These master schedule orders are then turned into specific material plans (Chapter 6) and typically represent the need for and the control of inventory, as discussed in Chapter 5.

Material plans are very important, but there are several system and managerial issues that must be addressed in order to execute these plans. Specifically, the proper amount of the right type of capacity is essential, as is discussed in detail in Chapter 7. Planning alone is not sufficient for most facilities. Once the plans have been finalized and released to production, they need to be carefully controlled in order to ensure customer requests are met with maximum efficiency and minimal operational disruption. The discussion of approaches for production control is included in Chapter 8.

Chapters 9 and 10 discuss alternative approaches to manage a production facility. Specifically, Chapter 9 discusses Just-in-Time (JIT) and Kanban systems, which has recently evolved into what is called "lean production." Chapter 10 discusses the fundamental approach of constraint theory.

Chapter 11 provides an overview of two of the critical "partnering" activities of planning and control, specifically the fundamental issues of purchasing and distribution. Purchasing represents an area where production often begins, specifically the procurement of the material and services needed as the "raw material" for production. Distribution, on the other hand, is concerned with the linkage between final production and delivery to the customer.

Finally, Chapter 12 provides a brief discussion of the overall approach to implementation of planning and control systems. It also examines the relationship between the production/market environment and the type of planning and control system selected. Additionally, it provides a brief overview of the highly integrated approach to these issues taken by many modern companies as facilitated by the development of large and comprehensive computer and hardware systems. A primary example of such extensive integration includes **Enterprise Requirement Planning** (ERP) systems and supply chains, where all flows of material and information from raw materials to final customer use are considered, evaluated, and planned. Such a cross-organizational level of planning and control requires extensive information sharing up and down the supply chain, and that assumes the information is accurate and timely. The internal planning and control systems that are the primary focus of this book are essential to provide that accurate and timely information.

KEY TERMS

Make-to-Stock (MTS)	Assemble-to-Order (ATO)	Project
Make-to-Order (MTO)	Engineer-to-Order (ETO)	Flow Processing
Job Shop	Batch Processing	Order Qualifier
Continuous Processing	Order Winner	
Kaizen	Package-to-Order	

SUMMARY

This chapter established several of the key environmental and organizational drivers that are used by managers to most effectively design and manage the planning and control systems used by their companies. Included in the discussion are the issues of organizational output (manufacturing vs. service), as well as the amount of customer influence in the design of the product or service. Also discussed are the categories of processing options, ranging from projects used for unique outputs with very low volume to flow production used for very high outputs of standard products. An additional aspect of customer influence is the dimension of competition by which the customer makes their purchasing decision (the order winner) from companies who have attained a basic level of performance in order-qualifying criteria. The dynamic nature of customer behavior and process change based on customer and technological issues are also discussed.

REFERENCES

Hayes, R. H., and S. C. Wheelwright, *Restoring Our Competitive Edge: Competing Through Manufacturing.* New York: John Wiley, 1984.

Hill, T. *Manufacturing Strategy.* New York: Irwin McGraw-Hill, 2000.

Vollmann, T. E., W. L. Berry, and D. C. Whybark, *Manufacturing Planning and Control Systems.* New York: Irwin McGraw-Hill, 1997.

Weiss, J. W., and R. K. Wysocki, *5-Phase Project Management.* Reading, MA: Addison-Wesley, 1992.

DISCUSSION QUESTIONS

1. Discuss the potential impact that each of the following may have on the design of a planning and control system. Will the impact change if the organization is more focused on products rather than services?
    a. Location proximity to customers
    b. The introduction of new technology impacting the design
    c. Customers demanding faster delivery
    d. Customers demanding lower prices
2. Discuss the potential impact that the evolution of "quasimanufacturing" organizations can have on planning and control. An example of quasimanufacturing is the development of large consumer credit organizations (typically classified as a service organization) within automobile manufactures.
3. What are the possible consequences on planning and control if the organization has a wide cross-section of product types (MTS, ATO, MTO) within the same organization?
4. Describe the possible cost implications of producing a standard product in a job-shop environment.

5. Discuss possible implications on planning and control if the customer base changes to the extent that an order qualifier has shifted to become an order winner.
6. Is it possible that there can be more than one order winner in a defined market? Why or why not?
7. What is the potential impact on planning and control if the organization has several types of customers, each with a different order-winning characteristic?
8. Discuss how a change in a product design could produce a change in the design of a planning and control system.
9. Would a change in process design necessarily imply a corresponding change in the design of a planning and control system? Why or why not?

CHAPTER 2

Forecasting Fundamentals

Chapter Outline

2.1   Fundamental Principles of Forecasting
2.2   Major Categories of Forecasts
2.3   Forecast Errors
2.4   Computer Assistance

Introduction—The starting point for virtually all planning systems is the actual or expected customer demand. In most cases, however, the time it takes to produce and deliver the product or service will exceed the customer expectation of delivery time. When that occurs, as is usually the case, then production will have to begin before the actual demand from the customer is known. That production will have to start from expected demand, which is generally a forecast of the demand. This chapter discusses some of the fundamental principles and approaches to forecasting for planning and control systems

2.1   FUNDAMENTAL PRINCIPLES OF FORECASTING

First, we begin with a basic definition of forecasting:

Forecasting *is a technique for using past experiences to project expectations for the future.*

Note that in this definition forecasting is not really a prediction, but a structured projection of past knowledge. There are several types of forecasts, used for different purposes and systems. Some are long-range, aggregated models used for long-range planning such as overall capacity needs, developing strategic plans, and making long-term strategic purchasing decisions. Others are short-range forecasts for particular product demand, used for scheduling and launching production prior to actual customer order recognition. Regardless of the purpose or system for which the forecast will be used, there are some fundamental characteristics that are very important to understand:

- ***Forecasts are almost always wrong.***   The issue is almost never about whether a forecast is correct or not, but instead the focus should be on "how wrong do we expect it to be" and on the issue of "how do we plan to accommodate the potential error in the forecast." Much of the discussion of buffer capacity and/or buffer stock the firm may use is directly related to the size of the forecast error.

- ***Forecasts are more accurate for groups or families of items.***   It is usually easier to develop a good forecast for a product line than it is for an individual product, as individual product forecasting errors tend to cancel each other out as they are aggregated. It is generally more accurate, for example, to forecast the demand for all family sedans than to forecast the demand for one particular model of sedan.

- ***Forecasts are more accurate for shorter time periods.***   In general, there are fewer potential disruptions in the near future to impact product demand. Demand for extended time periods far into the future are generally less reliable.

- ***Every forecast should include an estimate of error.***   The first principle indicated the importance to answer the question, "How wrong is the forecast?" Therefore, an important number that should accompany the forecast is an estimate of the forecast error. To be complete, a good forecast has both the forecast estimate and the estimate of the error.

- ***Forecasts are no substitute for calculated demand.***   If you have actual demand data for a given time period, you should never make calculations based on the forecast for that same time period. Always use the real data, when available.

2.2   MAJOR CATEGORIES OF FORECASTS

There are two basic types of forecasting: **qualitative** and **quantitative.** Under the quantitative types, there are two subcategories: time series and causal. While this chapter provides basic descriptions of many of the common types of forecasts in all the categories, the primary focus is discussing quantitative time series forecasts.

Qualitative Forecasting

Qualitative forecasting, as the name implies, are forecasts that are generated from information that does not have a well-defined analytic structure. They can be especially useful when no past data is available, such as when a product is new and has no sales history. To be more specific, some of the key characteristics of qualitative forecasting data include:

- The forecast is usually based on personal judgment or some external qualitative data.
- The forecast tends to be subjective and, since they tend to be developed from the experience of the people involved, will often be biased based on the potentially optimistic or pessimistic position of those people.
- An advantage is that this method often does allow for some fairly rapid results.
- In some cases, qualitative forecasts are especially important as they may be the only method available.
- These methods are usually used for individual products or product families, seldom for entire markets.

Some of the more common methods of qualitative forecasting include market surveys, Delphi or panel consensus, life-cycle analogies, and informed judgment.

Market surveys are generally structured questionnaires submitted to potential customers in the market. They solicit opinions about products or potential products, and also often attempt to get an understanding of the likelihood of customer demand for products or services. If structured well, administered to a good representative sample of the defined population, and analyzed correctly, they can be quite effective, especially for the short term. A major drawback is they are fairly expensive and time-consuming if done correctly.

Delphi or panel consensus forecasting uses panels of defined experts in the market or area for which the survey is being developed. The experts attempt to bring their individual knowledge of the factors that affect demand into the analysis, interacting with each other to attempt to develop a consensus as to the demand forecast for the products or product families in question. The major difference between the two methods is one of process. While panel forecasting tends to bring the experts together in a meeting format for the discussion, the Delphi method allows for a series of individual forecasts to be made by each expert. Each expert develops their own forecast with their own defined reasons. This collective set is then shared with all the experts, allowing each to then modify their forecast based on information from the other experts. Through a series of these steps, the idea is to obtain a consensus as to the forecast.

As one could probably imagine from the description of the process, these methods tend to be quite expensive, primarily due to the time requirements from a group of experts in the field. Such experts often charge fairly high fees for their time and observations. The advantage is that when done correctly, they do tend to be quite accurate.

Life cycle analogy forecasting is a rather special application used when the product or service is new. The concept is fairly simple. It is based on the fact that most products and services have a fairly well-defined life cycle. There is generally growth during the early stage after introduction to the market. At some point the product or service matures, implying little or no additional growth, until eventually the demand declines to the point where it is no longer offered. The major questions that arise with this life cycle include:

- What is the time frame? How long will growth and maturity last?
- How rapid will the growth be? How rapid will the decline be?
- How large will the overall demand be, especially during the mature phase?

One potentially effective method to answer these questions will be to link the demand for the new product or service to one in the past that is expected to be similar. This will be especially effective if the new product or service is essentially replacing another in the market, targeted to the same population. In that case the method assumes that the life cycle for the new product or service will essentially be roughly the same as for the old product or service it is replacing.

This method may not be particularly accurate, but may be a good starting point when no product demand history is available.

Informed judgment is among the most common forecasting methods used, but unfortunately is also among the worst methods to use. One common approach used is for a sales manager to ask each salesperson to develop a projection of sales for their area for some defined time period in the future. The sales manager then combines the individual sales projections into an overall sales forecast for the company.

Why does this method tend to be so poor? There are several things that will potentially alter the judgment of the individual salespeople, sometimes without them being consciously aware. For example:

- Sometimes salespeople will use the forecast as an opportunity for an optimistic goal. For example, if they feel they will really sell 5,000 of a certain product over the time period, they may give the forecast as 6,000 as a goal. This may also sometimes be prompted by their concern about the company planning to have adequate resources to produce enough product for them to sell. If they really give a forecast of 5,000 and the company makes only that amount, some salespeople feel they will be at a disadvantage if the market potential is really larger than they thought. Most salespeople want more than anything to have product available when a potential market for that product exists.
- On the other hand, some salespeople are fearful that the sales forecast will be used as a quota. If, for example, they feel they will really sell 5,000 in a given time period, they may give a much lower figure as a forecast. If, for example, they give a forecast of 4,000 and they really sell 5,000, they feel the sales above the forecast will make them look better as a salesperson. If they really do sell only 4,000, they can always say "See—I told you so!"

- Many salespeople really want to give the right figure, but are subconsciously impacted by recent events. If, for example, they had a very bad week of sales just prior to submitting the forecast, they may be pessimistic and lower the projection. The opposite can happen if they have a really good week.

ANECDOTAL EXAMPLE 2.1

The following is based on an actual situation recently experienced by a production control manager:

Joe, the production control manager, had just gotten the sales forecast for all the major products for the next year from Frank, the sales manager (the company does not use Sales and Operation planning). As Joe was developing his initial long-range production plans to meet the forecast, he noticed something that bothered him. For the past several years the company had sold roughly 10,000 product X per year. Product X was sold to a small group of about six companies that used it to make another product. The forecast for product X for next year was given as 16,000. Joe called Frank and the following conversation took place:

JOE: "Frank, we need to talk about product X. You gave me a forecast of 16,000 for next year. Why is that?"

FRANK: "Because that's what we project to sell."

JOE: "Do you have any new customers for the product, or do you expect to?"

FRANK: "No."

JOE: "Do any of your existing customers have new uses for the product?"

FRANK: "Not that I know of."

JOE: "Do any of your existing customers have expansion plans or expect to grow?"

FRANK: "Again, not that I know of."

JOE: "Do you or any of the customers for product X have any plans for new markets?"

FRANK: "I know we don't, and I don't think any of the customers do."

JOE: "Then I don't understand. Why the forecast of 16,000?"

FRANK: "Because that's what we say we will sell!"

Now Joe is faced with a major problem. How many should he plan to make? Product X uses some very expensive specialty steel that has a very long lead time. He needs to place an order for that steel soon to meet the needs for next year. He sees there are four scenarios, two of which are bad and two good:

- He makes 16,000 and the demand is 16,000—that's good
- He makes 16,000 and the demand is 10,000—that's bad, because a lot of expensive inventory is sitting around
- He makes 10,000 and the demand is 10,000—that's good

- He makes 10,000 and the demand is 16,000—that's bad, for a lot of obvious reasons.

What does he do? Sometimes people who hear this story say he should make 13,000 (hit the average), but that is likely bad for any of the four scenarios above.

The correct answer is, of course, to plan to make 10,000. Why? Go back to the conversation. What Joe was in fact doing is developing a forecast by asking the questions that Frank should have been using to make the forecast in the first place. Given the answers to the questions, Joe felt it was highly unlikely that the demand would be greater than it had been in the past. A year later Joe was proved correct, as the sales for product X roughly equaled 10,000 units.

Quantitative Forecasting—Causal

The first of the two types of quantitative forecasting methods we examine are called **causal.** Some of the key characteristics of these methods include:

- This method is based on the concept of relationship between variables, or the assumption that one measurable variable "causes" the other to change in a predictable fashion.
- There is an important assumption of causality and that the causal variable can be accurately measured. The measured variable that causes the other to change is frequently called a "leading indicator." As an example, new housing starts is often used as a leading indicator for developing forecasts for many sectors of the economy.
- If there are good leading indicators developed, these methods often bring excellent forecasting results.
- As somewhat of a side benefit, the process of developing the models will often allow the developers of the model to gain additional significant market knowledge. For example, if you are developing a causal model of vacation travel based on the leading indicator of gasoline prices, there is a good chance you will gain knowledge about both the mechanisms that control gasoline prices as well as the patterns of typical vacation travel.
- These methods are seldom used for product, but more commonly used for entire markets or industries.
- The methods are often time-consuming and very expensive to develop, primarily because of developing the relationships and obtaining the causal data.

Some of the more common methods of causal forecasting are given as:

Input–output models.   These can be very large and complex models, as they examine the flow of goods and services throughout the entire economy. As such, they require a substantial quantity of data, making them expensive and time-consuming to develop. They are generally used to project needs for entire markets or segments of the economy, and not for specific products.

Econometric models.   These models involve a statistical analysis of various sectors of the economy. Their use is similar to the input–output models.

Simulation models.   Simulating sectors of the economy on computers are growing in popularity and use with the development of ever more powerful and less expensive computers and computer simulation models. They can be used for individual products, but once again gathering the data tends to be expensive and time-consuming. The real value of these models is that they are fast and economical to use once the data has "populated" the model.

Regression.   A statistical method to develop a defined analytic relationship between two or more variables. The assumption, as with other causal models, is that one variable "causes" the other to move. Often the independent, or causal, variable is called a *leading indicator.* A common example is when the news reports on housing starts, since that is often a leading indicator of the amount of economic activity in several related markets (e.g., the lumber industry).

Since they are based on external data, causal forecasting methods are sometimes called **extrinsic forecasts.**

Quantitative Forecasting—Time Series

Time-series forecasts are among the most commonly used for forecasting packages linked to product demand forecasts. They all essentially have one common assumption. That assumption is that past demand follows some pattern, and that if that pattern can be analyzed it can be used to develop projections for future demand, assuming the pattern continues in roughly the same manner. Ultimately that implies the assumption that the only real independent variable in the time series forecast is time. Since they are based on internal data (sales), they are sometimes called **intrinsic forecasts.**

Time series are also the most commonly used by operations managers when they find they need to forecast in order to make reasonable production plans. The reason is simple: The other two major categories of forecasting (qualitative and causal) both require some knowledge of the external market and/or environment. Such knowledge is seldom easily available for an operations manager, who typically spends most of his or her attention focused internally. Previous demand is, however, often readily available for the operations manager.

Most time series forecasting models attempt to mathematically capture the underlying patterns of past demand. One is a **random pattern**—under the assumption that demand always has a random element. This implies what most people inherently know: the customers who demand goods and services from a company do not demand those goods and services in a completely uniform and predictable manner.

The second pattern is a **trend pattern.** The trends can either be increasing or decreasing, and they can be either linear or nonlinear in nature. Some examples of trends are illustrated in Figure 2.2.

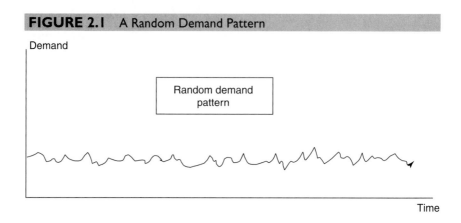

FIGURE 2.1 A Random Demand Pattern

The third major pattern is a cyclical pattern, of which a special but very common case is a **seasonal pattern** (see Figure 2.3). Even though called seasonal (since for many companies the most common pattern of this type follows the seasons of the year), these patterns are actually cyclical patterns, which may or may not be linked to the yearly seasons. Cyclical patterns then are demand patterns that follow some cycle of rising and falling demand. In the special case where the pattern follows the seasons of the year, the cyclical pattern is usually called seasonal.

If we were to put a random pattern together with a trend and a seasonal pattern, we could obtain a demand pattern that would look similar to the pat-

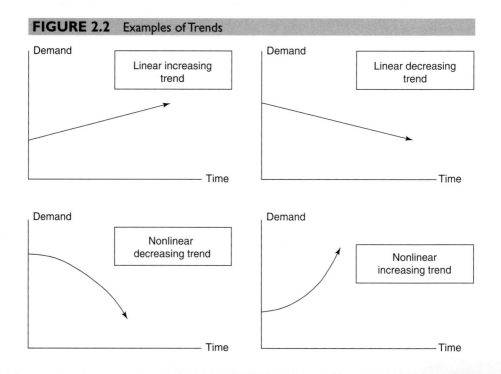

FIGURE 2.2 Examples of Trends

FIGURE 2.3   A Seasonal Demand Pattern

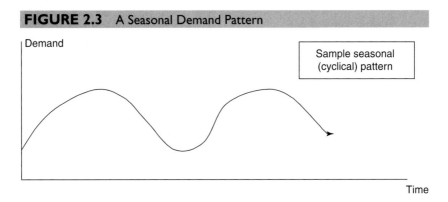

tern experienced by many companies for their products or services. For example, a random, seasonal pattern with a linear increasing trend might look something like Figure 2.4.

Now that the basic patterns are developed, we can examine some of the simpler time series methods that have been developed to forecast demand knowing these patterns exist. The first set of forecasting methods includes simple methods that are used to attempt to smooth the random demand patterns, assuming no trend or seasonal patterns exist. If no seasonal or trend patterns exist in the demand, one might be tempted to use the actual demand from the last period as the forecast for the next period. The problem with this approach is the organization would continually be increasing or decreasing production to accommodate the random pattern, and because of the randomness they would seldom be correct. For that reason the smoothing methods attempt to, as the name implies, smooth the ragged demand pattern.

There is an important trade-off in these approaches that needs to be realized. If the smoothing approach is minimal (allowing most of the randomness to remain), then there is little stability gained from the approach. On the other hand, if too much smoothing is done, then real potential changes in the demand are not captured in the forecast.

FIGURE 2.4   A Composite Demand with Seasonality, Trend, and Random Patterns

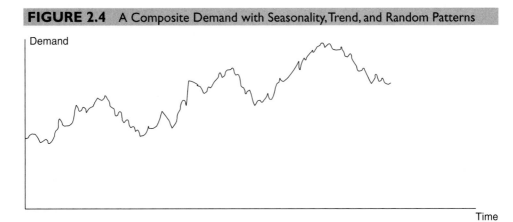

Simple moving averages are, as the name implies, nothing more than the mathematical average of the last several periods of actual demand. They take the form:

$$F_t = \frac{A_{t-n} + A_{t-n+1} + \ldots + A_{t-1}}{n}$$

Where: F is the forecast
t is the current time period, meaning F_t is the forecast for the current time period
A_t is the actual demand in period t, and
n is the number of periods being used.

The concept is much easier to see with an example. Suppose we are using a three-period moving average. The forecast for any time period then becomes the average of the actual demand for the three previous periods.

The calculations for the table are fairly easy. To get the forecast for period 4, take the actual demand for the three previous periods (periods 1 through 3) and find the average: (24+26+22)/3 = 24. The forecast for period 5 comes from the average of the demand for periods 2 through 4: (26+22+25)/3 = 24.3. The process is called *moving* average because as time progresses you always move to use the latest demand periods available. Graphically, the process looks as illustrated in Figure 2.5.

TABLE 2.1   A Three-Period Moving Average Forecast Example

Period	Demand	Three-period moving average forecast
1	24	
2	26	
3	22	
4	25	24.0
5	19	24.3
6	31	22.0
7	26	25.0
8	18	25.3
9	29	25.0
10	24	24.3
11	30	23.7
12	23	27.7
13		25.7

FIGURE 2.5   A Three-Period Moving Average Example

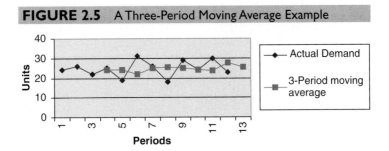

There are two important points that need to be made concerning the graph and the moving average method as well.

- First, it is fairly obvious to see that the forecast line is smoother than the demand line, showing the impact of taking an average. The more periods used in computing the moving average, the smoother this effect will be. The reason is that with more periods being used in the average, any one of the demand points will have less overall influence.
- Second, the forecast will always *lag behind* any actual demand. That is not so obvious in this graph, but suppose we use the same method to graph a demand pattern with an upward trend, as in Table 2.2.

The graph in Figure 2.6, shows clearly how the forecast is constantly lagging behind the trend in the data.

The implication of this lagging effect is that models such as simple moving averages should normally not be used to forecast demand when the data

TABLE 2.2   A Moving Average Forecast for Data with a Trend

Period	Demand	Three-period moving average forecast
1	13	
2	15	
3	18	
4	22	15.3
5	27	18.3
6	31	22.3
7	36	26.7
8	41	31.3
9	45	36.0
10	52	40.7
11	57	46.0
12		51.3

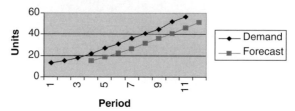

FIGURE 2.6   The Graph of the Moving Average Forecast of Data with a Trend

clearly follows any type of trend or regular cyclical pattern. It is important to note that forecasting methods should not be arbitrarily selected, but instead should be selected and developed to fit the existing data as closely as possible.

Weighted moving averages are basically the same as simple moving averages, with one major exception. With weighted moving averages the weight assigned to each past demand point used in the calculation can vary. In this way more influence can be given to some data points, typically the most recent demand point. They take the basic form (the W stands for the weight):

$$F_t = W_1 A_{t-1} + W_2 A_{t-2} + \ldots + W_n A_{t-n} \quad \text{where} \quad \sum_{i=1}^{n} W_i = 1$$

In simpler terms, each of the weights is less than one, but the total of all the weights must add to equal 1. Taking the same data points as in the first example (the three-period moving average data point from Table 2.1), we will apply a weighted moving average, with weights of $0.5, 0.3$, and 0.2 (with the 0.5 weight applied to the most recent demand data) (see Table 2.3).

The calculations are again fairly simple. For example, the period 4 forecast is calculated as $0.2(24) + 0.3(26) + 0.5(22) = 23.6$. Notice this value is smaller than the corresponding period 4 forecast using a simple moving average. The reason is, of course, that a larger weight is being put on the latest demand figure, which also happens to be the smallest of the three demand points being used.

Graphically, the data in the table appears in Figure 2.7.

As before, it is obvious that the forecast is smoothed, but also lags actual demand changes.

Simple exponential smoothing is another method used to smooth the random fluctuations in the demand pattern. There are two commonly used (mathematically equivalent) formulas:

$$F_t = F_{t-1} + \alpha(A_{t-1} - F_{t-1}) \text{ or } F_t = \alpha A_{t-1} + (1 - \alpha)F_{t-1} \text{ where } 0 \le \alpha \le 1$$

TABLE 2.3   A Weighted Moving Average Forecast Example

Period	Demand	Three-period weighted moving average forecast
1	24	
2	26	
3	22	
4	25	23.6
5	19	24.3
6	31	21.4
7	26	26.2
8	18	26.1
9	29	23
10	24	25.1
11	30	24.3
12	23	28
13		25.3

The second form shows that the exponential smoothed forecast incorporated a weighted average of past history $[(1 - \alpha)F_t]$. Since data from several periods early is still contained in the forecast, and was weighted numerous times as the forecast is developed period by period, one could consider it weighted exponentially, thus the name. The first form, however, is easiest to explain from the perspective of what the method does from a logical perspective. Essentially the forecast is found by taking the previous period's forecast (F_{t-1}) and adding a portion of the previous period's forecast error. The **forecast error** is, of course, the difference between the actual demand for any period and the forecast for that same period $(A_{t-1} - F_{t-1})$. The portion of the error term is found by multiplication by α, which is the Greek letter alpha, and is called a **smoothing constant.** The alpha value is always between zero and

FIGURE 2.7   Graph of the Weighted Moving Average Example

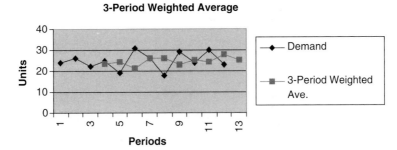

one, since if it equals zero you add no part of the error and your forecast is always the same number, while if equal to one you add the entire forecast error and do no smoothing at all. As you might expect, the larger the alpha value, the more of the forecast error is added. It makes the forecast more responsive to actual changes in the demand, but also can equate to more reaction (and disruption) in the organization as it constantly strives to react to a more erratic forecast. The impact of the alpha value on the forecast can clearly be seen by taking the same data set used earlier and finding exponentially smoothed forecasts using alpha values first of 0.2, then 0.5, and finally 0.8. The table uses simple moving average for the first two periods to develop an initial forecast of 25 units for period 3, after which exponential smoothing can be used to calculate the remaining forecasts.

Notice that exponential smoothing assumes you have a forecast quantity (F_{t-1}). When you initially start developing the forecast, however, you do not typically have such an initial forecast. This implies that you must start the process using another forecasting method, after which the forecast from that method can be used as the initial F_{t-1}.

The resulting graph showing the demand data and the forecast data is shown in Figure 2.8.

As can be seen, with such a small alpha, there is very little change in the forecast graph line. More responsiveness can be seen when alpha equals 0.5 (see Table 2.5).

TABLE 2.4 Example of Exponential Smoothing (α=0.2) with data from Table 2.1.

Period	Demand	Exponential smoothing with alpha = 0.2
1	24	
2	26	
3	22	
4	25	24.4
5	19	24.5
6	31	23.4
7	26	24.9
8	18	25.1
9	29	23.7
10	24	24.8
11	30	24.6
12	23	25.7
13		25.2

FIGURE 2.8   Exponential Smoothing with α = 0.2

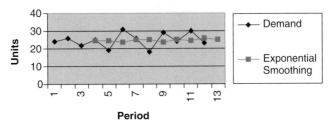

TABLE 2.5   Using α = 0.5 with Same Demand Data

Period	Demand	Exponential smoothing with alpha = 0.5
1	24	
2	26	
3	22	
4	25	23.5
5	19	24.3
6	31	21.6
7	26	26.3
8	18	26.2
9	29	22.1
10	24	25.5
11	30	24.8
12	23	27.4
13		25.2

The graph line for the forecast is obviously more responsive than it was for an alpha of 0.2, but shows even more responsiveness when the alpha is changed to 0.8, as in Table 2.6.

FIGURE 2.9   Graph of Demand Data with α = 0.5

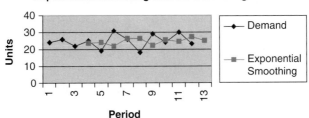

TABLE 2.6   Using α = 0.8 with Same Demand Data

Period	Demand	Exponential smoothing with alpha = 0.8
1	24	
2	26	
3	22	
4	25	22.6
5	19	24.5
6	31	20.1
7	26	28.8
8	18	26.6
9	29	19.7
10	24	27.1
11	30	24.6
12	23	28.9
13		24.2

FIGURE 2.10   Graph of Demand Data with α = 0.8

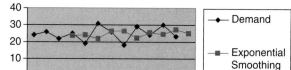

Exponential Smoothing with 0.8 Smoothing Constant

Regression has sometimes been called the "line of best fit." It is a statistical technique to try to fit a line from a set of points by using the smallest total squared error between the actual points and the points on the line. A particular value for regression is to determine trend line equations. The best way to show how it can be used is to illustrate with an example. In Table 2.7, we also add a seasonal aspect to the data so that we can illustrate an approach to deal with seasonal data using the same data set. We start with a data set that contains 2 years of demand data, listed by quarters. Notice that quarters 1 and 5 represent the same season, as do quarters 2 and 6, and so forth.

Placing the demand history in Microsoft Excel (or any of the multiple statistical packages that can calculate regressions) and applying the regression analysis, it was found the data had an intercept of 268.3 with an X-variable coefficient of 18.8. The general form of the regression equation is Y = aX + b, where 'a' is the slope of the line and 'b' is the X-intercept. This means the re-

TABLE 2.7   Demand History for Use with Regression

Quarter	Demand
1	256
2	312
3	426
4	278
5	298
6	387
7	517
8	349

TABLE 2.8   Regression Forecast with Data from Table 2.7

Quarter	Demand	Regression forecast
1	256	287.1
2	312	305.9
3	426	324.7
4	278	343.5
5	298	362.3
6	387	381.1
7	517	399.9
8	349	418.7
9		437.5

gression line has an equation of Y = 18.8(Quarter) + 268.3. Applying this formula, we obtain Table 2.8, including the regression forecast.

As you might expect, a straight-line forecast calculated by using a linear regression model does not show any of the seasonality of the data, as is clearly shown in Figure 2.11.

In order to pick up the seasonality for the forecast, we need to develop seasonal multipliers for each quarter. To do this we first find the ratio of the actual demand to the regression forecast in Table 2.9.

For example, in the first quarter the 0.89 comes from 256/287.1. Now an average for corresponding quarters is calculated. This means that for the first quarter of the year (as represented by quarter 1 and quarter 5) the seasonal multiplier is (0.89 +0.82)/2, which equals 0.86. Other multipliers are listed in Table 2.10.

Now the seasonal multipliers can be applied to the basic regression forecast to develop a seasonally adjusted regression forecast by simply multiplying the seasonal multipliers by the regression forecast, as in Table 2.11.

FIGURE 2.11 Graph of Data from Table 2.7 with Associated Linear Regression Line

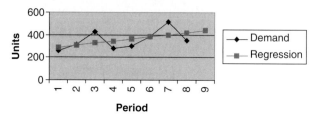

TABLE 2.9 Calculation of Seasonal Ratios

Quarter	Demand	Regression forecast	Ratio of demand to forecast
1	256	287.1	0.89
2	312	305.9	1.02
3	426	324.7	1.31
4	278	343.5	0.81
5	298	362.3	0.82
6	387	381.1	1.02
7	517	399.9	1.29
8	349	418.7	0.83
9		437.5	

TABLE 2.10 Final Seasonal Multipliers

Quarter	Demand	Regression forecast	Ratio of demand to forecast	Seasonal multipliers
1	256	287.1	0.89	0.86
2	312	305.9	1.02	1.02
3	426	324.7	1.31	1.30
4	278	343.5	0.81	0.82
5	298	362.3	0.82	0.86
6	387	381.1	1.02	1.02
7	517	399.9	1.29	1.30
8	349	418.7	0.83	0.82
9		437.5		0.86

TABLE 2.11   Seasonally Adjusted Regression Forecast

Quarter	Demand	Regression forecast	Seasonal multipliers	Seasonally adjusted regression forecast
1	256	287.1	0.86	246.1
2	312	305.9	1.02	311.3
3	426	324.7	1.30	422.9
4	278	343.5	0.82	282.2
5	298	362.3	0.86	310.5
6	387	381.1	1.02	387.8
7	517	399.9	1.30	520.8
8	349	418.7	0.82	343.9
9		437.5	0.86	376.3

Now if we look at the graphical comparison between the actual demand and the seasonally adjusted regression forecast in Figure 2.12, it can easily be seen how closely they compare. In addition, the forecast for period 9 will give us a fair confidence, given how closely other quarters track (in fact, on this graph it is very difficult to distinguish that there are in fact two separate lines).

To show how closely they track, Table 2.12 shows the percentage error between the seasonal forecast and the actual demand.

Before leaving the topic of regression, it may help to clear up any confusion that may exist because regression was classified as a forecasting methodology for both causal forecasting and time series. There is a fundamental difference, even though the mathematical computation of the regression lines is the same. The difference is that the independent variable in time series regression is always time, while the independent variable in causal regression is always some other variable, usually a leading indicator from the economy.

It also should be noted that even though the discussion of seasonal indexes was presented in the context of time series regression, the concept of developing and applying seasonal indexes can be used for virtually any of the time series models.

FIGURE 2.12   Seasonally Adjusted Regression Graphs

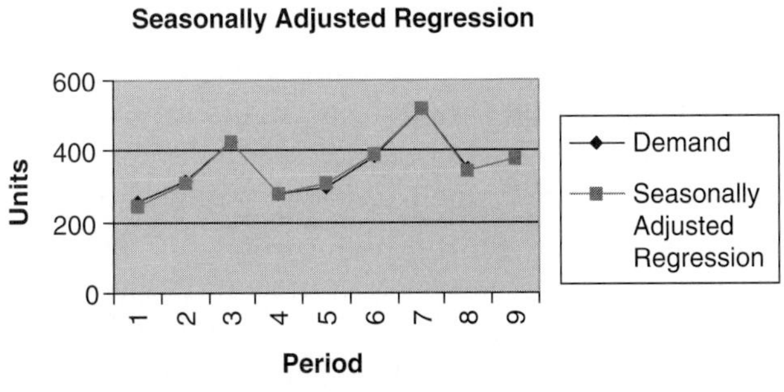

TABLE 2.12   Error Calculation for Seasonally Adjusted Regression Forecast

Quarter	Demand	Forecast	Error	Percentage error
1	256	246.1	9.9	4%
2	312	311.3	0.7	0%
3	426	422.9	3.1	1%
4	278	282.2	−4.2	−1%
5	298	310.5	−12.5	−4%
6	387	387.8	−0.8	0%
7	517	520.8	−3.8	−1%
8	349	343.9	5.1	1%

2.3   FORECAST ERRORS

Early in the chapter it was mentioned that every forecast should contain two numbers: the forecast and the error estimate. Since the first rule of forecasting is that the forecast is likely to be incorrect, a critical question is "How incorrect is it?" This is very important in planning and control since it represents a critical issue to run the business. Buffer inventory, buffer capacity, or other methods may be needed to be planned to accommodate actual demand that differs from that forecasted.

There are several important error calculations used. Among some of the most useful are included:

Mean Forecast Error (MFE).   As the name implies, this term is calculated as the mathematical average forecast error over a specified time period. The formula is:

$$MFE = \frac{\sum_{t=1}^{n}(A_t - F_t)}{n}$$

The $(A_t - F_t)$ has been encountered earlier in the chapter. It represents the difference between the forecast and the actual demand for any given time period, also called the **forecast error.** The MFE involves adding all the individual forecast errors and dividing by the total number of errors. This number is not as important for the actual value of the number, but instead for the sign of the number, whether it is positive or negative in value. If positive, it implies that over the range of numbers included, the actual demand was larger than the forecast. Another way of putting that is that the forecasting method was biased on the low side. If negative, of course, it means the forecasts were larger than the demand on average, implying the forecasting method was biased on the high side. For this reason, MFE is often referred to as forecast **bias.**

TABLE 2.13 Calculation of Forecast Errors

Period	Demand (A)	Forecast (F)	Error (A-F)
1	12	14	−2
2	15	13	2
3	13	12	1
4	16	13	3
5	14	15	−1
6	11	14	−3

There is a very good reason the MFE does not really represent the average forecast error, as can be shown in Table 2.13.

$$\text{MFE} = (-2 + 2 + 1 + 3 + -1 + -3)/6 = 0/6 = 0$$

Adding all the errors yields a zero, making the MFE equal zero. It is clear, however, that forecast errors do exist, so the MFE is not a good method to find those errors. It does show, however, that in this case the forecasting method was not biased, in that over the full range of the demand history the forecasting method did not over or under project the total demand.

Mean Absolute Deviation (MAD).   The formula is again given as the name of the term. It literally means the average of the mathematical absolute deviations of the forecast errors (deviations). The formula is, therefore:

$$MAD = \frac{\sum_{t=1}^{n}\left|A_t - F_t\right|}{n}$$

This represents a very important number, as it tells the average forecast error (always positive) over the time period in question. If we use the same basic data from the table above, we can calculate the true forecast error in Table 2.14.

TABLE 2.14 Calculation of the Absolute Value of Forecast Errors

Period	Demand (A)	Forecast (F)	$\left|A-F\right|$
1	12	14	2
2	15	13	2
3	13	12	1
4	16	13	3
5	14	15	1
6	11	14	3

$$MAD = (2 + 2 + 1 + 3 + 1 + 3)/6 = 12/6 = 2$$

From these calculations, we now know that for these six periods used the forecasting method was unbiased (MFE calculation) with an average forecast error of two units (from the MAD calculation).

Tracking Signal. Similar to the concept of control limits for statistical process control charts, the tracking signal provides a somewhat subjective limit for the forecasting method to go "off track" before some action is taken. It is calculated from the MFE and the MAD:

$$\text{Tracking Signal} = (n*\text{MFE})/\text{MAD}$$

In some cases this formula is written using the "running sum of the forecast errors," abbreviated as RSFE. The formula then becomes:

$$\text{Tracking Signal} = \text{RSFE}/\text{MAD}$$

This number is clearly a ratio that has no unit value—it is merely used as a signal. A rule of thumb for use of the tracking signal is that if the value of the tracking signal is larger than 4 or less than -4, the forecasting method may not be effective for tracking demand over the time period in question. It merely calls attention to investigate and adjust the forecasting method as necessary.

The tracking signal emphasizes an important trade-off: it would be time-consuming and possibly costly to evaluate and modify the forecasting method too frequently, but how often is too frequently? By the same token, to allow the method to proceed too long without evaluation could produce serious deterioration of the forecasts. The tracking signal, therefore, allows a systematic method to determine when the forecasting method should be evaluated or not.

2.4   COMPUTER ASSISTANCE

The speed, reliability, and relatively low cost of today's computers makes the use of very powerful computer packages utilizing time series formulas very attractive. Some modern packages come with several time series formulas built in with a variety of smoothing factors. Once demand data is input into the package, the system will find the best approach based on the lowest MAD (or some other error approach). The results from these packages can then become direct inputs into other planning and control systems, where they can be a great source to start the planning process.

These computer packages allow a fast and inexpensive approach to the process that should be followed with or without the computer package. Specifically, it is important to understand the use of the forecast, the past demand patterns (when they exist), and the need to seriously attempt to find or develop a forecasting method that will serve the purpose of the forecasting need the best. Once developed, the method should be tested against past data and modified as necessary.

SOLVED EXAMPLE

A demand pattern for 10 periods for a certain product was given as 127, 113, 121, 123, 117, 109, 131, 115, 127, and 118. Forecast the demand for period 11 using each of the following methods: a 3-month moving average; a 3-month weighted moving average using weights of 0.2, 0.3, and 0.5; exponential smoothing with a smoothing constant of 0.3; and linear regression. Compute the MAD for each method to determine which method would be preferable under the circumstances. Also calculate the bias in the data, if any, for all four methods, and explain the meaning.

Solution: An Excel spreadsheet was set up to calculate the forecasts for each method using the formulas and approaches outlined in the chapter. The following chart shows the result from that analysis. Notice that because the overall trend from the data was fairly "flat" and there appeared to be no seasonality or other cyclicality, the coefficient for the period in the regression equation was quite small (0.0182), making all the regression forecasts very close to each other. The starting exponential smoothing forecast value of 115 was selected as the actual demand from the previous period (not shown on the table) that was 115 units.

Period	Demand	3 Mo. MA	3 M. WMA	Expon. smooth.	Regression
1	127			115	120.0
2	113			118.6	120.0
3	121			116.9	120.1
4	123	120.3	119.8	118.1	120.1
5	117	119.0	120.4	119.6	120.1
6	109	120.3	119.6	118.8	120.1
7	131	116.3	114.2	115.9	120.1
8	115	119.0	121.6	120.4	120.1
9	127	118.3	118.6	118.8	120.2
10	118	124.3	124.2	121.3	120.2
11		120.0	120.1	120.3	120.2

The MADs for each of the forecasting methods were calculated using the formula presented in the chapter. The result was as follows:

Method	MAD
3-month moving average	7.1
3-month weighted moving average	7.9
Exponential smoothing	7.1
Linear regression	5.7

Given the data and information in the problem, regression should probably be used because of the relatively small MAD compared to the other methods. As more data is collected this could, of course, change.

Calculation of the MFE for each brought an interesting result. The first three methods (moving average, weighted moving average, and exponential smoothing) each brought a positive number (0.23, 0.16, and 1.76, respectively). The interpretation for those is that each of those three methods is biased, specifically producing forecasts that are forecasting too low for the demand over the range of data points given. That should not be too surprising, given that the regression coefficient is slightly positive—an indication that there is a slight upward slope to the data. Since it was discussed in the chapter how all three of these methods tend to lag behind and trend in the data, it is logical that the forecasting method is a bit behind (biased low).

By contrast, the regression method picks up this slight upward trend—so much so that the MFE equals zero, indicating the lack of bias in that method.

KEY TERMS

Forecasting	Qualitative Forecast	Quantitative Forecast
Market Surveys	Delphi Method	Panel Consensus
Life Cycle Analogy	Informed Judgment	Causal Forecasts
Input–Output Model	Econometric Model	Simulation
Regression	Intrinsic Forecasts	Extrinsic Forecasts
Random Pattern	Trend Pattern	Seasonality
Moving Averages	Weighted Moving Average	Exponential Smoothing
Forecast Error	Smoothing Constant	Mean Forecast Error
Tracking Signal	Mean Absolute Deviation	

SUMMARY

This chapter presents an overview of the some of the major characteristics of forecasting, and categorizes them into three major categories: qualitative, causal, and time series. Both qualitative and causal methods tend to require a great deal of information about external markets and environments. Since much of that information is not readily available to the operations manager, the time series methods (needing only past demand data) are appealing. Adding to their appeal is the relative ease of calculation, especially with computers. They tend to be primarily used for specific product demand, which is again useful for the detailed product planning activities required of operations managers.

A major characteristic of all forecasting methods is that they should be considered to be incorrect. The key to future planning methods is the issue of just how incorrect they really are. For this reason there should always be an error estimate presented with the forecast. Some of the more common methods for error calculation and use were also discussed.

REFERENCES

Fogarty, D. W., J. H. Blackstone, Jr., and T. R. Hoffmann. *Production and Inventory Management.* Cincinnati, OH: South-Western, 1991.

Willis, Raymond E., *A Guide to Forecasting for Planners and Managers.* Englewood Cliffs, NJ: Prentice-Hall, 1987.

DISCUSSION QUESTIONS

1. Think of some of the leading indicators that could be used as a major input to causal forecasts in the economy. Discuss their use.
2. Which type of forecasts would most likely be used for Sales and Operations Planning (S&OP), and why are they the most appropriate?
3. What value does it bring to an operation if a forecasting method is used that only forecasts for families of products?
4. Think of at least three products recently introduced that would probably use the life-cycle analogy. What products would they "copy"? Why is life-cycle appropriate for those products?
5. How should a company include information for their forecast that indicates the economy is headed for a recession? How, if at all, should that information impact time-series forecasting information?
6. Discuss the arguments for using a large smoothing constant for exponential smoothing instead of a small one. Under what conditions would each be better? Why?
7. Describe in your own words why using the MAD is better for describing the forecast error than is the MFE. What is the major use of each? Should they really be used together? Why or why not?

EXERCISES

1. Given the following data:

Period	Demand
1	43
2	37
3	55
4	48

   a. Calculate the three-period moving average for period 5.
   b. Calculate the exponential smoothed forecast for period 5 using an alpha value of 0.4. Assume the forecast for period 4 was the three-period moving average of the first three periods.
   c. Which method appeals the most for the data? Why?
2. Given the following demand data:

Period	1	2	3	4	5	6	7	8
Demand	17	22	18	27	14	18	20	25

   a. Calculate the four-period weighted moving average for period 9 using weights of 0.1, 0.2, 0.3, and 0.4 where the 0.4 is the weight for the most recent period.

b. Calculate the forecast for period 9 using a 3-month moving average forecasting method.
c. Which method would you recommend using and why?
3. Given the same data for the previous problem:

Period	1	2	3	4	5	6	7	8
Demand	17	22	18	27	14	18	20	25

a. Use Excel or some other statistical computer package to calculate the regression equation for the data.
b. Use the regression equation to forecast the demand for period 9.
4. A forecasting method resulted in the following forecasts shown by the data in the following table:

Period	Demand	Forecast
1	132	127
2	141	130
3	137	133
4	159	135
5	146	139
6	162	144
7	166	149
8	175	155
9	194	161
10	181	169

a. Use the data to calculate the MAD.
b. Find a regression equation for the demand data.
c. Use the regression equation to forecast demand for period 11.
d. Is the regression method preferred over the method used? Why or why not?
5. The following demand data was collected over a 3 year period for one product:

Month	Demand, year 1	Demand, year 2	Demand, year 3
1	72	84	97
2	67	98	119
3	85	86	138
4	99	113	124
5	87	121	143
6	135	140	162
7	127	133	157
8	131	156	178
9	102	125	136
10	96	134	141
11	88	118	122
12	79	102	120

Use the data to develop a regression-based forecast. Be sure to note that there is a seasonal factor to the demand.

6. The following information is presented for a product:

	1998		1999	
	Forecast	Demand	Forecast	Demand
Quarter I	212	232	222	245
Quarter II	341	318	316	351
Quarter III	157	169	160	145
Quarter IV	263	214	251	242

   a. What is the MAD for the data above?
   b. Given the information above, what should the forecast be for the first quarter of 2000 if the company switches to exponential smoothing with an alpha value of 0.3?

7. The following information is presented for a product:

	2001		2002	
	Forecast	Demand	Forecast	Demand
Quarter I	200	226	210	218
Quarter II	320	310	315	333
Quarter III	145	153	140	122
Quarter IV	230	212	240	231

   a. What are the seasonal indicies that should be used for each quarter?
   b. What is the MAD for the data above?

8. Consider the forecast results shown below. Calculate MAD and MFE using the data for months January through June. Does the forecast model under- or over-forecast?

Month	Actual Demand	Forecast
January	1040	1055
February	990	1052
March	980	900
April	1060	1025
May	1080	1100
June	1000	1050

CHAPTER 3

Sales and Operations Planning

Chapter Outline

Introduction—The strategic plans of the company and the more specific business plans derived from the strategic plans will specify the product and service mix that the company will pursue, and will also indicate planned changes in market penetration, market approaches, and other critical aspects of the business. Strategic and business plans tend to be too general to specify resource needs and the timing of those needs, however, and also tend to be too general to adequately coordinate action plans and resource needs of several of the key functions of the firm, including Operations, Marketing/Sales, Finance, Information Technology, and Human Resources.

Much of the more detailed planning of resources, including the type of resources, the quantity of resources, and the timing of those resources, is accomplished by **Sales and Operations Planning (S&OP).** This planning activity tends to go by several names, depending on the business and the type of production in which that business is involved. Other common names that have been used in the past include **aggregate planning, production planning,** and, in the case of operations focused more directly in services, **staffing planning.** Sales and operation planning (S&OP) is chosen as the preferred name in this book primarily because it more effectively indicates the trade-offs that are typically involved with those two major functions in a firm. In fact, production

Clearly these plans need to be carefully coordinated with whatever re-sources are needed to accomplish the plans. This coordination is a major function of the S&OP.

There are other issues in the design that need to be addressed, including the aggregation of time. For example, it is preferable to examine "buckets" of time that represent a week, a month, or some other unit of time. Again, the answer lies in a basic trade-off between the level of detail that is useful for planning and the amount of effort necessary to obtain information. The general rule is to aggregate as much as possible to the point where useful resource plans can be made. Aggregation of time and production units allow for ease of plan development and tend to be more accurate in the aggregate, but aggregation should not be done to the point where useful information is lost. The correct amount of aggregation is highly dependent on the type of product or service, the nature of the customers being served, and the processes being used to deliver the product or service.

3.3   APPROACHES TO SALES AND OPERATIONS PLANNING

The primary focus of developing S&OP is to establish decisions about sales volumes, customer service goals, rates of production, inventory levels, and order backlogs. In order to accomplish this process, it is important for Sales, Marketing, Operations, Finance, and Product Development to all work together, guided by the strategic plan and vision for the future of the firm.

Once the strategic planning process is completed in a firm, it is generally used to make a business plan, which is usually expressed in financial terms. Since many of the decisions made in the S&OP will impact the financial plans, it is important that these two planning processes are reconciled for agreement. Since in most firms the business plan is "owned" by top management, it is clear that those top managers must also be involved in the S&OP process. There are other reasons top management involvement is important—their involvement provides a clear "message" to all in the firm that the process and outcome of the process are important activities, and therefore the resulting plans should be followed.

The Make-to-Stock View of an S&OP

The diagram in Figure 3.1 provides a simple example of what the output from an S&OP process may look like.

There are several issues that should be noted on this sample. First, note that the sales history for the last 3 months shows that overall there were 11,000 more units sold than was called for in the plan, and the production was 4,000 less than called for in the plan. This meant that over the 3 months the inventory would have dropped by 15,000 units, since they would have used finished goods inventory to satisfy customer requirements. You can easily see the month-to-month calculations as well. For example, in the first month on the

FIGURE 3.1   Sample S&OP for Make-to-Stock

Family: Standard Polybobs

Unit of measure: 1,000 units

Target finished inventory: 15 days on hand

HISTORY

SALES	A	S	O	N	D	J	F	M	A	M	J	J
Forecast	300	310	300	320	300	310	310	310	320	320	320	320
Actual Sales	314	302	305									
Difference: Month	14	−8	5									
Cumulative		6	11									

PRODUCTION	A	S	O	N	D	J	F	M	A	M	J	J
Production Plan	300	310	300	325	310	310	310	310	320	320	320	320
Actual Production	303	305	298									
Difference: Month	3	−5	−2									
Cumulative		−2	−4									

INVENTORY	A	S	O	N	D	J	F	M	A	M	J	J
Plan	150	150	150	140	150	150	150	150	150	150	150	150
Actual	139	142	135									
Days on hand	14	14	13.5									

chart (August), sales were 314,000 while production was only 303,000 units—a difference of 11,000 units. That is what brought the planned inventory down from 150,000 units to 139,000 units.

You can also see how they plan to make up for the shortfall in their target level of 15 days (15,000 units) in inventory. In November they plan to produce 5,000 more than expected sales, and then produce 10,000 more than sales for December. By the end of December they should then be back on target.

Of course, these plans need to be reviewed and revised at the end of each month, since neither sales nor production are likely to exactly equal projections. In addition, conditions, policies, and other business plans may change. In this sense, the S&OP can be thought of as a dynamic plan, rolling through time to reflect conditions at the time. As each month passes, in fact, most companies will add an additional month to the end of the plan to maintain the same time horizon.

The Make-to-Order View of an S&OP

When the product is a make-to-order product, there is generally no finished goods inventory. The orders are taken and then production starts to that order. The orders that exist awaiting production are typically called a **backlog.** That produces a slight variation in the S&OP, illustrated in Figure 3.2.

FIGURE 3.2   Sample S&OP for Make-to-Order

Family: Deluxe Polybobs

Unit of measure: Each

Target Order Backlog: 3 weeks

HISTORY

SALES	A	S	O	N	D	J	F	M	A	M	J	J
Forecast	80	80	80	80	80	80	80	80	80	80	80	80
Actual Orders	82	79	81									
Difference: Month	2	-1	1									
Cumulative		1	2									

PRODUCTION	A	S	O	N	D	J	F	M	A	M	J	J
Production Plan	80	80	80	80	80	80	80	80	80	80	80	80
Actual Production	80	81	81									
Difference: Month	0	1	1									
Cumulative		1	2									

ORDER BACKLOG	A	S	O	N	D	J	F	M	A	M	J	J
Plan	60	60	60	60	60	60	60	60	60	60	60	60
Actual 62	64	62	62									
Weeks Backlog	3	3	3	3	3	3	3	3	3	3	3	3

3.4   STRATEGIES FOR SALES AND OPERATIONS PLANNING

While we now may have a "view" of the production requirements and how they "match" with sales, we need to develop more specific plans as to how the plan will most effectively and efficiently be accomplished. The rest of the chapter focuses on some of the approaches and trade-offs that can be used to more specifically look at production planning, keeping in mind that the major focus should be on planning resources.

Some Techniques

Mathematically, there are several approaches used to develop plans. In the past some companies would often try to put the major information into mathematical algorithms to search for an optimal combination of products to maximize an objective function, often defined in terms of profitability. While that approach is still taken in some environments where capacity and outputs are well defined and not too complex (such as in some process industries such as chemicals), many companies opt for different approaches for several reasons:

- Environments are often too complex to capture all the major variables and conditions adequately without making the model very difficult to set up, solve, and manage.

- When simplifying assumptions are made to make the mathematical model manageable, the simpler model often does not adequately reflect the environment itself.
- Many managers have not been adequately trained in modeling techniques to the point where they can understand how to manage the process.

In any case, the mathematical optimization techniques are beyond the intended scope of this book. If the reader is interested in learning more about them, they are urged to consult one of the several good books on management science or operations research.

A second approach is to simulate the production environment in a computer simulation, allowing rapid and effective solutions to scenarios that can be input into the program. This approach is gaining in popularity as fast and efficient computers become plentiful and inexpensive, and as the simulation programming packages become more powerful and easier to use. While it is often difficult to initially build the simulation model, once built the approach can be quite effective in developing "what if" approaches to the planning process.

The third popular approach is really a subset of the second. It involves simulating the demand on an production resource environment in the form of a computer spreadsheet. As with a simulation of the entire production environment, once the spreadsheet format has been established it becomes relatively easy to investigate various approaches in a "what if" format. A major difference in both the computer model simulation and the spreadsheet approach is that they usually do not give an optimal solution—merely a rapid and fairly simple approach to search for a satisfactory solution for the various combinations of conditions being input. This third approach, while not generally yielding an optimal solution, is heavily used because of the ease of use and the widespread knowledge and acceptance of spreadsheet software. It is therefore this approach that will be used in the remainder of the chapter.

Trade-off Approaches

The general objective of developing a good S&OP is to find the "best" alternative to align resources to meet the expected demand under certain operating conditions. Often "best" means an attempt to maximize firm profits, but other conditions can also be established to define "best" in the context of the firm's strategic plan. Examples of other conditions may be:

- Attempting to meet all expected customer demand
- Attempting to minimize inventory investment
- Attempting to minimize the adverse impact on people, often experienced with volatility in the workforce caused by frequent layoffs

It is frequently impossible to establish perfect conditions, so these trade-off criteria are important to understand as the plan is being developed. For example, under certain expected demand conditions very high levels of customer service may only be possible by having a very large inventory investment, sometimes to the point of having a negative impact on profitability for that period. In such a case the firm has to make a conscious decision as to whether it is better to allow customer service to fall or to accept the negative financial implications of attempting to meet customer demand. If the decision criteria used to make the final decision are established *before* the development of the plan, it often leads to a much smoother plan development with smaller probability for functional "battles" based on functionally focused criteria. In this context it must be noted that the S&OP planning process is for the *entire* business, not just for any one function.

There are three general categories of approaches used. They are:

- Level
- Chase
- Combination

Level.   As the name implies, a level planning approach establishes a level set of resources and implies the demand will fluctuate around those available resources, or, in some cases, attempts to alter the demand patterns themselves to more effectively match the resource levels established. This approach tends to be more common and certainly more appealing in environments where resources are difficult or expensive to alter. This also tends to be the approach used in many "lean production" environments. Examples include:

- Professional services, such as doctors and dentists. Professional services tend to use appointments to alter and smooth demand patterns around the availability of the relatively expensive and difficult-to-alter resource represented by the doctors and dentists themselves.
- Hotels and airlines. In both cases the resources (rooms and seats, respectively) are again expensive and difficult to alter in quantity. Appointments under a different name (reservations) are again used to alter demand patterns. In addition, pricing strategies (weekend rates and super-saver tickets, for example) are used to once again alter demand patterns to smooth out the demand closer to the resource availability. Many restaurants and automobile repair facilities also fit into this same category.
- Some manufacturing processes have similar characteristics. Some chemical processes cannot be turned off without expensive and time-consuming startup activities, and they additionally cannot be sped up or slowed down. An example is making certain glass products in large volume. The glass furnace may need to be continually run, as shutting it down implies cleaning out the entire furnace and starting it over. The one "luxury" that manufacturing processes have over the two previous examples is the ability to inventory the output as an alternative to altering the demand.

Level strategies have appeal from the perspective that they tend to provide highly stable production environments, but tend to put more pressure on the sales and marketing activities to alter the demand patterns in appropriate ways if the normal market demand does not tend to be level in a noninfluenced environment. The only alternative is to build an inventory in low demand times and use it when demand is high.

Chase.   This approach represents the other extreme, in that demand is not altered, but resources are. In fact in a "pure" chase environment the resources are continually being raised or lowered to meet the demand as it fluctuates under normal market conditions. As the approach is the opposite of level, so too are the typical characteristics of the environments where chase strategies may be appealing or, in some cases, the only alternative. These tend to be environments where demand is difficult or impossible to alter and where attractively simple and/or inexpensive methods to alter the resource base are available. Examples of such environments include:

- "Mid-tier" suppliers of manufactured products. The demand for such products are often resulting from customers two or more levels down the supply chain, making it difficult if not impossible to alter demand. For example, a supplier of light bulbs for automobiles is reacting to demand from the automobile manufacturers, which in turn are reacting to the consumers of the automobiles. The light bulb manufacturer has little ability to influence the demand for automobiles themselves.
- Service industries where demand is difficult to predict and equally difficult to alter. Some examples include:
  - Grocery stores and banks, where demand is often not recognized until the customer actually walks in and declares what they want.
  - Professional tax accounting services, which must attempt to deliver much of their service during the tax "season" with little opportunity to alter the demand pattern.
  - Some "process" industries such as electric utilities.

Combination.   This approach is by far the most common approach. As the name implies, companies using this approach will "mix and match," altering demand and resources in such a way to maximize performance to their established criteria, including profit, inventory investment, and the impact on people.

Graphically, the differences in the three approaches can be illustrated in Figures 3.3, 3.4, 3.5, 3.6, and 3.7.

In Figure 3.7, note that at point **A** the level production far exceeds the demand. It is at that point that inventory is being built at the maximum rate. The combination line also shows a building of inventory, but less than the level approach. By the time that point **B** is reached, demand exceeds the level production rate, and far exceeds the production rate for the combination approach. It is at that point that the inventory built in the low demand period will be used fairly rapidly. In the combination approach, far less inventory would have been built than with the level method. For that reason the production rate in

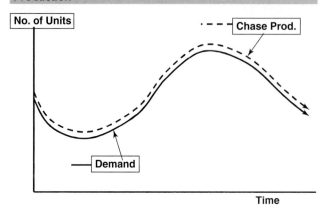

FIGURE 3.3   A Demand Pattern with Chase Production

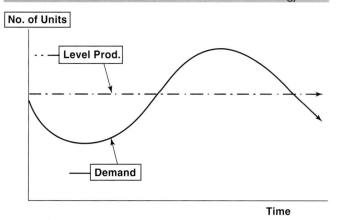

FIGURE 3.4   A Demand Pattern with Level Strategy

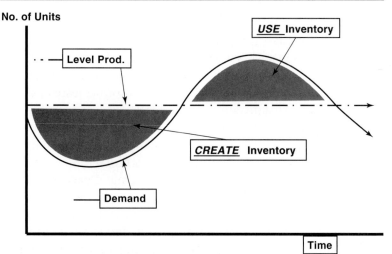

FIGURE 3.5   The Use of Inventory with a Level Strategy

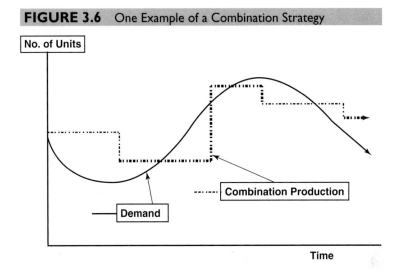

FIGURE 3.6 One Example of a Combination Strategy

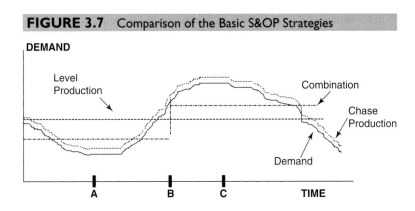

FIGURE 3.7 Comparison of the Basic S&OP Strategies

the combination approach needs to be increased or they will soon run out of inventory and fail to meet demand. At point **C,** therefore, note that the combination approach production rate exceeds that of the level, and is therefore using the relatively smaller amount of inventory less rapidly. Also note the combination method illustrated in the diagram is but one of what could be an infinite combination of production rates and timing changes for those rates.

3.5 BALANCING RESOURCES IN SALES AND OPERATIONS PLANNING

There are several options open to most companies for accomplishing the planning of resources. In general, they fall into two categories. One focuses on the supply side (Operations) to attempt to change the production supply. The other focuses on the demand side (Marketing and Sales) to attempt to alter demand patterns to meet production outputs. The strategies are summarized below.

Internal strategies (focusing on operations—the supply side):

- *Hire and fire*—As the name implies, this strategy focuses on altering the number of workers.
- *Temporary workers*—In some industries, this alternative is becoming increasingly popular.
- *Overtime/slack time*—The overtime alternative has been common in many companies for a number of years. Recently, companies in some environments are recognizing that it occasionally may be a wise move to continue to keep and pay workers, but to not expect them to produce product unless there is demand for that product.
- *Subcontracting*—Also called "outsourcing" in some environments, this option has also become popular in some companies in recent years. Basically, it means that the company will contract with a supplier or other contractor to produce some or all of a required output.
- *Inventory*—This is a very common option in manufacturing companies. Basically, the implication is that inventory will be produced during times of low demand and used to meet demand during times of high demand.
- *Backlog*—As the name implies, this means the company will take the customer order even if it does not have inventory or capacity to meet the immediate demand, but will promise delivery when capacity is available.
- *Do not meet demand*—Again, as the name implies, this options means the company will simply decline to take a customer order if they do not have the inventory or capacity to meet the order requirements.
- *Change production rates*—This option is rarely used, since it has a potentially negative impact on the workers. It implies the capability to slow down or speed up the rate of production. It can potentially have a negative impact on both morale and output quality.

External strategies (focusing on the customer to alter demand rates) include the following:

- *Pricing*—As the name implies, this involves changing the price of the product or service. Generally, lowering the price will increase demand while raising prices will decrease demand.
- *Promotions*—Offering special incentives ("rebates," for example) are occasionally used to increase demand.
- *Advertising*—A very common strategy used to increase customer awareness and increase demand.

- *Reservations*—Often used when capacity is scarce or very expensive (such as in some restaurants, in doctor's offices, dentist's offices, etc.), this approach smoothes demand, allowing both better customer service and more effective utilization of the scarce or expensive resource.
- *"Package" offerings*—A special type of promotion, the package offers tend to link popular items with less popular items to smooth the overall demand.

It can be said that in general the internal strategies are more commonly used in "chase" approaches, while the external strategies are more commonly used in "level" approaches. An exception to that may be the use of inventory.

3.6   DISCUSSION: A SIMPLE EXAMPLE

To illustrate a simple spreadsheet approach for each of these methods, let us examine a simple planning problem:

The Waldorf Sport Boat Company has a demand forecast for all its aluminum fishing boats under 15 feet for the next 6 months. The forecast is:

Month	Demand
January	250
February	300
March	420
April	560
May	610
June	580

There are currently 10 workers assigned to the production line, each capable of producing approximately 15 boats per month (December is typically the slowest month for sales). For this simple example we will assume each month has the same number of production days. They can hire more workers at a hiring and training cost of $400 per worker. If they lay off any workers, the unemployment cost is $1,000 per worker. The boats have a standard production cost (labor, material, and overhead) of $300 per boat. They can use overtime to produce boats, but a boat produced in overtime adds $60 in labor cost, and each worker can only produce an extra three boats per month using overtime. If they keep any boats in inventory it will cost them $6 per boat per month for any boat in inventory at the end of the month. Failure to meet market demand typically will imply the customer will buy from another supplier, and therefore cost the company $120 in profit. They recognize this lost profit (selling price less standard cost) as a stockout cost. They currently have no boats in inventory.

Using this simple data, the following tables will illustrate planning approaches using chase, level, and a combination strategy.

Chase

In this example, we will use a minimum number of workers to meet all demand. No inventory will be allowed, and overtime can be used if necessary rather than adding another worker who could potentially add inventory. Overtime production will be limited to 15 boats per month, for at that level it is better to hire another worker.

Month	Demand	Workers	Reg. produc.	OT produc.	Hire & fire	H/F cost	Reg. cost	OT cost
Jan.	250	16	240	10	+6	$2,400	$75,000	$600
Feb.	300	20	300	0	+4	$1,600	$90,000	0
Mar.	420	28	420	0	+8	$3,200	$126,000	0
Apr.	560	37	555	5	+9	$3,600	$168,000	$300
May	610	40	600	10	+3	$1,200	$183,000	$600
June	580	38	570	10	−2	$2,000	$174,000	$600
Total						**$14,000**	**$816,000**	**$2,100**

The number of workers necessary is calculated by dividing the demand by 15 (the regular production per worker per month). For example, in January, dividing the demand of 250 by 15 yields 16.67. That implies 16 workers are needed, giving a regular production of 240 and leaving the additional 10 to be produced in overtime. The grand total for hire/fire, regular production cost, and overtime cost is $832,100.

Level

In this strategy we try to establish a level workforce for the entire 6 months. If we divide the total 6 months' demand (2720 units) by 6, we see the average demand is about 453 boats. Establishing the level production at 450 (30 workers), we ensure that we will approximately meet the *average* demand, although it is obvious that inventory or shortages will occur since every month is not average. We will allow the inventory or shortage conditions, but will always have a constant, level production rate. At the end we will have to remember to add the one-time hiring cost of the additional 20 workers ($8,000):

Month	Demand	Production	Inventory	Shortage	Reg. produc. cost	Inventory cost	Shortage cost
January	250	450	200	0	$135,000	$1,200	0
February	300	450	350	0	$135,000	$2,100	0
March	420	450	380	0	$135,000	$2,280	0
April	560	450	270	0	$135,000	$1,620	0
May	610	450	110	0	$135,000	$660	0
June	580	450	0	20	$135,000	0	$2,400
Total					**$810,000**	**$7,860**	**$2,400**

This total cost (production plus inventory plus shortages plus the one-time hiring cost) is $828,260, or $3,840 less than the first alternative over the 6 months. On the negative side, however, there are 20 customers in June that did not get the boat they wanted. Note that to save space only columns that had relevant activity are included. We could have, for example, had a column for hire/fire cost, but since the only activity was in January we elected to add that cost at the end.

Combination

As mentioned before, there are numerous approaches that can be taken under the "combination" category. We will illustrate but one. In this alternative, we start with 25 workers—plenty of workers to meet early-year demand and build some inventory. As demand grows, we will use the inventory and start to authorize overtime. We want to meet all demand, so eventually we will have to add workers. With a three-boat limit per worker per month on overtime, the 25 workers will only be authorized to produce 75 extra boats on overtime, and this may not be enough for some months. It will be a policy to add the minimum number of workers, however.

Mnth	Dem.	Reg. prod	Inv.	OT prod	# wkrs	H/F	Reg. cost	H/F cost	Inv. cost	OT cost
Jan	250	375	125	0	25	+15	$112,500	$6,000	$750	0
Feb	300	375	200	0	25		$112,500		$1,200	0
Mar	420	375	155	0	25		$112,500		$930	0
Apr	560	375	0	30	25		$121,500		0	$1,800
May	610	510	0	100	34	+9	$183,000	$3,600	0	$6,000
June	580	495	0	85	33	−1	$174,000	$1,000	0	$5,100
Total							**$816,000**	**$10,600**	**$2,880**	**$12,900**

When we reached May we did not have enough capacity to meet demand even with overtime. The inventory was used up in April, and with 25 workers we could only produce 450 units (each worker can produce 18–15 in regular time and 3 in overtime). The decision was to hire nine workers. Recall they want to minimize the total number of workers. To come to the number of 34 workers, we divided the May demand of 610 by 18 to obtain 33.9. That implies that 34 workers could meet demand using almost all the authorized overtime. In June, the demand of 580 divided by the 18 gives 32.2, meaning they can meet demand with one less worker, but still with most working overtime. Note that the total cost of this alternative ($842,380) is the largest of the three examples, but does have the advantage of having little disruption of new workers and does meet all demand. Other alternatives may prove to be significantly cheaper.

Even once the plan is made and appears to be satisfactory, great care must be taken in using these plans. They must be considered as rough planning estimates only. Not only are some of the input numbers generalized and therefore lack precision, but there are several qualitative issues that may confound the plan as well. Some of those issues are described in the next section.

3.7   QUALITATIVE ISSUES

The quantitative approach described above focuses essentially on one aspect: financial. There are several other issues that must be examined as well. The discussion below summarizes some of those qualitative issues:

1. *The "human" factor.* Some of these approaches imply the "manipulation" of humans in the operation. The most obvious is the use of layoffs and/or hiring, as well as overtime.

   - Layoffs will often impact the morale of the people. Clearly that will often be the case for those laid off, but also for those that remain on the job—sometimes called "survivor guilt." Many will start to worry if they are next. Others will have friends or relatives who were laid off. This condition can have negative impacts on efficiency and effectiveness. Also, once those on layoff are called back, many will have not only lost some of the "edge" on their skill, but will often have less of a feeling of dedication toward the company. This, too, may affect their approach to the job in a negative fashion.

   - Hiring, too, has implications. The learning curve is a well-documented phenomenon that implies the efficiency level of those newly hired people will often be quite a bit lower. These new people may also adversely impact the efficiency of the existing personnel as the new people attempt to learn by asking existing personnel, "Can you show me how to do something?"

   - The use of temporary workers can also cause some problems, not only with the obvious impact of learning curve, but also cost efficiencies for full-time workers. As an extreme example, one company with very seasonal demand patterns built two identical production processes. In periods of high demand, both processes were run, each staffed with a combination of regular, highly skilled workers and low-skilled temporary workers. Clearly the processes had to be carefully designed to allow for rapid "insertion" of the temporary workers with little skill. When the low demand periods came, the company merely shut down one of the processes and staffed the remaining one with just the highly skilled regular workers. The implication is that the positions normally taken by a low-skilled temporary worker was now being filled by a highly skilled (and highly paid) regular worker. The company avoided the problem of having to lay off their regular workforce, which had some clear advantages—but the cost was a severe underutilization of the skilled workers staffing the unskilled positions in the process.

- Even with a stable workforce, the assumption of a fixed output per worker built in to the sample model clearly may not hold due to the impact of learning and experience.

2. *The customer factor.* The model almost assumes that customer-based actions (price changes, promotions, etc.) can be taken easily without any lasting impact. Such actions can have longer-range impressions on customers or potential customers, however, and as such may not be wisely used without discretion. Even some approaches typically viewed as operational (backordering and planned stockouts) can impact customer impressions and buying habits.

3. *The forecast factor.* One of the most important characteristics of forecasting, described earlier in Chapter 2, is that a forecast should always be considered to be incorrect. It is for that reason that a good forecasting model should give both the forecast and the error estimate. Notice that the model development earlier in this chapter does nothing about the expected error. What this implies is that the company needs to make (depending on the flexibility inherent in the process) some specific contingency plans to deal with incorrect forecasts. Generally, this contingency planning will use buffer inventory, buffer capacity, or both. The size of the buffer is generally based on the size of the forecast error.

4. *External environmental factors.* There are often constraints or pressures from the environment outside the organization that will constrain or at least impact the ability to create an ideal S&OP. Some of the more common of these include:

- Labor contracts or union activities that can constrain the ability to obtain the right number of people with the right skills. Also, the cost of these resources will potentially be impacted. Even without union activity the size and/or cost of the labor pool can be impacted by availability of labor skills due to location.
- Government regulation, especially concerning environmental, health, and safety issues, can impact both costs and resources.
- Competitive forces in the market can always impact demand. The forecast, which is the usual starting point for making the S&OP, is based on a projection of demand from past data, but clearly strategic moves by competitors in the market are sometimes hard to project and their impact on the market difficult to estimate.

The important overriding message in the uncertainty of the model based on both quantitative and qualitative factors points again to the key point in developing these higher-level plans for the operation. The purpose is to make general decisions about the use of resources to produce to the level of anticipated customer demand in the most effective manner for both the firm and the customers. The type of resources, the quantity needed, and the timing of the need are the major focus of this planning activity, but management must be prepared to be flexible in this planning to adjust to the reality of the unknown factors in the process.

To illustrate the potential application in a more service-oriented setting, consider Example 3.1 below.

EXAMPLE 3.1

The Acme Accounting Partners are a local CPA firm. They are relatively small, with only 15 full-time accountants. The accountants are highly trained, and any layoffs are out of the question for the firm. They also believe that for now the staff of 15 is as many as they can afford to keep on a full-time basis. During the tax season (January through April) the demand on the accountant's time is very heavy. They are paid on the basis of a 40-hour work week, but during tax season they can be expected to work a maximum of 60 hours per week. The partners believe that any more hours than that will hurt productivity and concentration to the point where major mistakes and inefficiencies are probable. Luckily, they have an agreement with a temporary employment service that can supply temporary clerical help at the rate of $25 per hour. When they use the clerical help, they merely adjust the workload so the accountants can do the technical work while the clerks can concentrate on more structured tasks.

The company will save the overtime hours for the accountants in an "inventory" of hours. The accountants are then expected to use those hours to take time off during the period of light demand (usually in the summer). Since their fiscal year ends August 31, any hours left in "inventory" are paid in monetary compensation to the accountants at the rate of $50 per hour.

The partners have developed a forecast of demand (in hours) for the next 8 months based on past experience of client tax needs.

Month	Demand (Hours)	Weeks in Month
January	5000	4.5
February	5500	4
March	6000	4.5
April	4000	4
May	2000	5
June	1500	4
July	1000	4.5
August	1000	4.5

The partners need an estimate of the financial impact to determine if their decision to keep the staff at 15 is a good one. They also need to determine if it may be feasible to take on additional work, should a new client request their services.

Solution: The following table shows the financial impact of their aggregated demand.

Month	Demand (hours)	Reg. time avail.	Total time needed (reg. + OT)	Temp. hours needed	Cumul. OT hours	Temp. $
Jan.	5,000	2,700	4,050	950	1,350	$23,750
Feb.	5,500	2,400	3,600	1,900	2,550	$47,500
March	6,000	2,700	4,050	1,950	3,900	$48,750
April	4,000	2,400	3,600	400	5,100	$10,000
May	2,000	3,000	2,000		4,100	
June	1,500	2,400	1,500		3,200	
July	1,500	2,700	1,500		2,000	
Aug.	1,500	2,700	1,500		800	
						$130,000

Using this projection, the partners can now see they need approximately $170,000 beyond their normal salary expectations — $130,000 for temporary workers plus $40,000 (800 hours at $50 per hour) to compensate for unused overtime at the end of August.

3.8   SOME BUSINESS ENVIRONMENT ISSUES

Clearly there are many issues that must be considered when designing the approach to be used for this level of planning. They include the level of detail (the level of aggregation) and the length of the planning horizon. To provide a brief synopsis:

- *Level of detail.* The issue here is first to determine whether the time aggregation should be in weeks, months, quarters, or some other unit of time. The general rule to dictate the logical time aggregation is to link it to the volatility in the market the company is serving. Keeping in mind that the primary purpose of this level of planning is to plan resources, one must first determine how quickly change is likely to occur in the market, and how much such a change is likely to impact the resources that are being planned. Also at issue is whether the operation can or chooses to react to changes quickly. A highly capital-intensive operation producing a high-volume standard product, for example, is more likely to look at quarterly figures instead of monthly, especially if their strategy is largely based on level planning.

  The level of aggregation of products or services must also be addressed. The general rule of thumb here is to aggregate whatever products or services that utilize the same basic category of resources being planned as long as it is possible to generate a projection of total demand on those resources. In other words, if two or more products use the same set of people and/or equipment, they can be aggregated for planning those resources if it makes sense to aggregate them when projecting total market demand for the time horizon in question.

- *Time horizon.* The next question is how far into the future should the plan go? The general answer is that the plan should have a horizon at least as long as the time it takes to make the change in the resource base being planned. For example, if the resources are workers, we must know how long it will take to hire and train (if necessary) the workers necessary. The same is true for equipment—how long will it take to obtain and implement any equipment changes necessary? When making these determinations, one must have some ideas as to the present conditions, including:
  - Flexibility of the existing workforce—can they be moved from one resource base to another with relative ease?
  - Flexibility of the existing equipment—can it be used for producing multiple categories of aggregated outputs?
  - Ease of obtaining capital and the amount of time it takes to obtain the capital—most resource changes (especially resource additions) will require financing, and the company must know how that will be done and how long it will take to obtain.

KEY TERMS

Sales and Operations Plan	Level Strategy	Chase Strategy
Staffing Plan	Internal Strategies	External Strategies
Combination Strategy	Production Plan	Backlog
Aggregate Plan		

SUMMARY

This chapter focuses on the approach to developing intermediate-term strategies for the best use of resources to meet the expected customer demand. There are three basic approaches—level, chase, and combination—each with a number of substrategies that can be applied, and each with certain environments with which they fit more appropriately. The key issue is to recognize that planning at this level focuses on the "best" plan for the use of resources, and does not plan specific production output.

REFERENCES

Fogarty, D. W., J. H. Blackstone, Jr., and T. R. Hoffmann, *Production and Inventory Management.* Cincinnati, OH: South-Western, 1991.

Ling, Richard C., "How to Implement Sales and Operations Planning." *1992 APICS International Conference Proceedings.*

Vollmann, T. E., W. L. Berry, and D. C. Whybark, *Manufacturing Planning and Control Systems.* New York: Irwin
McGraw-Hill, 1997.

Wallace, T. F., *Sales & Operation Planning.*
Cincinnati, OH: T.F. Wallace & Company,
2000.

DISCUSSION QUESTIONS

1. Discuss the approach to Sales and Operations Planning that might be the most
   appropriate for the following companies. Explain your reasoning:
   - A bank
   - A fast-food restaurant
   - An automobile service center attached to a dealership
   - A hotel
   - An attorney's office
   - A retail clothing store
2. Discuss the potential impact that an especially militant labor union can have on
   the strategic approach to S&OP.
3. A company has traditionally used a level strategy for planning for several years.
   Discuss the potential changes in their environment that could make them consider using more chase tactics.
4. What changes, if any, will the perishability of the inventory have on the capability
   of a company in using a level strategy. Consider, for example, a meat market and a
   fast-food restaurant.
5. How, if at all, will the overall strategic plan of the company alter its approach to
   S&OP?
6. How, if at all, will the overall economic conditions in a company's environment
   alter their approach to S&OP? Give several examples.
7. Discuss the potential pros and cons of the aggregation process that must be done
   prior to developing the S&OP. For example, what are the trade-offs when deciding
   to aggregate the data into quarters instead of by month? What are the trade-offs
   when deciding how many product definitions to include in a "product family"?

EXERCISES

1. The ABC Company has recognized the following demand for the next four quarters:

Quarter	Demand
1	3,000 units
2	4,000 units
3	4,500 units
4	3,500 units

   ABC has traditionally used the hiring and firing of workers to accommodate the
   changes in demand for their products, but is considering maintaining a stable
   workforce and subcontracting production when demand exceeds the capability of
   the workforce. They currently have 30 workers, each capable of producing 100
   units per quarter. It costs them $3,000 to hire a worker and $5,000 to fire a worker.

If they subcontract the work, it will cost them $30 per unit above their normal production cost. Given this information, should they continue their current practice or move to subcontracting the production over what their current workforce can produce?

2. Use the data from exercise #1 to consider another possibility: They could hire a set of workers at the beginning of the year and build inventory. They could then use the inventory (and some subcontracting, if necessary) to deal with the quarters where demand exceeds production. Using this method, the inventory will cost them $15 per quarter based on the inventory on hand at the end of the quarter. Will this option be more or less attractive than the alternatives considered in exercise #1?

3. The Icanride Bicycle Company has the following projected sales demand for the next 6 months (assume each month has the same number of production days):

Month	Demand
1	2,500
2	3,600
3	2,900
4	3,300
5	4,000
6	3,500

Inventory costs them $10 per month per bike based on average monthly inventory (beginning plus ending inventory divided by 2), and any shortage costs them $15 in lost profit. They currently have 30 workers, each capable of producing 100 bikes per month. The workers can produce 20 extra bikes per month on overtime, but it costs an additional $14 in overtime cost per bike produced in overtime.

a. Compute the cost of using overtime and inventory production without shortages. Can they accomplish that goal under current circumstances?

b. Compute the cost of producing only using overtime and shortages (if necessary).

c. Which alternative is better? Discuss.

4. The Mesa Table Company has projected the following demand for their dining room table line:

Month	Demand
1	740
2	720
3	860
4	900
5	810
6	700

There are currently 20 workers on the line, each capable of producing 10 tables per week on regular time, and an extra two tables per week using overtime. A table produced using overtime costs an additional $40 per unit in overtime pay. They also have the option of using a local subcontractor, but to do so costs an additional $50 per table. They can also hire workers at a hiring cost of $2,000 per worker hired, and if a worker is fired or laid off there is a cost of $3,000 per worker. Any table remaining in inventory at the end of a month costs $10 per month based on the quantity at the end of the month (assume 4 weeks per month).

a. Compute the extra cost to meet all demand by using overtime and inventory. Subcontracting is to be used only if absolutely necessary. Hiring and firing of workers is not allowed.

b. Compare the extra cost in (a) with the cost of using hiring/firing and subcontracting, with no overtime and minimal inventory.

5. Another family of products for Mesa Table Company has the following projected monthly demand:

Month	Demand
1	1,000
2	850
3	600
4	500
5	650
6	700

There are currently 30 workers each capable of producing 50 tables per month. They have a no-inventory policy in this area because of lack of space. There is also no subcontractor for this line. They can lay off workers at a cost of $5,000 per worker. To bring them back costs an additional $4,000 per worker. The marketing department has suggested that if they start a promotion campaign immediately they can increase the demand during the last 4 months to 750 per month. The promotional campaign will cost the company $35,000. The company recognizes a cost of $300 per table in the event of a shortage. Based on financial considerations, should they give the marketing department permission to start the campaign?

6. The Imsocool Refrigerator Company has projected the following demand for their family of specialty refrigerators:

Month	Demand
1	200
2	250
3	400
4	510
5	500
6	450

There are currently 10 workers on the production line, and there is no physical space to have any more. Each of the workers can produce 20 of the refrigerators per month, with the capability to produce an additional four per worker per month on overtime. A unit produced by overtime costs an additional $30. The company can also use a subcontractor, but to do so will increase the cost $34 over the normal cost. The current price of the refrigerator allows for a profit of $40 per unit over normal cost. The marketing department announces that they can project that if they raise the price by $15, the demand during the last 4 months with high demand can be reduced to only 300 per month demand. Financially, should they consider the price increase or not?

7. The Cramer Computer Company has the following projected demand for the next 6 months:

Month	No. of Working days in Month	Demand
1	20	2,600
2	21	3,100
3	21	3,700
4	22	4,300
5	19	3,500
6	20	3,300

There are currently 100 workers, each working a normal 8-hour shift, 5 days a week. They can work an extra 10 hours a week in overtime, but it costs the company an extra $10 per hour in overtime costs. One of the computers takes 5 hours of worker time to produce. They can hire more workers at a cost of $3,000, with an additional cost of $5,000 if they lay off a worker. The company has a policy of not allowing shortages, but they are allowed inventory. Inventory costs $15 per month per unit based on average inventory levels for the month. There are no subcontractors for the units. There is a starting inventory of 60 units. Even though they have the "no shortage" policy, if one does happen to occur they charge $150 per unit due to lost profit.

Space will only allow them to have 110 workers. If they need more, they need to start a second shift. To do so increases the cost per worker by $1.50 per hour for a shift premium. A second shift also requires hiring support personnel (a supervisor, maintenance person, and material handler) at an additional cost of $20,000 per month.

Given all these conditions, find a satisfactory solution to help them minimize cost. (Hint: Do not look for an optimal solution. Instead try to set up the problem on a spreadsheet and look for patterns toward a good solution.)

8. The Biloxi Baby Buggy Company is preparing to develop a production plan for the next four quarters. They have a history of poor planning and they want to improve by using a structured approach. They currently have eight employees in their premium baby buggy (leather sides, stereo sound, and air conditioning) area, each of which is skilled and can perform virtually any of the tasks required to make the premium buggies. In order to plan better, they have gathered some data. They have found that it costs $800 to hire a new employee, but costs $1,200 to place an employee on layoff. Each employee can produce an average of 50 premium baby buggies each quarter. If they use overtime to produce, the overtime charges add an additional $200 to the cost of a buggy. Any buggies left in inventory cost them about $10 per buggy per quarter, based on the number in inventory at the end of the quarter. There are currently none in stock. The forecasted demand is for 700 in quarter I, 300 in quarter II, 900 in quarter III, and 500 in quarter IV.

a. Suppose they were to use a pure "chase" strategy with a no-inventory policy. What would the additional cost (over normal labor and material costs) be for the full year?

b. Suppose they were to use a level strategy where they had enough people at the start of the year to cover average quarterly demand, and then used overtime and inventory to accommodate the variations. What would the additional cost of such a plan be?

c. What additional considerations should be taken into account before making the final choice between the two plans? Which would you be likely to select and why?

9. The Whoareyoukidding TV Company has just completed the demand forecast for their 85-inch TV for the next year. The demand forecast is:

Quarter	Demand
1	350
2	480
3	400
4	370

The following policies are in place:

- They are not allowed to use overtime to build inventory
- They must use the maximum overtime before they can hire a new person
- They must stop all overtime before they let any employee go
- They must fill all customer demand (no stockouts)

The other data about the company:

- Each employee can produce 25 TVs per quarter
- The hire cost is $3,000
- The fire cost is $5,000
- The extra cost to produce one unit on overtime is $300
- The inventory cost is $40 per unit per quarter based on the number of units in inventory at the end of the quarter
- The maximum overtime is five units per quarter per employee
- There are now 11 employees
- There are now 20 units in inventory
  a. Develop a plan that uses Hire/Fire with minimal inventory. Determine the *extra cost* (above normal cost of labor, materials, and overhead).
  b. Develop a plan that hires employees only at the beginning of the first quarter, and after that neither hires nor fires anyone. All demand is met using overtime and inventory. Again, determine the extra cost of that plan.

10. The Shine-on Specialty Lamp Company has made the following quarterly forecast for aggregate specialty lamps requirements for the next four quarters (it may look like a lot, but it's really light work):

Quarter	Forecast
1	2,900
2	5,200
3	3,500
4	4,400

Each employee currently averages 300 lamps per quarter. To avoid hiring and associated benefit costs, they will authorize each employee to produce up to 30 lamps per quarter on overtime, although they will never authorize using overtime to build inventory. They want to avoid stockouts or backorders at all costs, so if regular work and overtime fail to produce enough, they will hire new workers. Any new hire can also be assumed to be able to work the overtime. Once they do have a new person, they will stop all overtime before they will consider putting anyone on layoff, but have no problem with a layoff if necessary. The current cost to hire a new employee is $2,000 and the layoff cost is $1,200. If they do use over-time, each lamp will cost an additional $40. If inventory is built up, they will incur a $3 per lamp per quarter inventory cost for each lamp in inventory at the end of the quarter.

a. Develop a modified chase strategy where overtime and inventory can be used, but the approach is to minimize inventory levels. Assume there are currently 10 employees. What is the total extra (inventory, hire/layoff, and overtime) cost of the plan?

b. Now develop a modified level strategy where you can hire (or lay off) at the beginning of the year only. There are to be no backorders, but inventory and overtime is allowed. What is the total additional cost of this plan?

11. The Shafer Company has the following demand data for the last 2 years of sales for all models of their popular Polybob product:

Month	2000 Demand	2001 Demand
January	233	254
February	301	325
March	421	398
April	355	369
May	296	324
June	288	297
July	232	255
August	194	241
September	273	256
October	243	266
November	221	235
December	247	249

The Shafer Company currently has five employees on the Polybob line, each capable of producing approximately two polybobs per day (assume 25 days per month). It costs them $4,000 per person to hire a new person, and $6,000 to lay a person off. The employees each earn $20 per hour for the standard 8-hour day, with $10 extra per hour premium for each hour of overtime. Each employee is limited to no more than 5 days of overtime per month. They can subcontract the production of the polybob, but to do so costs them $42 per unit above the normal standard cost. They can use inventory, but inventory holding costs are $25 per month per unit, based on the number of units in inventory at the end of the month. They have room for only 200 units in inventory, after which they must use a public storage facility, which adds another $15 per month to the inventory holding cost. They currently have (as of the end of December 2001) 29 units in inventory.

a. Use the demand data to develop a forecast for 2002 annual demand (month by month). What method did you use and why?

b. Use your forecast data to develop the "best" aggregate plan you can with the data given. Discuss why you think your method is the best, and also discuss the pros and cons of using your method over alternative approaches.

CHAPTER 4

The Master Schedule

Chapter Outline

Introduction—This chapter summarizes the concepts of developing and managing the master schedule. It is the next logical step in production planning, and assumes the proper resources have been planned, as is usually done in the Sales and Operations Plan (S&OP). It usually contains more detail than does the S&OP, but the typical time horizon is shorter than that of the S&OP.

Another important distinction between the master schedule and the S&OP is that while the S&OP is usually planned in terms of product families, the master schedule often represents final, sellable products. As a result, the master schedule represents a critical part of the planning process, in that it usually serves as the major "interface" between the production system and the external customers.

While some firms, especially small firms or firms primarily offering a pure service, do not have a formal master schedule, it could be said that every company has one. Even if done informally, every company has to have some method to promise customer orders and to translate customer order require-ments into a production schedule. Regardless of the formality or the name given to it, that mechanism is really a master schedule.

4.1   BACKGROUND AND LINKS TO THE S&OP

The S&OP "lines up" the proper resources in a very aggregate fashion, but only uses aggregate forecast data as demand input. While the S&OP serves a very important function in planning for long-range resource needs, there are usually no inputs from actual customer orders, and the planning is not typi-cally done at the final product level. As a result, there needs to be some addi-tional planning in more detail but for a shorter time horizon that allows the firm to:

- "Break down" the aggregated plans made in the S&OP into information more focused on specific, "buildable" products.
- Serve as a plan that uses actual customer orders in addition to forecast data.
- Serve as a source of information by which to develop much more specific capacity and resource plans.
- Serve as a method to effectively translate customer orders into effectively timed production orders for the facility.
- Serve as an effective tool for planning inventory levels, particularly at the finished goods level.

The planning activity that allows such planning to occur is typically called the master schedule. It is really a process that starts with (typically) a fairly de-tailed product forecast and, using a specified set of "rules," allows the actual customer orders to "consume" that forecast. Those rules then allow the trans-lation of the actual and projected customer orders into specific production or-ders—which may or may not reflect the customer purchase pattern, depending on the environment.

The master schedule typically has a great deal more detail than does the S&OP, and will typically have a shorter time horizon than does the S&OP. As stated in the S&OP chapter, the S&OP must extend far enough into the future to adequately address the resource issues for production, based on the lead times to obtain those resources. In addition, the master schedule values should add up to the values developed in the S&OP, since the S&OP was the agreed-upon plan developed at the high level to reflect the business strategy and busi-ness plan. The master schedule, on the other hand, only has to extend far enough into the future to address the cumulative lead time of the product or service being scheduled. The resources, assuming the S&OP has been man-aged properly, can be expected to be available already, at least in the aggre-gate. One way to view the relationship between S&OP and master scheduling is that the S&OP activity develops capacity constraints that serve as boundaries for master schedule planning.

4.2   MASTER SCHEDULE HORIZON

In order to be effective, it is ***extremely important*** that the master schedule needs to have a planning horizon equal to or longer than the cumulative lead time of the product or service being planned. In order to establish the planning horizon, we first need to look at a *bill of material* (also called a product structure). The bill of material shows all the components used to assemble a product. It typically will show not only the relationships between all components (which components are used to make which assembly), but will also show quantities needed for each component. Bills of material and their use will be explained in more detail in Chapter 6. The bill of material file that contains component relationship information will also typically contain lead times for purchase or production of each component or assembly. It is this lead time data that is used for calculation of cumulative lead time. As an example of cumulative lead time, take a product with a bill of materials four levels deep. Finding the longest lead time for each level, we discover the diagram in Figure 4.1.

Now assume that it takes

- 2 weeks to assemble product A from subassemblies B and C
- 3 weeks to assemble subassembly B from components D and E
- 4 weeks to assemble subassembly C from component F and subassembly G
- 5 weeks to produce subassembly G from component H
- 3 weeks to obtain component D from a supplier
- 2 weeks to obtain component E from a supplier
- 4 weeks to obtain component F from a supplier
- 7 weeks to obtain component H from a supplier.

FIGURE 4.1   A Sample Bill of Materials

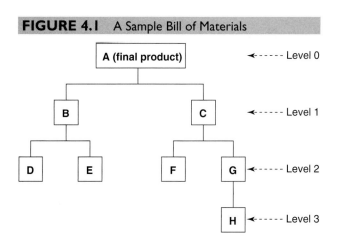

Going level by level, we can see the longest lead time for each level:

Level	Longest lead time
0 (end product)	2 weeks
1	4 weeks
2	5 weeks
3	7 weeks

The cumulative lead time of this product (A) is 18 weeks (2+4+5+7). If we don't plan out at least 18 weeks, we have little chance of delivering a customer order. As an example, suppose we had no master schedule. A customer ordered one of the products for delivery in week 14. We had no problem promising delivery, since the lead time for making the end product A is only 2 weeks. That will, in fact, be the case *assuming adequate inventory exists at the lower levels.* If we have not planned the lower levels, however, why would we have that inventory? If we do not have adequate inventory, follow what would happen:

- Since the customer wants the product in week 14 and it takes 2 weeks to build, we would need to start the end product production in week 12.
- Since the level 1 subassembly (C) takes 4 weeks to build and we need it to build the end product starting in week 12, we will need to start the production for subassembly C in week 8.
- Since the level 2 subassembly (G) takes 5 weeks to build and we need to have it completed by week 8 to use it for the level 1 component, we will need to start its production in week 3.
- Since the level 3 component (H, a purchased part) has a 7-week lead time, and we need it in week 3 to use it to build the level 2 subassembly (G), we will need to order it 7 weeks before week 3, or *OOPS*—4 weeks ago!

What this scenario above implies is the need to plan the production of product A at least 18 weeks into the future, and a plan made that far out may not have the benefit of knowing actual customer orders. We will, therefore, often have to build the master schedule initially with forecasts. As time progresses and we know the actual order, however, we can see that those actual customer orders will "consume" the forecast quantities, much as is shown in the diagram in Figure 4.2.

4.3   TIME FENCES

There is at least one potentially troublesome issue with the concept of using forecasts to plan production—it is a well-known principle of forecasting that forecasts are almost always wrong. Most people do not count on a forecast

FIGURE 4.2   Customer Orders "Consuming" the Forecast

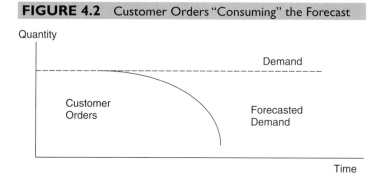

being correct, they are primarily concerned with "how wrong is it?" and "how do we deal with the anticipated error?"

For that reason some master schedules use **time fences** to establish rules for managing the master schedule. The two most common time fences are:

Demand Time Fence.   "Inside" the **demand time fence** the forecast data is often ignored, and only customer order quantities are used to make master schedule computations. For example, if a demand time fence is set at week 2 for the master schedule, the forecast data for weeks 1 and 2 are ignored for calculation purposes, regardless of how they may or may not agree with actual order data. In some cases the master production schedule for the weeks inside the demand time fence is considered "frozen," in that production has probably progressed to the point where it is either impossible or impractical to make any real change in quantity or timing. It should be clearly stated that the demand time fence is the one closest to the present time in the schedule.

Planning Time Fence.   This time fence is usually set equal to or slightly larger than the cumulative lead time for the product. In our earlier example of product A with four material levels, the planning time fence could be set at the 18-week mark. Beyond the time fence (19 weeks and beyond), there is adequate time to react to new orders, even if there will be a requirement to order the purchased items in the bill of materials, so the master production schedule values are very "free" to be changed. In fact, some master schedulers allow the computer to have control of master schedule actions beyond that time fence.

Between the demand time fence and the planning time fence (from 3 weeks to 18 weeks out in our example), there may be time to react in small ways to customer orders, changing both quantities and timing to a small extent based on the nature of the product and the environment. On the other hand, changes can be limited since there is inadequate time to order long lead-time purchased items (at least without incurring expediting expenses). Changes of this type are usually not allowed to be in the control of the computer, with the exception of offering exception messages and recommendations. Since some call the zone within the demand time fence "frozen" and outside the planning

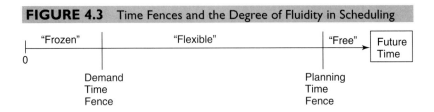

FIGURE 4.3   Time Fences and the Degree of Fluidity in Scheduling

time fence "free," this zone between the two time fences is then sometimes called "flexible." The general "rule of thumb" here is that the closer the schedule is to the present time, the less flexibility there will be to make changes without the potential to incur major problems. See Figure 4.3.

4.4   SOURCES OF DEMAND

Sometimes the master schedule is said to be a **disaggregation** of the Sales and Operation Plan (breaking down S&OP product family numbers into specific product numbers), but typically that activity is not a true numerical disaggregation. Usually what happens is that the master schedule is developed somewhat independently of the S&OP, but once developed it should be able to be aggregated back to S&OP values. This means that it is important that the master schedule numbers must agree with the S&OP production plan numbers, since the production plan numbers were agreed to at the high level during the S&OP process.

It should also be noted that the forecasting methods used for demand forecasting are often different for the master schedule when compared to the S&OP. S&OP forecasts are long-range, aggregate forecasts, often generated from causal methods (see the discussion in Chapter 2). While master schedule forecasts can be generated using those methods, they are more often generated from qualitative or time series methods, also discussed in Chapter 2.

Another major source of demand numbers for the master schedule is the actual customer orders. This is an issue that substantially sets the master schedule apart from other planning approaches, and also makes it a planning tool of critical importance for the firm. In many companies it is the only place in the planning system where actual customer orders represent the major input, and it becomes, therefore, a critical system for establishing and obtaining good customer service.

4.5   BASIC METHODOLOGY

Using demand (both forecast and customer orders) as input, the objective is to develop a preliminary master schedule to fit certain established priorities within the firm (many of which have been established as approaches toward production in the S&OP). For example, there are typically inventory plans, labor plans, plans for phasing in new products, and so forth. In addition, the master schedule has to accommodate additional constraints as seen in the S&OP, but now at a different level of detail:

- Meeting the customer needs for delivery as established in the S&OP
- Balancing the preliminary master schedule numbers against available capacity
- Establishing inventory levels according to the S&OP

Figure 4.4 shows a simple master schedule. It should be noted that the entire planning tool is called a master schedule, while the specific schedule production quantities and times are called the **master production schedule (MPS).**

The calculations are quite simple in this example. Note that we start with an on-hand quantity of 70 units. The demand in period 1 is 40 units, leaving us with 30 projected available at the end of that period. In period 2 we will expect to make 80 units (from the MPS value) and have a demand of 50 units. The difference between those, 30 units, will be added to the 30 units left after period 1 to give us a projected 60 units available in period 2.

This simple example shows all "sources" of demand (forecast and/or customer orders) lumped together. It also shows a case where there is obviously no existing plan to build inventory. Note also one major difference between the master schedule and the more detailed material requirement planning record (covered in detail in Chapter 6). In this case the MPS shows the *completion date* of the order, where as we will see in Chapter 6 that material requirements planning uses the last row of the record to show the projected *start date* of the order. Also, lot sizing is often done using the basic trade-off between the cost to set up and run the order and the cost of holding inventory above immediate demand. These trade-off issues are discussed in much more detail in Chapter 5.

FIGURE 4.4 A Sample Master Schedule

On hand = 70
Lot size = 80

Period	1	2	3	4	5	6	7	8	9	10
Demand	40	50	45	50	50	50	50	50	50	50
Projected Available	30	60	15	45	75	25	55	5	35	65
MPS		80		80	80		80		80	80

FIGURE 4.8   Sample Planning Bill of Materials

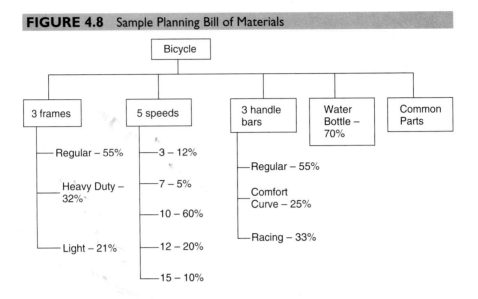

tion. Historic sales, however, may or may not capture current sales trends—especially if there are plans for advertising and/or promotional campaigns to promote certain options. Much in the same way safety stock of certain inventories are kept to accommodate unanticipated sales demand, in this case the **percentage overplanning** will accommodate extra demand for options. In this case, for example, the real historic sales percentages for the frames may have been 51% for regular, 30% for heavy-duty, and 19% for light. Sometimes this *option overplanning* is sometimes called a *mix hedge*—meaning a hedge against a higher than historical average demand for a certain mix of options.

- The percentage for the water bottle, too, may be inflated with a mix hedge. In this case, however, the customer does not have to select an option (such as in the case with frames and handle bars), but simply selects to have the option or not.

- The common parts are all those parts that are not options, but must be planned in the bill of materials if the product is to be made. The common parts list is not a buildable assembly, but merely reflects all those parts that are needed to make any of the bicycles, yet are not part of any option subassembly. There is no percentage here, as in you need as many parts as you plan to make bicycles, as is reflected in the end product forecast. Sometimes you may wish to overplan the real forecasted amount, which is an alternative to maintaining a specific safety stock of final product. For example, the actual forecast for any week of the bicycle may be 50 units, but you may input a forecast of 53. The extra three units are a final product overplanning, much like a safety stock. Since it is a hedge against overall market demand, it is sometimes called a *market hedge*.

4.10   THE TWO-LEVEL MASTER SCHEDULE

In those cases where a planning bill such as the one above is used, a two-level master schedule is sometimes used. The top level is where the projected demand forecast for the final product is input, and is also the source of MPS requirements for the common assemblies for the product, since the demand for those common assemblies equal the production of the product itself. The options, however, are a different story. To illustrate how the two-level master schedule works for our simple example above, we will examine the master schedule for the final product (the bicycle) and three of the options: The regular frame, the 10-speed option, and the water bottle. In this case assume there is no demand time fence, and a planning time fence of 10 (see Figure 4.9).

There are several numbers and other issues on the charts in Figure 4.9 that need explanation:

- The forecasts for options are really the expected amount to be sold given the condition of sales for the final product. For example, in the case of the regular frame, the forecast for week 1 is zero since there are none of the parent bicycles that can be sold. In week 2, the forecast for the frame is 10 units, which is (rounded off) 55% of the unconsumed 18 units of forecast of the final product ($100 - 82 = 18$). There are other approaches that some master schedules use (there is not one standard method). Some are very optimistic, some very pessimistic. The "middle of the road" method shown here is an illustrative example. To see other approaches, the reader is encouraged to consult more comprehensive sources on master scheduling. Many are available from the American Production and Inventory Control Society (APICS), and can be found by going to their website at *www.apics.org*.

- Even though available to promise is shown in week 1 for all the options, none of these will be sold in week 1 since there are no final products that can be sold that week. The ATP method shown here is noncumulative, so the ATP method is linked to a specific MPS quantity. In some systems a cumulative ATP is shown in which each ATP is calculated as the sum of the ATP for the MPS quantity for a specific time period added to the previous ATP. In other words, the cumulative ATP for period 2 would be the Single ATP from period 2 plus the single ATP from period 1. The cumulative ATP for period 3 would then be the single ATP for period 3 plus the cumulative ATP from period 2, and so on. Working the way backward from the last week of the record, the cumulative ATP is sometimes deemed to be easier to follow in two-level master schedules.

- In any case it does little good to show an option forecast in excess of the final product unconsumed forecast for any given week. It is impossible to sell more options than final product, unless the option also has independent demand. It is, of course, sometimes possible and desirable to sell more final product than forecast, in which case each option availability needs to be assessed individually.

FIGURE 4.9 Sample Two-Level Master Schedule

Assembly: Bicycle On-hand: 100 Lot size: 150

Week	1	2	3	4	5	6	7	8	9
Forecast	100	100	100	100	100	100	100	100	100
Customer orders	100	82	70	52	23	12	0	0	0
Projected available	0	50	100	0	50	100	0	50	100
Available to promise	0	68	28		127	138		150	150
MPS		150	150		150	150		150	150

Assembly: Regular Frame On-hand: 20 Lot size: 100

Week	1	2	3	4	5	6	7	8	9
Option Forecast	0	10	17	26	42	48	55	55	55
Booked orders	51	49	15	20	15	9	0	0	0
Projected available	69	10	78	32	75	18	63	8	53
Available to promise	20		65		76		100		100
MPS	100		100		100		100		100

Assembly: 10- speed On-hand: 5 Lot size: 90

Week	1	2	3	4	5	6	7	8	9
Forecast	0	11	18	29	46	53	60	60	60
Customer orders	70	2	52	45	13	6	0	0	0
Projected available	25	12	32	48	79	20	50	80	20
Available to promise	23		38	45	71		90	90	
MPS	90		90	90	90		90	90	

Assembly: Water bottle On-hand: 100 Lot size: 100

Week	1	2	3	4	5	6	7	8	9
Forecast	0	13	21	34	54	62	70	70	70
Customer orders	65	50	42	30	15	3	0	0	0
Projected available	25	62	99	35	66	1	31	61	91
Available to promise	25	50	28		82		100	100	100
MPS		100	100		100		100	100	100

- There are many different approaches to the two-level master schedule. Only one is shown here just to introduce the concept as a potentially valuable tool for certain ATO and MTO environments. A more complete analysis needs to be done prior to selecting a method.
- The potential power of the method is obvious. Suppose, for example, a customer wants 30 bicycles in week 2, all with regular frames, all with 10 speeds, and all with a water bottle. In that case we could promise delivery of 20 in week 2 and the rest in week 3. The reason: there are plenty of final products (ATP in week 2, even though the demand will cause final sales for week 2 to exceed the forecast. The only consequence is that if sales of later weeks equal forecast, an additional MPS may be needed). The problem is in the options. Water bottles are no problem, but the ATP for week 2 for the 10-speed is only 23 (borrowing from week 1—there will be no more sales for week 1 and there is no MPS in week 2 to replenish the supply). Similarly, the ATP for the frame is only 20, also with no MPS in week 2 to replenish. The customer will probably have to order different options or be content with getting 20 of their order in week 2 and the rest in week 3.

4.11   SOME NOTES ON THE MASTER SCHEDULING RESPONSIBILITY

The job of the master scheduler is a highly visible and important position, and every business—no matter how large or small, manufacturing or service—has a master schedule. It may be very informal and may even exist only in one person's head, but it is there. Key issues to keep in mind:

- The master schedule (even if an FAS is used) is the major link to customer orders.
- The master schedule should basically reflect the policy issues and constraints developed in the S&OP, including chase, level, or combination approaches to demand.
- MPS values are a reflection of the *completion* of the order.
- If the company is to operate effectively and efficiently, the master schedule must be developed in a realistic manner. Too often companies will fail to complete a plan made for one week and "roll" the uncompleted portions of the plan into the next week with no regard for capacity or other impacts. These "overloaded" master schedules are more indicative of an optimistic dreamer than they are of an effective planner. The proper approach is to update the entire master schedule as new information is received. Often this is done in a similar manner to the S&OP. Specifically, when the current time period reflected in the master schedule has passed, the schedule is rolled forward, implying the current period information is deleted and a new period is added to the end of the planning horizon, meaning the total planning horizon would remain the same. This is not done, of course, with-

out incorporating all relevant new information received since the last schedule was made, including inventory balances, forecast quantities, customer orders, and any other information that could impact the plan.

- Lot sizes are usually established much as they are for other items—basically involving a trade-off of inventory holding costs against the order cost. In cases where there is little or no order cost, often the lot size is to order just what is needed (often called *lot-for-lot*). In other cases, lot sizes are calculated or estimated as quantities where the total cost (holding cost and order cost) are minimized. In some cases, other conditions will impact the lot sizing decision. Examples might be limitations on storage space, concerns about spoilage or obsolescence, transportation issues, or perhaps restrictions on package ordering quantities from suppliers.

- Safety stocks, when desired, can be planned as an absolute number or a percentage of the forecast. Many people feel safety stocks (marketing hedges) are much more appropriate at the master schedule level, since the major uncertainty is external demand. In that way safety stocks can be minimized or avoided at a lower level and more detailed planning approaches where the predictability is much higher. With adequate safety protection at the master schedule level, numerous changes and replanning of MPS quantities can be avoided. This is desirable, since any change at the MPS level "ripples" its way through the entire bill of materials and may impact numerous components. This rippling effect is often called **system "nervousness."** The major decision that must be made here is another basic trade-off in business: cost versus flexibility.

- Sometimes the MPS values can be considered as a series of **firm planned orders,** especially within the planning time fence. A planned order is one that has not been released for production, meaning no actual company resources have been committed. Often a planned order, because it does not represent committed resources, can be allowed to be freely moved by the computer. A firm planned order, on the other hand, implies that even though there are no resources yet committed, the computer is *not* allowed to change the order, but only to recommend a change to the planner. In this respect the computer should never be allowed to move them or change quantity without an evaluation by the master scheduler. It must be remembered that if the MPS is within the planning time fence that numerous purchasing and production orders may have already been released for lower level components. A good general "rule of thumb" is to never allow a computer to have completely free rein on decisions that represent actual committed resources of the firm.

- Even though any changes should be carefully evaluated, the master schedule can still be very effectively used to evaluate "what if" scenarios. This can not only be valuable to evaluate production issues (e.g., equipment breakdown, supplier problems), but also can be effectively used to communicate possible order availability for customers.

- The master schedule generally represents an extremely vital part of the planning system for any company. Not only does it often represent the major interface with customer orders, but initiates the generation of production and purchasing orders that represent a major financial commitment for most firms. For that reason, it is highly recommended that control of the master schedule never be abdicated to computer control, even if the computer system is being used. It is just good business practice to always have a person responsible for any large asset use (as well as customer service) for the firm. Few things can make a top manager more frustrated than to investigate a major failure of the firm to plan adequately only to be told "the computer did it."

4.12   DEMAND MANAGEMENT OVERVIEW

At first it may appear an infringement on another function for planning and control functions to talk about "managing demand." After all, isn't that the responsibility of Marketing and Sales? In truth, there is clearly an overlap, but it falls (or should fall) under the heading of cross-functional communication or joint responsibility rather than infringement.

Why must we manage demand? Clearly an operation cannot simply become a passive order-taker, merely taking every order that any customer wants and promising delivery whenever the customer wants it. There must be coordination between Marketing, Sales, and Operations beyond the S&OP and more than just making a master schedule. There are two very important reasons that demand management is a significant topic for planning and control professionals to understand:

- Some demand is *internal to the company itself.* This may take several forms, including:
  - Service requirements, especially for field repairs
  - Requirements for new product engineering to build prototypes
  - Requirements for quality assurance for testing
  - Internal repairs or replacements for work-in-process
  - Distribution requirements
- Marketing and Sales tend to be much more flexible and can often change "direction" much more quickly than a typical operation can. It is often a fairly quick process to develop new marketing plans and identify new potential sources of customer demand—at least in comparison to the time it often takes an operation. Most operations are subjected to much longer lead times in several areas:
  - Changing capacity. Equipment, either in obtaining new equipment or developing new tooling for existing equipment

- Changing human capacity. Even if only people are involved, there are often issues of hiring and/or training
- Lining up suppliers, either with changes in product or quantity of product. Even altering the timing of purchase orders can be difficult, costly, or time-consuming
- Inventory considerations
- Phase in/phase out of designs

4.13   ELEMENTS OF DEMAND MANAGEMENT

There are at least four major aspects of demand management. They include:

1. **Prediction.**   This is essentially the forecasting of anticipated customer demand. There are, however, several issues that surround the forecasting issue. Most of those deal with the fact that forecasts are, almost by definition, incorrect. The issue for demand management is "how wrong are they" and "how do we cope with the incorrect information."

   - First, it must be realized that there are different forecasting methods for different purposes. Selecting the forecasting method that best serves demand projection for a given business system is a primary starting point.
   - Next, the forecast must be tracked and evaluated, both to help refine and improve the methods used and also to gain information as to expected forecast error.
   - Finally, we must find methods to cope with and lessen the impact of the expected error. Some of those methods include:
      - **Communication.**   This implies opening more effective lines of communication with customers, Marketing, and Sales in order to more rapidly and accurately understand the demand patterns. The communication channels can be written, voice, or electronic in nature.
      - **Influence.**   When the forecast is different from the resource availability, there is often a trade-off involved as to whether it is better to change resources or try to influence the demand with marketing tools. This is similar to the trade-off issues discussed and resolved at the S&OP level.
      - **Lead time reduction.**   If the lead time to produce an item and get it to the customer is less than the delivery time expected by the customer, then you can start production with close to perfect customer demand information. That is almost never the case, however, and the larger the time difference between total delivery lead time and customer expected lead time, the more you must start production well in advance of known demand. A well-known characteristic of forecasting is that the further out into the future you forecast, the greater the expected forecast error. The major implication of this is that if work is done to substantially reduce lead time, the forecast error and subse-

quent coping mechanisms can be significantly reduced, even if the lead time can never be equal to the customer delivery time.

- ***Production flexibility.***   This issue is highly related to lead time reduction, since both are impacted by process setup reduction. Basically, if the production processes are very flexible then the operation is more capable of easily and quickly shifting production to meet changing demand patterns.

- ***Policies guiding the development of both the S&OP and the master schedule.***   When the "higher-level" plans are made, they are often done so under explicit policies regarding desired customer service levels, inventory policies, policies toward using temporary workers, and so forth. The nature of these plans represent a major source of the ability of the organization to cope with unexpected demand.

- ***Safety stock or MPS overplanning.***   These are really a special case of master planning policies, specifically designed to cope with forecast errors.

Tracking demand.   Policies, safety stocks, and most of the other issues described under the coping mechanisms must have information in order to establish effective coping mechanisms, both in quantity and timing. That information comes from tracking and analyzing the nature of demand and comparing it carefully with forecasting methods. Not only will this lead to refinement of forecasting methods, but will also allow for careful development of methods and policies to cope with error and manage demand more effectively.

Service levels.   Most companies will, as a matter of strategy or policy, have some "target" level for their desired customer service often measured by order fill rates. These target levels need to be clearly understood by all involved with demand management, since they provide a major influence on the extent of use of these management mechanisms. For example, if safety stock is used as a major coping mechanism, a critical decision must be "how much safety stock and at what level in the bill of material structure?" There is a fundamental trade-off here, for larger customer service levels imply larger safety stocks for a given level of demand variability within lead time. This has clear cost implications, which in turn often have some influence on pricing policies. This same type of trade-off analysis is appropriate for virtually each of the coping mechanisms described above.

2. *Communication.*   The second element of demand management is effective two-way communication, especially with customers. Again, this may take several forms:

- Order entry. Clearly, this is an opportunity to obtain specific information from the customer as well as an opportunity to communicate specific order details and updates back to the customer.

- Order delivery date promising. Sometimes order delivery promises are given during order entry using standard lead times, but in some cases only after ATP logic or certain delivery constraints are examined. Some of these constraints include internal resources (equipment, people, etc.) while some are external to the company, such as suppliers, distributors, or material/capacity evaluations.
- Customer order servicing. Once the order is entered and promised, there is, in some companies, a need to continually communicate order status and other issues to the customer. In some cases, for example, the customer expects to inspect the product themselves before shipment.

3. *Influence.*   The ability to influence demand is one of the primary responsibilities of the Sales and Marketing function. To effectively manage the demand, however, the Sales and Marketing function must work closely with the Operations Planning function in order to understand both constraints and opportunities.

4. *Prioritization and allocation.*   Once the order is entered, it must take the proper position with respect to all other orders for products or services from the company. In some cases this is done naturally as part of the order promising activity, but in other cases orders are promised with a standard lead time, forcing the facility to continually prioritize the order bank and allocate resources accordingly. To do this there should be guidelines and rules established to ensure proper allocation of resources based on the priorities established as being appropriate for the business.

Impact of Operation Environments

If a generalization can be made as to the effect of environments on demand management activities, it would primarily be on customer communication and on the type of forecasting activity used. More specifically, the more the customer preferences are allowed to move backward into the production activity (from MTS to MTO), the more there is a need for customer communication of various types. Since forecasting is tightly linked to master scheduling, *what* is being forecasted and *how* will also be influenced (see Figure 4.10).

Make-to-Stock.   There is virtually no order promising, prioritization, or order servicing in a MTS environment. Communication is often at a minimum, as the customer will usually satisfy their needs from finished good stock. The only exception may be in cases where customers are willing to file backorders and backorders are a policy of the operation. In those cases, backorder information will need to be taken and communication channels designed.

In most facilities, however, the primary focus on demand management for MTS environments tends to be forecasting, inventory, and safety stock policies. Influence activities tend to be less visible in this environment, especially if the stock item is a standard commodity type. When it is not

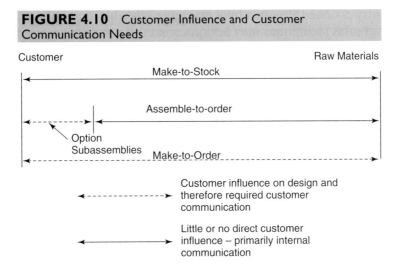

FIGURE 4.10   Customer Influence and Customer Communication Needs

standard, typical approaches to influence demand do tend to be used, ranging from pricing to advertising and promotional activity.

Since the primary operations function is to replenish stock, the forecasting is often done at the finished product level, as is the master scheduling activity.

Assemble-to-Order.   The ATO environment has more customer influence, in that the customer can order various combinations of standard subassemblies or options. Clearly in this environment there is order entry and order promising, with much of the focus on order promising made through the Available-to-Promise (ATP) logic of the master schedule.

Customer communication should be both ways, at least up to the point of influencing the design of the final product. As discussed earlier in the chapter, master scheduling is typically done at the option level, as is the forecasting. Order entry is primarily done through the final assembly schedule (FAS).

While flexibility tends to be fairly good in this environment with good planning and demand management actions, it must be remembered that flexibility steadily decreases as demand activity moves closer to the present time. For that reason, customer influence actions are both appropriate and frequently used.

Make-to-Order.   The MTO environment has an extensive amount of customer influence, forcing the master schedule and the forecasting to be done at or very close to the raw material level. Customer communication and order promising are very important, in that those actions influence virtually the entire production operation. The critical factor for order promising tends to shift from inventory to capacity management. Again, order

5.1   BASIC CONCEPTS OF INVENTORY

There are two important concepts that need to be clearly understood if one is to really take the proper perspective on managing inventory in a firm.

The first of these concepts is that much of a firm's inventory is really *stored capacity.* That means that most inventory represents the use of the firm's capacity to create a product ahead of the actual demand of that product. That concept is one of the major issues that makes the planning and control for a pure service firm so different from a manufacturing firm. The average service firm does not have the luxury of planning and using the capacity ahead of the demand for its use, but instead must use the capacity only once the demand is created.

The second concept is that inventory is almost never a problem in any company, in spite of the fact that it is often mentioned that "one of our problems is too much inventory." In most firms, *inventory exists as a symptom of the way the business is run.* While inventory is often claimed as a problem, it is a symptom, not the problem—albeit a very visible and expensive symptom in many cases. If one really wants to control inventory, they need to examine the managerial approaches to the business that will cause the inventory to exist. At least part of the chapter is devoted to explaining those relationships, and subsequent chapters will help highlight approaches to control them more effectively.

Most people think of inventory as physical goods, yet it does not have to be in some cases. An example may illustrate. Public accounting firms employ highly well-trained and valuable professional CPAs. They know that they must not have any layoffs without risking losing these people, which they do not like to see. The demand for services, however, tends to be highly seasonal—with the biggest demand being "tax season" (January through April in the United States). For many firms, the staff accountants work exceptionally long hours in the tax season, yet have little to do during the summer months. Some firms, therefore, "save" the extra hours spent during tax season in an hour "bank" instead of paying the accountant for the overtime (see Example 3–1). This bank of hours can then be used during the summer when the demand for their services is light, allowing the staff accountant to have an extended vacation period by using hours in their bank. In a sense, these hours are really an inventory, in that they represent using capacity ahead of demand. They use the capacity in January through April for the demand (for vacation time) later in the summer.

ANECDOTAL EXAMPLE (A TRUE STORY):

One production planning and control manager recently discussed one example from his early career, prior to his full understanding of inventory as a symptom of the way the business was being run. The company he worked for had experienced a slowdown in sales. The general manager of the company, concerned about profitability, asked the production planning and control manager to cut 15% of the inventory in order to bring inventory expense in line with the lower level of sales.

Without understanding, the production planning and control manager did what was asked of him—except that without a good understanding of the relationships between managerial approaches and inventory, he merely cut the inventory level without making any changes in the business processes. About 3 months after the initial request from the general manager, the planning and control manager was again approached by the general manager. The conversation went something like this:

GENERAL MANAGER: "What are you doing to my production facility?"

PLANNING AND CONTROL MANAGER: "What do you mean?"

GENERAL MANAGER: "We have all kinds of new problems—lots of premium freight shipments from suppliers in response to all kinds of part shortages, split lots being frequently run on the equipment—which are drastically increasing our setup costs, a major falloff in labor efficiency, and other similar problems—what *are* you doing?"

PLANNING AND CONTROL MANAGER: "I'm getting rid of 15% of the inventory."

GENERAL MANAGER: "Well, then, put it BACK!"

The point of this is that the Planning and Control Manager focused on the inventory as the problem and the focus of his efforts, not recognizing that it existed symptomatically. What he should have done was to first "fix" the system.

Keeping these two major points in mind, we need to first look at the reasons inventory exists before we can really understand well how to manage it. To the untrained eye, inventory looks like inventory ("stuff" sitting around), to the accountant it is cost and money "tied up," to the salespeople it is an opportunity, but to a good planning and control person it is a symptom of the way the business has been designed and is being managed. Once we understand *WHY* it is there (as a symptom), we can better understand *HOW* to manage and control it properly. Many of these reasons why inventory exists have categorical names related to several issues, including company policies, flexibilities, designs, customer responsiveness issues, and seasonal patterns. Specific explanations of these issues are in the next section.

5.2   CATEGORIES OF INVENTORY

The first categorical division of inventory is based on the *source of demand*. There are essentially two ways to categorize inventory based on the source of demand:

- *Independent demand inventory.*   The source of demand for this type of inventory is typically from sources outside the company itself, usually emanating from an external customer. It is called independent since the demand for it is essentially independent of any internal actions of the firm.

In many cases these items are the end items of production, often a "sellable" finished good.

- ***Dependent demand inventory.*** The source of dependent demand inventory is directly dependent on internal decisions, primarily on the decision of how many of which product to produce at what time. It should be noticed that some may think this is still dependent on customers, but in fact many firms can decide to produce at far different times and at different rates than what represents the external customer demand. This goes back to the concept of inventory as stored capacity.

An example may help clarify the difference. Suppose the company makes chairs. The demand for the finished chairs comes from external customers, and is independent demand. On the other hand, the demand for the seats, backs, and legs is dependent on the internal decision of how many chairs to make and when to make them.

The distinction between independent and dependent inventory is a very important distinction for production planning and control. The approaches and systems used to plan and control independent inventory are very different from those used for dependent inventory, and result in systems that are also often quite different from each other. Even the approach to capture the demand of each type is different. Independent demand is usually forecasted and then captured through sales order entry. Dependent demand, on the other hand, can be calculated based on the schedule of what to make and when.

The second categorical division is based on *the position of the inventory in the process*. The four general categories include:

- **Raw materials** represent inventory that has been purchased for use in the production process, but have had no value added by the company's production process.
- **Work in process *(WIP)*** represent inventory that has had some value added, but still has additional processing to be completed before it can be used to meet customer demand.
- **Finished goods** represent inventory that has completed all the processing from the firm. It is generally ready to be used to meet customer demand, with the possible exception of packaging.
- **Maintenance, repair, and operations (MRO)** inventory is material used to support the company's business and production processes, but typically will never be directly sold to a customer. It is made up of spare parts, machine oil, cleaning supplies, office supplies, and so forth.

The third and final categorical division is the *function or use of inventory in the process*. The most common categories in this area include:

- **Transit inventory** is inventory in motion from one activity to another. Inventory in the transportation system is the most common form.

- **Cycle inventory** is inventory that exists because for any time period the rate of replenishment exceeds the demand—a situation often caused because of order costs, setup costs, or packaging considerations. An example may clarify. Suppose an office supply store sells approximately 10 pens of a certain style per day, on average. When they order a replenishment supply from their distributor, the pens can only be shipped in packages of 500. When a shipment arrives, there are 500 (assuming that none of the old supply remain) in inventory. The next day there will be approximately 490, the day after that 480, and so forth. The inventory left from the shipment of 500 day after day for the next 50 days is called cycle inventory.

- **Buffer inventory** is also called **safety stock,** and exists "just in case." There are many situations that can occur in a firm that can disrupt the normal flow of work in the operation. Workers can fail to come to work, suppliers can be late with shipments or ship the wrong product, quality problems can occur, machines can break down, and so forth. Inventory that is maintained explicitly to protect the organization just in case one or more of these problems occur is called buffer inventory or safety stock.

- **Anticipation inventory** is inventory built up on purpose in anticipation of some demand in excess of the usual production output. The two most common uses for this are to accommodate seasonal demand or marketing promotions. Products that have highly seasonal demand will often have inventory built up during the periods of low demand in order to meet customer demand during the peak season. Also, if the marketing group is planning a special promotion or a sale of a product, the demand can (if the program is successful) be expected to rise significantly. As some firms have found out the hard way, planning a promotion without adequate product to meet the demand generated can be quite damaging to customer relations.

- **Decoupling inventory** is inventory that is purposely placed between operations to allow them to operate independently of one another. Again, an example may illustrate this function the best. Suppose we have two operations, A and B. Operation B uses the output from operation A. The capacity of A is 90 per hour while the capacity of B is 100 per hour (see Figure 5.1).

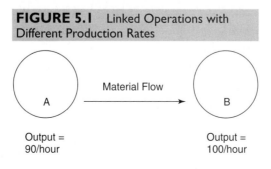

FIGURE 5.1 Linked Operations with Different Production Rates

A   Material Flow   B

Output = 90/hour   Output = 100/hour

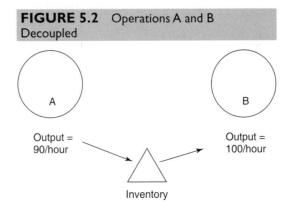

FIGURE 5.2 Operations A and B Decoupled

The problem with this situation occurs when the operators and the processes are measured by the typical approach used for many facilities, efficiency and utilization. In this case the operator for operation B is waiting for the output from operation A 10% of the time, impacting the efficiency of the operation negatively—and the poor efficiency is totally out of their control. If the facility wants to maximize efficiency of all operations, they may want to alter the situation to look like the following (Figure 5.2).

In this second situation illustrated by Figure 5.2, the inventory between the operations (decoupling inventory) serves to allow each operation to operate more independent of each other. Operation A can produce without worrying about B, by merely putting the output into inventory. Operation B can be run efficiently by using the inventory rather than waiting for the output from A. Operation A may need to work more hours than B, since B uses the inventory faster than A can replace it, but they can still be more independent of each other. One interesting fact should be noted in this discussion that may have impact in discussions in later chapters: *any inventory in the system, regardless of the reason for its existence, can serve as decoupling inventory, even if that is not the intention.*

5.3 THE BASIC INVENTORY LOT SIZING MODEL— ECONOMIC ORDER QUANTITY (EOQ)

The basic economic order quantity model attempts to balance the costs of having inventory against the costs of not having the inventory, with the overall objective to *minimize TOTAL cost.* The following list outlines some of the more significant costs of having and not having inventory.

COSTS OF HAVING INVENTORY:

- Storage, such as warehouse or stockroom expenses (in some cases this is not included because it may be considered a fixed cost of the operation)

$$EOQ = \sqrt{\frac{2DS}{H}}$$

One of the big disadvantages with this model is that it assumes near perfect conditions that are seldom if ever met. Some of the key conditions include:

- Demand is constant and uniform
- Lead time is constant
- Price per unit is constant
- Inventory holding cost is based on average inventory
- Ordering and setup costs are constant
- No backorders are allowed

If these conditions are seldom met (which is the case), one may wonder why the model is used (or at least cited) so frequently. There are two important reasons. The first is that most other inventory models are based at least in part on the concepts of the EOQ. Relaxing one or more of the basic simplifying assumptions of the basic model in fact develops many of the more complex models. The second reason is that the total cost curve in the relative vicinity of the EOQ is fairly "flat." That means that the "true" economic quantity can be violated by a fair amount before significantly higher costs are incurred. Another way of stating this is that the EOQ formula and concept are quite robust.

5.4   BASIC INDEPENDENT DEMAND INVENTORY REORDER MODELS

There are two basic categories of independent demand inventory replenishment models. They fall into the categories of quantity-based models and time-based models.

Quantity-based (continuous review) inventory models assume that a perpetual inventory position is monitored, so the inventory control system at any time can be used to tell exactly what the inventory position is. Given that these are models used for independent demand conditions, the basic assumption is that the demand is relatively uniform over time, producing the classic "sawtooth" pattern of demand over time, as shown in Figure 5.4.

The diagram in Figure 5.4 shows the gradual usage of the inventory until none is left. At that point the inventory is replenished with an amount equal to the EOQ. One unrealistic condition should be immediately evident in this discussion. That condition is that the model above assumes that when the zero quantity point is reached that an immediate replenishment can occur. In practice, of course, that is virtually impossible. It takes time to replenishment, regardless of whether the replenishment comes from an internal source (via

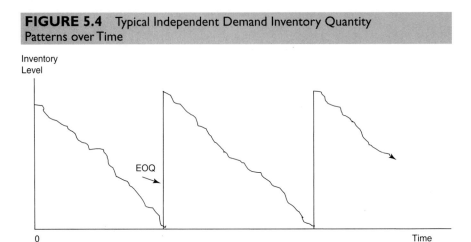

FIGURE 5.4 Typical Independent Demand Inventory Quantity Patterns over Time

production) or from an external supplier. The time it takes to make that replenishment is called the **replenishment lead time.**

Because of that replenishment lead time, we clearly need to place the order for replacement inventory before the zero point is reached. But how much before? The reason this is called a quantity-based system is that the decision to reorder is made when a certain quantity remains. That quantity is called the reorder point, and is determined by finding the amount of inventory that should cover demand during the time it takes to replenish the inventory. As an example, suppose we have customers buying an average of five units of some item per day. Also assume the supplier for the item will take 10 days to replenish the inventory after the order is made. Under those conditions, we will need 50 units in inventory at the time the order to the supplier is made or we will not have adequate inventory to cover customer demand while the supplier replaces the inventory.

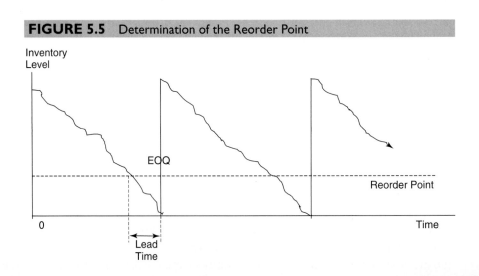

FIGURE 5.5 Determination of the Reorder Point

The formula for the reorder point is fairly simple:

$$R = \bar{d}L$$

Where R is the reorder point, $\bar{d}$ is the average daily demand, and L is the lead time in days. The same formula works if the unit of time is anything other than days, as long as the unit of time for average demand and lead time are the same.

One common problem many people notice immediately with this model is that several things can happen to disrupt the conditions established. The two most common are that the supplier is late with the replenishment of supply and/or the demand for the item during the replenishment lead time can exceed that which is expected. Either condition can cause a stockout, which is clearly a potential problem for the maintenance of good customer service.

The approach to deal with the customer service issues in an environment of uncertainty is to maintain safety stock (buffer inventory). The amount of safety stock is generally dependent on two issues. First is the standard deviation of the demand during the lead time. The second issue is the level of customer service desired. The standard deviation can be calculated from past experience, but the customer service level desired is established by the management of the company, usually based on the probability of meeting customer demand during the order cycle. The standard safety stock assumes a normal distribution of demand during lead time, with the formula typically given as:

$$SS = z\sigma_L$$

Where SS is safety stock, z is the statistical z-score corresponding to the stated customer service level, and σ_L is the standard deviation of demand during lead time. Some typical values for z are:

90% customer service level, $z = 1.29$
95% customer service level, $z = 1.65$
99% customer service level, $z = 2.33$

Clearly, the larger the desired customer service level, the larger the safety stock for any given variability in customer demand during lead time.

Occasionally the variability (standard deviation) of demand is given for a different time period than the lead time. In those cases an extra calculation has to be made in order to determine the standard deviation of demand during lead time. Suppose, for example, the lead time is given in days and the standard deviation of demand is found for a single day. In that case the standard deviation of demand during lead time, σ_L, would be found using the following formula:

$$\sigma_L = \sigma_d \sqrt{LT}$$

where σ_d is the standard deviation of demand for a day and LT is the lead time in days. This will also work for weeks, months, or any other time period under one condition: the lead time $MUST$ be expressed in the same time period units as is the standard deviation of demand during lead time.

When the typical reorder point is combined with safety stock, we have a new formula for the reorder point, taking into account the safety stock:

$$R = \bar{d}L + z\sigma_L$$

As stated earlier, it should be noted that the model in this form still has several simplifying assumptions, including a known and fixed supplier replenishment lead time, perfect quality for incoming material, and the capability to replenish the entire EOQ quantity at one time. Additional inventory models have been developed to deal with these and other assumed conditions, but those are beyond the scope of this book. In spite of these simplifying assumptions, one must always keep in mind that the model is robust enough to provide a reasonable approximation of the best replenishment quantity even under less than ideal conditions of stability.

We can now see how all these concepts work together with a simple example:

EXAMPLE

The XYZ outlet has a certain item, "A," that they sell. It has an average weekly demand of 50 units and a weekly standard deviation of demand of six units. The supplier quotes them a lead time of 3 weeks to replenish the stock of A with a unit price of $12. XYZ figures that it costs them $40 in total administrative costs each time they order the item. They also have estimated that the annual cost of holding inventory is 20% of the item cost. Management has stated that they would like to maintain a 95% customer service level. Using this information and assuming 52 weeks per year, develop the most appropriate inventory ordering policy.

Solution: Usually an inventory ordering policy for independent inventory consists of the quantity to order and the reorder point. Let's start with the order quantity. We use the EOQ to determine a reasonable estimate for that quantity:

$$EOQ = \sqrt{\frac{(52)(50)(40)}{(0.2)(12)}} = 208.17 \text{ or } 208 \text{ units}$$

Keep in mind that the EOQ is usually expressed as an annualized formula, so the weekly demand of 50 units has to be multiplied by 52, the number of weeks in a year.

The safety stock will be:

$$1.65(6)\sqrt{3} = 17.14, \text{ or } 18 \text{ units}$$

The total reorder point will then be the demand during lead time (50)(3) = 150 plus the 18 units safety stock, or a total of 158 units. Note that the 17.14 units was rounded up to ensure that under the conditions the 95% customer service level would be maintained.

The least expensive inventory policy is then (under the conditions given) to order 208 units from the supplier every time the inventory level reaches 158 units.

It should be noted that the EOQ formula can also be used to make the decision whether or not to accept a quantity discount price from a supplier. An example of that analysis is shown and discussed in Chapter 11, which deals more directly with purchasing issues.

Time-based inventory models have the advantage of not requiring a perpetual inventory balance being maintained. As the name suggests, these models merely allow the inventory to be used without keeping records updated until a certain time has elapsed. When that time has elapsed, the approach is to count the inventory remaining and then determine the appropriate replenishment quantity, again taking into effect the lead time.

If we assume the EOQ calculations are essentially correct, we can use the EOQ to determine the time intervals involved. For example, if we use an average of 2,400 units in a year, and the EOQ is 200 units, then we should expect to order 12 times per year on average (2400/200 = 12). That means the time interval should equal one order per month. If the demand does follow a relatively constant pattern, then the time interval associated with (D/Q) orders per year will usually mean the correct order quantity will roughly equal the EOQ.

Figure 5.6 shows a sample of what might be a time-based inventory model.

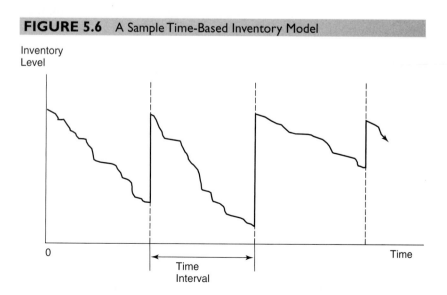

FIGURE 5.6   A Sample Time-Based Inventory Model

Time-based ordering is being used less frequently in practice for at least two reasons. First, there is greater risk involved. During the time period between checking the inventory it is possible that the demand could greatly exceed the normal pattern. In such a case, it is possible to run out of inventory before the time has elapsed to review, and many times people in the company do not even realize there is a potential problem. This generally implies the call for larger levels of safety stock, which will increase the overall inventory expense.

The second reason is that with new computer-based systems and bar coding, the task of keeping good perpetual records is becoming easier and less expensive. For example, the cash registers in many large retail establishments will often double as point-of-sale computer terminals, allowing the retail business to automatically deduct any sold item from perpetual inventory at the same time the receipt is generated for the customer.

5.5   INVENTORY CONTROL

Methods for properly controlling inventory are often ignored or given little exposure in many operations management books, yet remain a critical issue for many modern planning and control systems. These modern planning and control systems (such as ERP systems) are highly integrated computer-based systems that can be extremely effective and provide great benefits for a company using them properly. Unfortunately, they are also extremely sensitive to the accuracy and timeliness of the data used to generate their information. Far too many companies achieve far less benefit than is possible due to basic control problems, and inventory control is one of the most critical.

What level of accuracy is necessary? Clearly that is a matter of opinion, but most agree that an ongoing accuracy level in the very high 90 percentile range is required in order to maintain confidence in the accuracy of the information from modern planning and control systems. This is also dependent, of course, on the basic business policies of the firm, but if the accuracy levels are allowed to decline much below this high level, people will increasingly become skeptical regarding the information being generated by the system. Two clear symptoms of inaccurate information are growth in inventory levels (as people bring more in "just in case" the records are incorrect) and a corresponding growth in expediting activity as people are caught with inventory shortages when they thought adequate inventory existed for their need.

The right perspective.   The first issue that should be clearly understood is how to measure the accuracy level. Some take the accounting perspective resulting from the annual physical inventory. The following example illustrates the potential problem with that perspective. Suppose a firm has four items in their inventory — A, B, C, and D. The information they have on the item cost of those items and the number in inventory is given as follows:

Item	Cost	Quantity
A	$2	10
B	$5	4
C	$1	22
D	$3	8

The total value of the inventory is $86, found by taking [10($2) + 4($5) + 22($1) + 8($3)]. Now, suppose a physical inventory is taken. The actual count shows the following:

RECORD

Item	Cost	Quantity	Actual Count
A	$2	10	15
B	$5	4	0
C	$1	22	17
D	$3	8	13

The total value of the actual inventory based on the count is $86, again found by [15($2) + 0($5) + 17($1) + 13($3)]. From a pure financial perspective the inventory accuracy was 100%, in that the records showed $86 in inventory and the actual count confirmed that.

Unfortunately, from a planning and control perspective the actual record accuracy was 0%, in that not one single record was correct in the quantity of items. If someone claims the inventory records are correct, they should try to convince the person who counted on using the four units of item B for an immediate customer requirement! The message here is clear—from the perspective of planning and control, only the actual item count should be used to determine record accuracy. In fact, item count alone is NOT sufficient. In addition, the location of the items are just as important. Knowing a certain quantity of inventory is available does little good if someone does not know where the inventory is located.

Location Approaches for Stockrooms and Warehouses

There are three basic approaches for locating items in a stockroom or warehouse, each with certain advantages and disadvantages. The three are **home base, random,** and **zoned random.**

Home base implies that each item has its own distinctive location, and that the item is always stored in just that location. *The location is, therefore, dedicated to that specific item.* The advantage of this approach is that the location is always known and therefore easy to find. The disadvantage is one of space. The location needs to be kept open for that item even if there are currently none in stock. The problem gets much worse if new items are added to the system as products are added or engineering changes impact existing products. The number of locations will grow as new items are added, making an ever-growing demand for space. Clearly this approach works best when the items to be kept in inventory are quite stable in number and design.

Random is just the opposite approach. Whenever a new item is entered into the stockroom or warehouse, it is placed in whatever location is available (open space) *anywhere in the storage area.* This approach will generally maximize the efficient use of space, but there is one major disadvantage — namely, the location must be carefully noted and accurately placed into the location database. Any item that has any mistake in noting or recording the location may become almost completely lost, forcing a massive search of the entire storage area. This system is most commonly used where products are rapidly changing in design, making the home base approach far less practical.

Zoned random is a "hybrid" approach that attempts to combine the best of both approaches, and is generally applicable in all but the most extreme situations. The concept here is to identify a zone where items belonging to some defined class of goods (often commodity based) will all be stored. For example, there may be one zone for fasteners, another for electronic components, and so forth. *Within the zone, the items may be stored in a random fashion.* The advantage is as follows — the random storage of parts within the zone allows for efficient use of space, while the zone concept allows for easier investigation should the location be in error on the system. If a location is incorrect, only the zone needs to be checked – not the entire stockroom.

Maintaining Inventory Data Accuracy

One area of inventory control that is often underappreciated and sometimes even overlooked is that of keeping the inventory database accurate and timely. People will often either assume that the information in the system is accurate or else fail to realize how much poor accuracy will adversely impact the entire planning system. This section describes the importance of such data and some of the more common methods used to obtain and maintain the accuracy level needed for effective planning.

The risky approach is that some companies regard inventory control and stockroom or warehouse work as a mundane activity requiring little skill or responsibility. In these environments the workers in the inventory control area are often low paid and given little training or education. Often the workers in these companies view the inventory job as a "foot in the door," allowing them to later move into a "better" job as a machine operator, assembly worker, or some other job requiring more skill and better pay.

Whether that type of approach to inventory control is the cause or not, the fact remains that the costs of having poor inventory records will typically far exceed that of correcting the records and keeping them correct. Unfortunately, many companies will not realize the costs of poor records and attribute the problems to other causes. Some of the symptoms of poor inventory records include:

- Excessively high inventory levels. The more that people using the records to make decisions and plans suspect the accuracy of those records, the more they will have the tendency to request excessive amounts of inventory "just in case" the records are incorrect. One question commonly asked with respect to the issue of too much inventory is how can one tell that the level of inventory is excessively high? The starting point to answer that question begins with an analysis of the inventory turns. Turns are commonly calculated by taking the cost of goods sold for the year (from the income statement) and dividing it by the dollar value of the inventory on the books from the balance sheet. This figure can then be converted into the amount of inventory available in a time basis. For example, if the inventory turns are 3, that implies 4 months of inventory (12 months divided by 3 turns).

  That figure needs to be compared with what a reasonable level of inventory should be. That number can be calculated by looking at the routing information for a typical product. Add the total of all the times (processing, setup, move, etc.) and then consider the run time as a multiple of the lot size. Add in a reasonable allowance for queue time and other factors as appropriate (inspection and kitting, for example). Then compare that figure with the inventory turn figure. As an example, one company recently wanted to reduce their inventory so the inventory turns would change from 4 turns to 6 turns. The question was raised, "Is 6 turns reasonable? That represents only two months worth of inventory." After an examination of the routing for their major product, it was noticed that the total setup and processing time was only 4 hours! Even with a very liberal allotment for non-value-added activities, the 2 months of inventory turns represented by the 6 turns appeared to be far too much. This issue of "too much" is, of course, also related to business policies concerning inventory levels, but at least the analysis suggests that such policies should be reviewed to determine if they are reasonable. If so, then the focus for improvement should be on the causes of such levels of inventory.

- Premium freight shipments. These commonly occur when the records indicate that a certain item supplied by an outside supplier is in stock and not in need of replenishment, and then the discovery is made that the stock position is much smaller than indicated. In these cases the firm often needs to place a rush order, and usually has to request shipment by the fastest means possible. The fastest method of shipment is often not the least expensive, causing excessive shipping costs.

- Expediting. Expediting can occur for both internally produced and supplier products. While it is sometimes done in response to a customer request, it also often occurs when the actual inventory position is much less than indicated on the records. Expediting causes many people to bypass systems, create inefficiency, and in general expend a great deal of extra time and money to try to get the inventory replenished in a time frame much shorter than the usual replenishment time.

- Split lots. Often a result of expediting, split lots can occur when a normal production run has its setup broken to use the equipment to produce another part in short supply. Often the original setup has to be redone after the expedited run is complete so the rest of the normal production lot can be finished. The activity of setting up equipment twice for a single production run costs the company both time and money.

The Structured Approach

The first thing that should be understood is that all inventory accuracy is not alike. If you have some inventory that is worth several thousand dollars each, then even missing one unit is serious. On the other hand, a small screw worth $0.005 is not worth bothering with. The process used to establish the relative importance of an item is called ABC inventory distribution. The concept is to separate the inventory based on the annual dollar usage. Annual dollar usage is, of course, the dollar value per item times the average number of items used per year.

There is no hard rule for the separation of A, B, and C items, but the "rule of thumb" that is often used is to list all items in order of highest annual dollar usage to lowest. The top 20% of the items will often represent the A items, those between 20 and 50% will be the B items, and the lowest 50% will be the C items. It is often found, as indicated in the generic distribution graph shown in Figure 5.7, that the A items, while representing only 20% of the total items, may represent from 70 to 80% of the annual dollar investment of the firm.

Once the items have been classified, the attention paid to the control of an item will be based on that classification. "A" items, for example, will often be monitored very closely and have the accuracy of the data checked as often as once a month (in some cases more frequently). If the "A" items can be easily moved, they are often kept in a locked storage area or tightly controlled in other ways. "C" items, on the other hand, will often have far less control. In some cases they are treated like independent inventory (using a reorder point) even if they are dependent demand items. They will often have a large amount of safety stock, as the inaccuracy of the records has a far greater tolerance. These records are also checked far less often—usually only once a year. The "B" items, as one would suspect, are treated more carefully than "C" items, but not monitored as closely as are the "A" items.

There are some cases when a low-cost item may be artificially elevated to an "A" classification. Suppose, for example, that a low-cost item has a very long replenishment lead time and there is a very large penalty for a stockout. This may come from the part being a required part for a large assembly and there are no substitutes. Missing the one part can cause delay of a major high-value shipment while replenishment is underway, and if that delay is long it

FIGURE 5.7   A Sample ABC Inventory Distribution

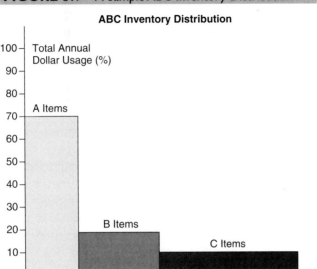

could cause serious erosion of customer confidence and loyalty. Under those circumstances the firm may elect to purposely elevate that item to an "A" classification, even though the quantitative analysis would normally classify the item as a "C" item.

As is suggested by the above discussion, one of the major purposes of the ABC classification is to indicate those items that deserve closer attention and a higher level of inventory accuracy because of the financial implications to the firm of an inaccurate record.

Obtaining Accurate Inventory Records

There are basically two methods to check records for accuracy and correct those found to be incorrect. Those methods are a **complete ("wall-to-wall") physical inventory** and **cycle counting.**

"Wall-to-wall" physical inventory. This process involves establishing a fixed time period to physically count all the items in inventory for the entire operation. Often the production processes may need to be suspended for several days while this is being done, especially since the production workers are sometimes called on to assist with the count.

This process is often done at least once per year, often in conjunction with the accounting fiscal year cycle. The accounting system will typically require an accurate dollar value of the inventory, as it usually appears as a major asset on the accounting balance sheet of the firm.

The problem with this approach goes well beyond the obvious problem of the loss of production while the count proceeds. Counting parts for several hours over several days is tiring and boring, especially for production people not used to doing that type of work. Human fatigue and apathy will often produce new inaccuracies in the count. In addition, so many people handling parts in this manner increases the risk of damage or mislocating the parts after the count is made. In addition, since this process is typically done only once per year, the inaccuracies will build over time, especially if the transaction system recording the inventory usage and flows has any flaws.

Cycle counting.   Cycle counting is often used as a highly preferable alternative to the wall-to-wall physical inventory approach by many companies. As the name implies, this approach is to count each item on a defined cycle throughout the year. Specific individuals are trained and assigned (often as a full-time job) to perform the cycle counts throughout the year. This is often done instead of, not in addition to, the annual physical inventory count.

Each day there are certain items identified to cycle count. These items are counted and inaccurate records corrected. Record correction is, however, not the primary purpose of the approach. *The primary purpose of cycle counting is to track down the cause of the incorrect record and fix the process so that the records have a better chance of being maintained correctly between count periods.* Essentially, if an incorrect record is discovered, all transactions for the record since the last time the record was known to be correct are listed. The cycle counters then try to discover which of the transactions caused the accuracy problem and why. The process can then be corrected. Many cycle counters in companies that use the process correctly have to be knowledgeable people that understand the systems and processes of the company. They clearly have to have many skills beyond just their ability to count parts.

The primary purposes of cycle counting are, then, to:

- Identify the causes of record errors
- Correct the conditions in the processes that cause the errors
- Maintain a high level of inventory record accuracy for both count and location
- Provide a correct statement of assets for the accounting system

There are several approaches that can be taken to identify the items that need to be counted during the cycle count on any given day. The more common methods include:

- *The ABC system.* This implies the frequency and the definition of "accurate" will depend on whether the item has been classified as an A, B, or C item as described earlier. There is no hard and fast rule, but most will use something like the following:

Classification	Frequency of count	Accuracy level
A	Once a month or more frequent	1%
B	Every 3 months	5%
C	Once a year	10%

What this shows is the "A" items are counted more often and a much lower tolerance of inaccuracy is acceptable. This is, of course, because of the much higher dollar value of those items. There is sometimes an issue raised as to what to do if the record and the count are different, but still within the accuracy tolerance. For example, suppose the record for a "C" item shows 920 in inventory but the count shows 905. The percentage difference is only 1.6% (15/920), which is far less than the 10% allowable accuracy percentage. Should the record be changed to show the 905 or left at 920? Again, approaches differ in practice, but the position of many companies is to leave the record alone since it is within the tolerance level. This is because the cycle count itself may be somewhat off. Sometimes companies will require a double count in the case of an inaccurate record just to confirm that it is the record and not the first count that was in error. While this method provides a good opportunity to obtain the most accurate record, it is costly in both time and money, and is usually not worth the expense, especially for "C" items.

- *The reorder system.* This approach is to count items at the time when they are reordered, meaning their inventory is likely at a very low point and therefore much easier and quicker to count.
- *The receiver system.* Similar to the reorder point approach, the inventory is likely to be low when new items are received, making the counting process easier.
- *The zero or negative balance system.* When the record indicated a zero balance or a negative balance, it would be quite easy to check, since again the inventory should be quite low (if it exists at all). This becomes especially important if the record indicates a large negative balance.
- *The transaction system.* Count when a specified number of transactions have occurred. The idea here is if there has to be some "detective" work done to find out the cause of any errors, the detection of the cause will be easier if there are not too many transactions involved.
- *The zone system.* If the zone random system of location is used, sometimes a complete zone is targeted for a cycle count. This makes it easy to determine location identification problems.

Cycle count advantages.   There are numerous advantages to using an effective cycle count program. They include:

- Operations do not have to be suspended
- The annual physical inventory can be eliminated

- Errors can be more quickly discovered
- The causes of errors can be tracked more effectively and quickly, and processes can be corrected more effectively
- Records can be adjusted as necessary throughout the year
- Overall record accuracy generally improves greatly
- Correct statements of assets can be obtained throughout the year—no big year-end inventory "shrinkage" surprises
- Improvement efforts can be concentrated in problem areas
- Specialists (cycle counters) become effective in getting good counts and count procedures and can become effective problem solvers for process problems.

KEY TERMS

Independent Demand Inventory
Work in Process
Maintenance, Repair, and Operations (MRO) Inventory
Anticipation Inventory
Decoupling Inventory
Replenishment Lead Time

Zoned Random Location
Cycle Counting
Dependent Demand Inventory
Finished Goods
Buffer Inventory
Economic Order Quantity (EOQ)
Home Base Location

ABC Inventory Model
Shrinkage
Raw Materials
Transit Inventory
Cycle Inventory
Random Location
Physical Inventory

SUMMARY

This chapter describes the functions and importance of inventory, and discusses some of the more common approaches to plan and control inventory levels. One of the most common tools to use for establishing inventory order quantities is the economic order quantity (EOQ), and the development and potential use of the EOQ is discussed. In addition, alternative control methods for inventory are introduced and discussed.

Probably the most important considerations for planning and control of inventory are given by two simple but critical observations. First is that inventory should be considered to be stored capacity, and should be treated as such. The second is that inventory always exists as a symptom of the way the business is designed and managed. It should never be considered a problem, but can be viewed as an extremely valuable asset, can be used to determine how the overall operation is being planned and managed, and can also be used as an ongoing measure for the effectiveness of the operational planning and control systems.

REFERENCES

Bernard, P., *Integrated Inventory Management.* New York: John Wiley, 1999.

Fogarty, D. W., J. H. Blackstone, Jr., and T. R. Hoffmann, *Production and Inventory Management.* Cincinnati, OH: South-Western, 1991.

Schönsleben, P., *Integral Logistics Management.* Boca Raton, FL: St. Lucie Press, 2004.

DISCUSSION QUESTIONS AND PROBLEMS

1. The basic reorder point assumes you will order as soon as you reach the reorder point. What happens if the item is only one of several that is ordered from the same supplier? Discuss how joint replenishment from a single supplier might alter your inventory model.

2. Describe the type of inventory policy you might find in each of the following operations, and describe why—a hospital, a cafeteria, an automobile repair facility, a bakery, and a dental office.

3. One of the products stocked by Joe's Club is *JoesCola,* which is sold in cases. The demand level for *JoesCola* is highly seasonal.
   - During the *slow season,* the demand rate is approximately 650 cases a month, which is the same as a yearly demand rate of 650*12 = 7,800 cases.
   - During the *busy season,* the demand rate is approximately 1,300 cases a month, or 15,600 cases a year.
   - The cost to place an order is $5, and the yearly holding cost for a case of *JoesCola* is $12.
     a. According to the EOQ formula, how many cases of *JoesCola* should be ordered at a time during the *slow season*? How many cases of *JoesCola* should be ordered during the *busy season*?
     b. Suppose Joe's Club decides to use the same order quantity throughout the year, resulting in an order quantity of 150 units. Calculate total holding and ordering costs for the year. Do *not* consider safety stock in your calculations. To do your calculations, annual demand can be calculated as an average of the slow and busy rates given above.

4. Continuing with the basic information in problem 3, during the busy season, the store manager has decided that 98% of the time, he does not want to run out of *JoesCola* before the next order arrives. Use the following data to *calculate the reorder point* for *JoesCola.*

Weekly demand during the busy season:	325 cases per week
Lead time:	0.5 weeks
Standard deviation of weekly demand:	5.25
No. of standard deviations above the mean needed to provide a 98% service level:	2.05

5. Because computer technologies become obsolete so quickly, a well-known computer manufacturer is thinking about raising holding costs from 30% of item cost

to some **higher** percentage. What will be the impact on the economic order quantity for monitors? You **must** explain your answer using any formulas or examples you think are helpful.

6. The following data exists for the computer manufacturer in problem #5:

Estimated annual demand:	15,376 monitors (50 weeks per year)
Cost:	$640 per monitor
Lead time:	2 weeks
Standard deviation of weekly demand:	16 monitors
Holding cost per unit per year:	40% of item cost
Ordering cost:	$25 per order
Desired service level:	95% (z = 1.65)

a. Calculate the economic order quantity for the monitor. Round your answer to the nearest whole number.

b. Suppose the company decides to order **64 monitors at a time.** What would their yearly holding and ordering costs for the monitor be?

c. Based on the data, what should the **reorder point** be for the Viewsonic monitor?

7. The Ajex Company has several items they store in inventory. The table below shows the annual demand and the item cost. Develop a logical classification for the inventory based on ABC:

Item	Item Cost	Annual Usage (# units)
C34	$12	4,000
B99	$23	8,000
V94	$19	5,500
H64	$41	1,200
P77	$72	400
Y12	$62	1,100
R74	$33	1,440

One additional item, the M22, has a very low usage (300 per year) and a low item cost ($3 per unit), but has a very long lead time and is often difficult to obtain. How should that item be handled and why?

8. The Polybob Company is looking at total inventory costs for some of their "A" items in inventory. They cycle count all the "A" items four times a year, and given that they use only skilled people, they estimate that each "A" item costs an average of $0.12 in labor costs to cycle count. They currently use a customer service level of 99% (z = 2.33) to establish safety stock, but are considering moving to 90% (z = 1.29). One product they are evaluating has an item cost of $53.50, an annual demand of 1,500, and a weekly standard deviation of demand of 6. They recognize an order cost of $21 per order, and a holding cost of 23% per year. The replenishment lead time is 3 weeks. Using a cost analysis only, should they change the customer service level or not? What other considerations should be made before making the final decision?

9. You are in charge of inventory for Bongo's Appliance Outlet. The recent demand for the Gremlin brand of microwave ovens has followed the following pattern:

Week	1	2	3	4	5	6	7	8	9	10
Demand	53	22	32	61	17	37	43	24	53	30

Bongo's recognizes a carrying cost of 23% per year for their inventory. They purchase the ovens from the manufacturer for a wholesale price of $163 each. It costs them $200 to make one order, including purchase and shipping costs. There is a 2 week lead time for delivery once the order is made. Bongo's also has a policy of maintaining a 95% customer service level.

a. What should the inventory policy be (order quantity and reorder point)? Discuss any implications or problems you might see with the inventory policy.
b. The manufacturer has approached Bongo's with an offer to negotiate a price discount if Bongo's will order 500 ovens at a time. They said they would be able to keep the purchase and shipping costs the same. What is the highest the wholesale price can be and still make the offer an attractive one financially?
c. The person responsible for forecasting demand for appliances has just sent you a note. It states that the market appears to be changing and they offer as evidence that the MAD for the forecast for microwave ovens has gone from 12 to 23 units in only 6 months. How would you interpret this and what would your response be?

CHAPTER 6

Material Requirements Planning

Chapter Outline

Introduction—The fundamental concept behind material requirements planning (MRP) is really quite simple. As an analogy, suppose you have been assigned by your family to plan the meals this week. Probably the first thing you would do is to fill out a menu. To continue, suppose that for dinner tonight you have planned lasagna as a main dish. Now what? You would start to answer the question by counting how many people you need to serve, thereby figuring out how much lasagna to make. Logically, you would then need to find out what ingredients are used to make the lasagna, and then find the process steps to prepare the ingredients. Both of these are typically found on the recipe. Once you know the ingredients, you need to figure how much of each do you need for the amount of lasagna you plan to make. Then you would typically find out how much you need to buy, given that you may already have some of the ingredients on hand. For example, if you need three boxes of lasagna noodles and you already have one, you only need to buy two. You also need to figure timing. If, for example, it takes 90 minutes to bake the lasagna, 1 hour to prepare the ingredients, and 2 hours to shop for the necessary ingredients, you would need to start the process at least 4.5 hours prior to the scheduled meal time.

The process described above is precisely how basic MRP works. The major difference is in the terminology and the structured formality associated with MRP. The following are the associated MRP terms with the examples above:

- The menu calling for the lasagna—called the **master schedule**
- The list of ingredients—called the **bill of materials**
- The process steps to make the lasagna—called the **process routing**
- The total amount needed of any ingredient—called the **gross requirement**
- The amount needed to buy, after subtracting inventory—called the **net requirements**
- The time it takes to perform all the steps—called the **lead time**
- The time to start the buying process offset for lead time—called the **planned order release.**

6.1   BACKGROUND AND FUNDAMENTAL CONCEPTS

The fundamental concepts inherent with MRP have been known for many years before those concepts were effectively used. Prior to MRP use, most companies used variations of the reorder point system, where inventory was allowed to shrink to a certain critical reorder quantity, at which time a standard replenishment quantity was ordered—in other words, the basic reorder point model commonly used for independent inventory (see the detailed discussion in the chapter on inventory management).

The major reason MRP was not used was the very significant quantity of calculations required. It was not until the availability of relatively powerful, reliable, and cost-effective computers that an MRP system really became viable.

The Problem with Reorder Points

The reorder points described above are typically found with independent demand inventory. **Independent demand inventory** is inventory whose demand is independent of internal operational decisions. The typical dependency is only on external customer demand. Independent demand inventory is therefore typically the finished goods of the operation or customer demand for spare parts used to service a product. **Dependent demand inventory,** on the other hand, is inventory whose demand is based on internal decisions—usually how much of a product we choose to make and when we choose to make it. This may or may not equal the external customer demand for the product.

To return to the earlier analogy, suppose we recognize the need to feed six people with our lasagna dinner, with each person expected to eat about 0.4 kg of lasagna. That would call for 2.4 kg to be made. Dinner time is at 6:00 P.M., meaning we should start the preparations at 1:30 P.M. Our decision, however, is to make 4 kg (we like leftovers), and because we would like to do something else in the afternoon, we will start the preparation at 8:00 A.M. and just plan on reheating the meal at the proper time. The 2.4 kg represents the independent demand for our meal, but the demand for timing and quantity of lasagna noodles (dependent demand) is based on the need to make 4 kg with the process starting at 8:00 A.M., because that was our internal decision.

To return to the major discussion, reorder points do not work well in most dependent demand situations because of order quantities and lead times. To illustrate the point, let's examine a simple product, a two-drawer filing cabinet. The finished product, sold in office supply stores, clearly has independent demand. To help illustrate the point, we will assume constant demand over time. We have some inventory, Q, at time zero in the diagram in Figure 6.1. Over time as customers purchase the cabinets, the inventory drops in a uniform fashion.

Eventually, of course, we will run out of cabinets if we don't reorder. Given that there is some lead time to replace the cabinets, we will order when the quantity gets low enough to just be able to satisfy our needs for sales until the next shipment arrives. This is the most basic reorder point, reflecting a quantity represented by demand during replenishment lead time, as illustrated in Figure 6.2.

The diagram in Figure 6.2 shows the quantity drops until it reaches the reorder point (A), at which time the replenishment quantity (typically the EOQ) will be ordered. The quantity in inventory continues to decline during the lead time required to replenish the stock. Finally at point B the new stock comes in, and the quantity in inventory returns to the original level. This "sawtooth" pattern is very typical of independent inventory with relatively constant demand, as was discussed in the previous chapter.

If the replenishment quantity is ordered from an outside supplier, the lead time is often quoted by the supplier. The issue is different if the replenishment quantity is being produced in the company's operation, however. Calculating or estimating lead time can be a somewhat complex issue for most operations. The elapsed time comes from several sources, including:

- **Purchasing lead time (raw material delivery lead time)** — the time it takes a supplier to deliver the part, if it is purchased from an outside source.
- **Move time** — the time it takes to move a job from one operation to another.
- **Setup time** — the time to set up the equipment to perform a defined job.

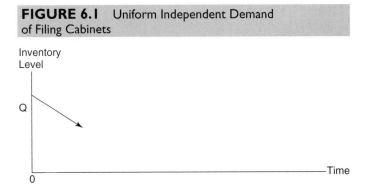

FIGURE 6.1   Uniform Independent Demand of Filing Cabinets

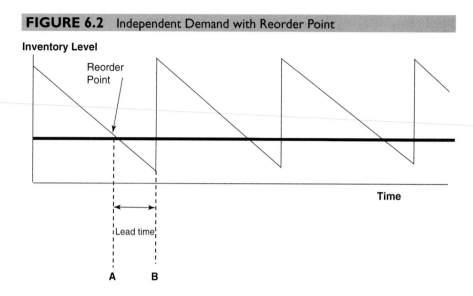

FIGURE 6.2 Independent Demand with Reorder Point

- **Processing time**—the time it actually takes to perform the defined operation on the part.
- **Wait time**—the time a job has to wait to be moved after it has been processed on a given operation.
- **Queue time**—the time a job must wait to be processed once it has been moved to the operation.

It is interesting to note that for most manufactured items the queue time often represents the *major portion of lead time by a large margin.* That fact will become an important consideration when we discuss just-in-time or "lean" production in a future chapter.

Now let's examine the usage pattern for one of the component parts, the cabinet drawers. Even though there may be some independent demand for the drawers, clearly the demand for drawers comes almost exclusively from the demand to make and replenish the supply of the finished cabinets. Figure 6.3 shows the relationship between the demand for the drawers and the reorder point for the cabinets.

In Figure 6.3, reaching the reorder point for the cabinets (A) triggers an order for the factory to replenish the finished cabinets. The bottom portion of the diagram shows the demand for the drawers. At time zero there is no demand for the drawers. There is no demand to make finished cabinets (only sell from inventory), and since in this figure the only demand for the drawers comes from the need to make the cabinets, the demand for drawers is zero. This demand stays zero (showing as a flat demand line) until the reorder point (A) for the cabinets is reached. That reorder point triggers the demand to make a new batch of finished cabinets. Suddenly the demand for drawers is

FIGURE 6.3   Cabinet Reorders Impacting Drawer Demand

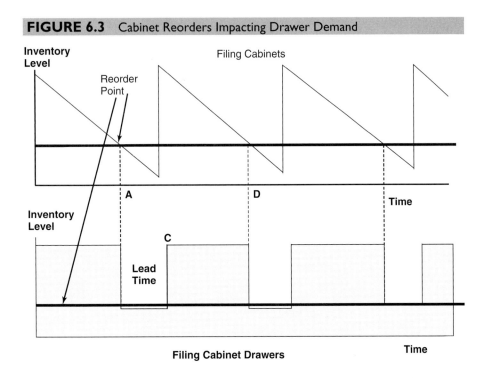

Filing Cabinet Drawers

very large. For example, if the order is to replenish 100 of the finished cabinets, there is a virtually instant demand for 200 of the drawers, shown in the diagram as a vertical drop in drawer quantity.

Since the inventory of the drawers has now fallen below its reorder point, an order to replenish the drawers is generated. After the lead time has elapsed, the drawers have now been replenished at point C. The inventory will again stay constant until demand hits again, which won't happen until the call comes to build and replenish the supply of the finished cabinets, shown on the diagram as point D.

The problem with this "lumpy" demand for the dependent demand inventory items comes primarily from batch lot sizes, and the reason it is not desirable is clear from Figure 6.3. All the material in stock of the drawers (shown in the diagram as the shaded area under the drawer quantity line) *represents inventory—costly, difficult to store inventory.* This pattern is repeated for other dependent components (for example, raw steel, locks, handles, etc.).

The MRP solution comes from a simple premise: If we can project requirements, then with knowledge of the starting inventory we should be able to predict or calculate when the reorder point for the finished cabinets will take place. Knowing that, we should be able to keep the inventory of the drawers low until just before we need them to build the next batch of finished cabinets. That situation is shown in Figure 6.4.

FIGURE 6.4   Keeping Drawer Inventory Low until Needed

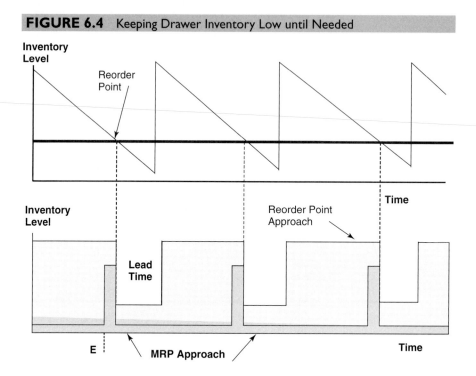

In the diagram in Figure 6.4, the inventory of the drawers is very low (shown in the darker shaded part of the curve). Since we now have a prediction of the timing and quantity of the reorder point, we can build up the supply of drawers just prior to their need, as shown as point E. That inventory is used very quickly. Clearly the cost associated with the darker shaded area above is significantly less than the old approach. This is the purpose and principle behind MRP, with the projection of finished goods (filing cabinets) timing and quantity being projected in the master production schedule (MPS).

6.2   BILLS OF MATERIAL

At this point it will be helpful to examine the structure and use of the bills of material in more detail. They are also sometimes called a **product structure** since that is what they indicate, much as the recipe list in our lasagna example. We can start with a very simple example, a skateboard.

The skateboard has a very simple bill of materials, especially if we assume we purchase the wheels ready for mounting on the axles (see Figure 6.5).

This bill of materials is classified as *three levels deep*. The first level, designated by the final product, is often called *level zero*. The next level, with the board and wheel assemblies, is called level one, and the level with the axle and wheels is level two. This shows the relationship graphically, but in most systems this data is stored as a list, with the various levels indented (called an ***indented bill of materials***). In our example, the indented bill would be:

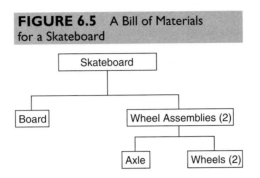

FIGURE 6.5   A Bill of Materials for a Skateboard

COMPONENT	QUANTITY REQUIRED
Skateboard	1
Board	1
Wheel assemblies	2
Wheels	2
Axle	1

The product or subassembly that uses a given component is often called a **parent.** In this example, the wheel assembly is the parent of the wheels and axle. The skateboard itself is the parent of the board and the two wheel assemblies. Also note that there is a multiplicative relationship. In the finished skateboard there are four wheels. The bill of materials shows two wheels for each wheel assembly and two wheel assemblies for each finished skateboard, making a total of four wheels.

6.3   THE MRP "EXPLOSION"

With the MPS (the menu), the bills of material (the recipe), and existing inventory, there is almost enough information to calculate the planned orders for the components. Some additional information is needed, often found on a data file called the **item master.** Along with other useful information, the item master typically will contain information on the lead times and lot sizes. There is almost always exactly one item master file for each component used in the facility.

The calculation that takes all this information and computes planned orders for the components is often called an **explosion,** because as the calculation starts at the parent level it "fans out" into lower levels of the bill of materials, looking like an explosion of calculations.

Probably the easiest way to explain the process is through an example. The calculations shown here are almost always done on a computer using one of the many good software programs available. Some people may ask, "Why bother learning the method if the computer does the calculation?" There is a fundamental reason that is at the heart of any managerial responsibility when using a computer. It is very important that a manager understands the methods used by the computer to obtain critical planning and decision numbers. Otherwise, if a problem occurs the manager may not understand how to solve it since they do not understand how the values were obtained. It must be remembered that a computer is generally nothing more (at least so far) than a very large and very fast calculator. A wise manager will understand basically how the computer is obtaining planning numbers, will understand how to make decisions using those numbers, but will never let the computer make critical business decisions by itself. Even with today's sophisticated systems, there are almost no circumstances where a computer can possibly have all the information necessary to make a complex business decision.

As an example, let's look at the product structure for an assembly we call X. For convenience, we will assume that X is used in another product in the facility, for which a master schedule has been developed. As you can see in the data below, we have listed both the bill of material and also the information from the database, including existing inventory levels, lead times, and lot sizes. The lot size "lot for lot" essentially implies that the order size will equal the exact quantity needed for the stated time period. It means if you need 20 you order 20, if you need 55 you order 55, and so forth. Most other lot sizes are *minimal* lot sizes. For example, if the lot size is 100 and you need 78, you will order 100. On the other hand, if you need 127, you can order 127. In some cases, especially if the items are purchased, the lot sizes may be multiples. This often occurs if products can only be made or delivered in set sizes or packaging. In this case if the lot size is 100 and you need 127, you would order 200, or two lots (packages). See Figure 6.6 (adapted from slides accompanying

FIGURE 6.6   Product "X" Example

ITEM	On-Hand	Lead Time (Wks)	Lot Size
X	50	2	Lot for lot
A	75	3	100
B	35	1	50
C	100	2	300
D	20	2	300

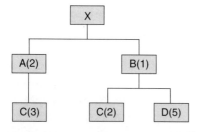

Production and Operations Management by Chase and Aquilano, 7th edition).

The basic MRP record appears as follows. Notice that although variations exist, a common approach is to show requirements in weekly "buckets." The explanation of each row is:

- **Gross requirements** represent the total needed quantity for the item on a week-by-week basis—they are the quantity to be used during the period. At the top level of the bill of materials the gross requirements usually represent the primary input for generating most component requirements. If the item being planned is one level below the product planned in the master schedule, the gross requirements for that item are primarily the MPS values for the product planned by a master schedule.

- **Scheduled receipts** represent orders that have already been committed, either as a production order or a purchasing order. They are important because they represent actual commitment of resources from the firm. The quantity and timing are, as the name indicated, what you are scheduled to receive, and assumed to be available at the beginning of the period. Because these do represent firm commitments, generally they *cannot* be freely moved by the computer logic. If the logic does show they should be moved or changed in quantity, generally the system will generate an exception message suggesting the move. The general "rule of thumb" is to not let a computer commit the resources of the firm without human review.

- **Projected available** represents the inventory available of the component at the end of the weekly bucket.

- **Net requirements** are the amount needed for the week after the gross requirements have been netted against available inventory and/or scheduled receipts.

- **Planned order releases** are the quantity of net requirements that are planned to be ordered or released at the beginning of the period, taking into account lot sizes and offsetting for lead times. Planned order releases are usually calculated by the computer, and the computer logic is free to move them or change quantity based on the programmed rules (such as lot size). Unlike scheduled receipts, they do not represent actual resource commitments from the firm, merely when you *plan* to release an order based on the information available at the present time. The planned order releases represent the primary output of MRP, as they represent what must be purchased or produced in both quantity and timing. They therefore represent primary input into detailed capacity planning, the purchasing system, and the production activity control systems that schedule and control the actual production of the orders.

Using this information, let us proceed with filling out the MRP record. We always start at the top of the bill of materials—in this case, assembly X. Since assembly X is used in another product, the demand that becomes the gross requirements for X most likely comes directly from the MPS values of the parent product.

Item: X   On-hand: 50   Lot size: Lot-for-lot   Lead time: 2

Week		1	2	3	4	5	6	7	8	9	10
Gross requirement		20	20	20	10	10	20		40		40
Scheduled receipts											
Projected available	50										
Net requirements											
Planned order release											

We have now filled in the demand, and note that we also filled in the on-hand inventory in the "projected available" space prior to week 1. We also have no scheduled receipts for this item. Given the information, we are ready to calculate the net requirements based on the gross requirements and the on-hand inventory:

Item: X   On-hand: 50   Lot size: Lot-for-lot   Lead time: 2

Week		1	2	3	4	5	6	7	8	9	10
Gross requirement		20	20	20	10	10	20		40		40
Scheduled receipts											
Projected available	50	30	10	0	0	0	0	0	0	0	0
Net requirements		0	0	10	10	10	20	0	40	0	40
Planned order release											

To explain the logic, go first to week 1. Starting week 1 there is a requirement of 20 with a starting inventory of 50. Using 20 of the inventory to satisfy demand, there will be 30 left in inventory at the end of the week, and the net requirements are zero since there was enough inventory to satisfy demand. This logic continued until week 3. At the end of week 2 there are only 10 units left in inventory, but there are requirements for 20 in week 3. That will leave no units left in inventory at the end of week 3 and an additional requirement above available inventory of 10 units (net requirements). Since the lot size is lot-for-lot, we will only build what we need, leaving our projected available as zero and the net requirements equaling gross requirements for the rest of the record.

Some may wonder how we started with inventory at all if the lot sizing rule is lot-for-lot. Anyone spending any time in a business knows that customer demand is very dynamic. Customers change their minds constantly about both quantity and timing of product need. In this case, the 50 units in inventory could have easily been an order that was generated to meet a customer demand, but after the items were already being built the customer cancelled the order.

Now that we have generated the net requirements, we are ready to proceed with the planned order releases:

Item: X   On-hand: 50   Lot Size: Lot-for-lot   Lead time: 2

Week	1	2	3	4	5	6	7	8	9	10
Gross requirement	20	20	20	10	10	20		40		40
Scheduled receipts										
Projected available 50	30	10	0	0	0	0	0	0	0	0
Net requirements	0	0	10	10	10	20	0	40	0	40
Planned order release	10	10	10	20		40		40		

Notice that the "planned order release" row has all the net requirements, but 2 weeks earlier. That is the lead time offset. In other words, given a lead time of 2 weeks, we need to release an order and start making the product in week 1 if we are to use that product to meet a net requirement for week 3.

Now let's review the remaining lot sizes and look for existing scheduled receipts:

COMPONENT	LOT SIZE	SCHEDULED RECEIPTS
A	100	None
B	50	None
C	300	300, week 1
D	300	None

With this information, we are ready to generate the record for part A. Notice on the bill of materials that part A is used to build part X, and that there are two part As required to make one part X. The first thing we need to look for is the gross requirements for part A. Note that part A is *not* sold to the customer. *The only requirement for part A comes from the need to build X.* For that reason we look for when we plan to *BUILD* X and the quantity needed to *BUILD* X, *NOT* when we sell X or how many we sell. The timing and the quantity of the gross requirements for A comes, therefore, from when we plan to build X, which is found in the *planned order release row of the item X record.* This then represents a fundamental principle of MRP:

The gross requirements for any component come directly from the planned order releases of the parent component.

In this case, of course, there are two As required every time we build an X. Therefore, the gross requirements for A are the same as the planned order release row of X, only doubled:

Item: A On-hand: 75 Lot size: 100						Lead time: 3				
Week	1	2	3	4	5	6	7	8	9	10
Gross requirement	20	20	20	40		80		80		
Scheduled receipts										
Projected available 75										
Net requirements										
Planned order release										

Now we can use the same logic used in the record for X to complete the record for item A:

Item: A On-hand: 75 Lot size: 100						Lead time: 3				
Week	1	2	3	4	5	6	7	8	9	10
Gross requirement	20	20	20	40		80		80		
Scheduled receipts										
Projected available 75	55	35	15	75	75	95	95	15	15	15
Net requirements	0	0	0	25	0	5	0	0	0	0
Planned order release	100		100							

To explain some of these numbers, let's follow the logic. The existing inventory of 75 will satisfy all the need until week 4, when the 15 left from week 3 will not satisfy the demand of 40. The net requirement of 25 will generate a planned order 3 weeks earlier (lead time is 3 weeks), but the order size will be 100 because of the lot size rule. Assuming the lot of 100 will be ready at the beginning of week 4 (which is the underlying assumption in MRP), the lot of 100 combined with the 15 left in inventory means there will be 115 available at the beginning of week 4. Subtracting the requirement of 40 from the 115, we are left with 75 at the end of week 4, as shown in the "Projected available" row.

This happens again in week 6. The 75 left after week 5 are not enough to satisfy the requirement of 80 for week 6, yielding a net requirement of 5. That will generate the planned order release of 100 for week 3, giving you a projected 175 available at the beginning of week 6. Taking the requirement of 80 away from the 175 gives a projected available balance of 95 at the end of week 6.

Now let's look at component B. As in the case of component A, component B is only used to make X. Unlike A, however, there is but one B required for each X. The gross requirements for B, therefore, become exactly equal to the planned order releases for X. The completed record, using the same logic, becomes:

Item: B   On-hand: 35   Lot size: 50   Lead time: 1

Week	1	2	3	4	5	6	7	8	9	10
Gross requirement	10	10	10	20		40		40		
Scheduled receipts										
Projected available 35	25	15	5	35	35	45	45	5	5	5
Net requirements	0	0	0	15	0	5	0	0	0	0
Planned order release			50		50					

Next we look at part C. The bill of materials has been recreated here:

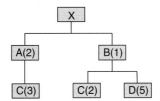

There are two issues that need special discussion concerning part C. First, C is the first component we look at that is NOT used to build part X—at least not directly. Instead part C has *TWO* parents in the bill of materials—part A and part B. Three part Cs are needed every time A is built, and two part Cs are needed each time part B is built. To obtain the gross requirement for C, therefore, we need to access the records for both parts A and B. Note that because we are only interested in the need to build A and B, we no longer look for X. Only A and B are used to build X, and if we have enough of those we would need no Cs at all. We only need C to build A and B. This is another important principle:

We only examine the DIRECT parent(s) for any component to obtain the dependent demand requirements for a component of interest.

To illustrate how the planned orders of A and B become the gross requirements for C, we will recreate the records for A and B, as well as generate the gross requirements for C and complete the record for C:

Item: A   On-hand: 75   Lot size: 100   Lead time: 3

Week	1	2	3	4	5	6	7	8	9	10
Gross requirement	20	20	20	40		80		80		
Scheduled receipts										
Projected available 75	55	35	15	75	75	95	95	15	15	15
Net requirements	0	0	0	25	0	5	0	0	0	0
Planned order release	100		100							

Item: B   On-hand: 35   Lot size: 50   Lead time: 1

Week		1	2	3	4	5	6	7	8	9	10
Gross requirement		10	10	10	20		40		40		
Scheduled receipts											
Projected available	35	25	15	5	35	35	45	45	5	5	5
Net requirements		0	0	0	15	0	5	0	0	0	0
Planned order release				50		50					

Item: C   On-hand: 100   Lot size: 300   Lead time: 2

Week		1	2	3	4	5	6	7	8	9	10
Gross requirement		300		400		100					
Scheduled receipts		300									
Projected available	100	100	100	0	0	200	200	200	200	200	200
Net requirements		0	0	300	0	100	0	0	0	0	0
Planned order release		300		300							

To obtain the gross requirements, as stated earlier, we need the records for both A and B. The requirement for 300 Cs in week 1 comes directly from the need to make 100 As in week 1 (the planned order release). Recall that three Cs are needed for each A. The requirement for 400 Cs in week 3 comes from the need to make 100 As (needing 300 Cs) and the need to make 50 Bs (needing 100 Cs).

It is also easy to see the result of the scheduled receipt. We are scheduled to receive 300 Cs in week 1, which we immediately need for the gross requirement of 300. That means the inventory of 100 when we start is still there at the end of week 1.

Finally, we need to create the record for item D. Its only requirement comes from the need to build component B, and the bill of material shows that we need 5 Ds for each B. The record is shown:

Item: D   On-hand: 20   Lot size: 300   Lead time: 2

Week		1	2	3	4	5	6	7	8	9	10
Gross requirement				250		250					
Scheduled receipts											
Projected available	20	20	20	70	70	120	120	120	120	120	120
Net requirements		0	0	230	0	180	0	0	0	0	0
Planned order release		300		300							

Before finishing this discussion, it should be pointed out that in our numeric example we can see the same aspect of dependent demand "lumpiness" that the earlier graph illustrates. Notice the difference in planned orders that exist in components A, B, C, and D when compared to the gross requirements for part X, for which the components are used. It is the lot sizing rules that tend to produce these "lumpy" demand conditions and resulting inventory for the lower-level components. Given that, it will be instructive to summarize some of the most commonly used lot sizing "rules."

Common Lot Sizing Rules

While there are several lot sizing rules that have been developed, some that are seldom are beyond the scope of this book. The more common rules are:

- *Lot for lot.*   This rule was described earlier in the example. It basically says you order the exact quantity needed to meet the net requirements for the period being evaluated

- *Fixed quantity.*   As the name implies, this rule says you order the same quantity each time you order. The most common reasons would be that the quantity results from an economic analysis showing that quantity is the lowest total cost to produce or procure or that there is some standard packaging used and therefore all orders need to be in multiples of that package quantity. If the quantity comes from the economic analysis case, often the fixed lot size represents the minimum quantity that must be ordered, while in the packaging case the quantity implies that any requirement above the stated lot size must be ordered in integer multiples of the stated lot size.

- *Least unit cost.*   This method tries to evaluate ordering several periods' worth of requirements in order to possibly take advantage of a quantity discount for the item. Perhaps the easiest way to illustrate is with an example. An item has an order cost of $50 per order, a base price of $300 each, but a quantity discount price of $270 per item is offered if the quantity purchased is 500 or more units. There is an inventory carrying cost of $1 per item for every period the item is held in inventory. The per period requirements for the item over the next six periods are given as:

Period	1	2	3	4	5	6
Requirements	120	80	100	150	100	200

Based on the information above, the following table shows the least unit cost analysis:

Period	Requir.	Cumul. Req.	Order Cost	Inven. Cost	Unit Price	Cumulative Total Cost	Cost per Unit
1	120	120	$50	0	$300	$36,050	$300.42
2	80	200	$50	$80	$300	$60,130	$300.65
3	100	300	$50	$280	$300	$90,330	$301.11
4	150	450	$50	$730	$300	$135,780	$301.73
4q	50	500	$50	$930	$270	$135,980	$271.96
5	100	550	$50	$1130	$270	$149,680	$272.15
6	200	750	$50	$2130	$270	$204,680	$272.91

Some of these calculations and rows need further explanation. The inventory cost column, for example, uses the carrying cost of $1 per unit per period. The $730 carrying cost for period 4, for example, comes from the fact that to order 450 units (the cumulative amount for periods 1 through 4) means that the 80 required in period 2 would be held for one period until used ($80), the 100 required for period 3 would be held for two periods ($200), and the 150 required for period 4 would be held for three periods ($450). The sum of the $450 + $200 + $80 gives the $730 carrying cost value. Looking at the cumulative total cost for the same period, it comes from ordering 450 units at $300 (total of $135,000) and then adding the order cost of $50 and the carrying cost of $730.

The period labeled "4q" also needs explanation. Some time during period 5 we will reach the cumulative target of 500 units for the quantity discount. This is because the cumulative amount required through period 4 is 450 units, and the requirement in period 5 is 100 units. For analysis, we look at that point during period 5 when we "hit" that 500 requirement boundary (requiring 50 units above those required in period 4), and call that point period "4q." Note that in that row the unit price changes to the discount price of $270. The inventory carrying cost comes from the fact that those extra 50 units would not be used until period 5, meaning they are held for four periods at a total carrying cost of $200. Adding that $200 to the $730 cost for period 4 gives the $930 carrying cost in that row.

This table clearly shows in the "cost per unit" column that it is worthwhile to purchase the quantity discount quantity, but no more. Notice that if more are purchased than the 500 units the cost per unit starts to rise because of the carrying cost.

- **Least Period Cost.** This method is very closely related to the least unit cost method, but evaluates on the basis of cost per period rather than cost per unit. Taking the data from the least unit cost example above, we can see how this calculation works:

PERIOD	CUMULATIVE REQUIREMENTS	CUMULATIVE TOTAL COST	COST PER PERIOD
1	120	$36,050	$36,050
2	200	$60,130	$30,065
3	300	$90,330	$30,110
4	450	$135,780	$33,945
4q	500	$135,980	$30,218
5	550	$149,680	$29,936
6	750	$204,680	$34,113

The number used to divide the $135,980 in period "4q" was 4.5. That value came from noting that the 50 units more than the total required for period

4 was exactly a proportion of .5 of the 100 units required for period 5 (50/100 = 0.5). Using this analysis, one would select a lot size of 550 units, since that gives the least period cost.

6.4   OTHER MRP ISSUES

The discussion above illustrates the basic approach to MRP. There are, however, several additional issues that must be discussed to understand the dynamic nature of MRP systems.

Generation of Data

The calculation of all this data for all the products in a dynamic manufacturing environment is almost always an issue. There are two basic approaches, with variations:

- **Regeneration.**   This process involves taking all the necessary data (MPS, inventory data, bill of materials [BOMs], item master data) and doing the calculations completely. This method takes a very large amount of computation time, but since the output is usually printed and typically not stored on the computer, it does save on computer memory. This method was the original method used by many companies when computer memories were small and purchasing additional memory was very expensive. Many modern systems do not use regeneration unless policies emanating from the business environment dictate its use. It does tend to take a fairly long time in many environments and the dynamic nature of most operations imply that the data starts to become old and irrelevant almost as soon as it is generated, especially since many companies will only regenerate about once a week.

- **Net Change.**   This process means that all data (inventory, order completion, customer orders, etc.) are input into the computer and process as soon as they occur. This takes very little time to do, but requires a very large amount of computer memory, as all the information is kept online and in real-time.

- **Batch.**   This approach really combines the two approaches. It keeps most of the information online for immediate access, but does not immediately update changes. Instead, data changes are kept in a subfile and periodically all the information is used to update the records. The time between batch updates is dictated by the facility, and many systems today use batch updates so effectively that there is little substantial difference between batch and net change to the user. It does make a great deal of difference in the computer memory demand, however.

Updating Information

As time passes and production activity occurs, the records should be updated in order to ensure correct information is being used for decision making. As an example, let us look again at the record for item X in our example above:

Item: X   On-hand: 50   Lot size: Lot-for-lot   Lead time: 2

Week		1	2	3	4	5	6	7	8	9	10
Gross requirement		20	20	20	10	10	20		40		40
Scheduled receipts											
Projected available	50	30	10	0	0	0	0	0	0	0	0
Net requirements		0	0	10	10	10	20	0	40	0	40
Planned order release		10	10	10	20		40		40		

Now let's assume that week 1 has passed. The demand for 20 units in week 1 did occur, and the planned order release for 10 units in week 1 was released by the planner. Let's also assume that in week 11 (from the original record) a customer demand of 20 units was generated. Now in the next week the record would change as follows. Note that the week 1 in the record below is really the week 2 information from the record above, since the "old" week 1 has passed and the new week 1 is really the same as the "old" week 2.

Item: X   On-hand: 30   Lot size: Lot-for-lot   Lead time: 2

Week		1	2	3	4	5	6	7	8	9	10
Gross requirement		20	20	10	10	20		40		40	20
Scheduled receipts			10								
Projected available	30	10	0	0	0	0	0	0	0	0	0
Net requirements		0	0	10	10	20	0	40	0	40	20
Planned order release		10	10	20		40		40	20		

Note the changes. The on-hand is now 30 because you used 20 in the "old" week 1. The planned order release of 10 in the "old" week 1 was released, and has now become a scheduled receipt for the new week 2. Everything else has moved by one week, and the new order for 20 in week 10 (the "old" week 11) has been generated.

It is possible that the original plans will have changed for some reason. Let's take the same record and assume that instead of the 20 we expected as demand for week 1 that the customers only took 15. In that case the new record would appear as follows:

Item: X   On-hand: 35   Lot size: Lot-for-lot   Lead time: 2

Week		1	2	3	4	5	6	7	8	9	10
Gross requirement		20	20	10	10	20		40		40	20
Scheduled receipts			10								
Projected available	35	15	5	0	0	0	0	0	0	0	0
Net requirements		0		5	10	20	0	40	0	40	20
Planned order release		5	10	20		40		40	20		

Exception Messages

Most MRP systems generate so much data that any planner would find it difficult to evaluate it all. To assist, the system usually will generate exception messages, which basically are messages that call attention for some suggested planner actions. The most common of these is the message to release an order. The two major types of order releases are for purchase orders or production orders. Items on the bill of materials that have no components below them are typically purchased, while components or subassemblies that are parents to some components are usually produced in the facility.

As mentioned before, the computer will typically take control of items that do not represent actual resource commitments (planned order releases, for example), while it is often recommended that the system only generate exception messages for those areas that do represent actual resources, such as scheduled receipts. As an example, let us look once again at the record for item C:

Item: C   On-hand: 100   Lot size: 300   Lead time: 2

Week		1	2	3	4	5	6	7	8	9	10
Gross requirement		300		400		100					
Scheduled receipts		300									
Projected available	100	100	100	0	0	200	200	200	200	200	200
Net requirements		0	0	300	0	100	0	0	0	0	0
Planned order release		300		300							

Let's suppose that for some reason (e.g., a customer order cancellation) the 300 called for as gross requirements in week 1 are not needed. The record will then look as follows:

Item: C   On-hand: 100   Lot size: 300   Lead time: 2

Week		1	2	3	4	5	6	7	8	9	10
Gross requirement				400		100					
Scheduled receipts		300									
Projected available	100	400	400	0	0	200	200	200	200	200	200
Net requirements		0	0	0	0	100	0	0	0	0	0
Planned order release				300							

Note that the computer recognized it no longer needed the planned order release for week 1 and eliminated it. That is perfectly acceptable since it is only a planning number with no real resources committed. The scheduled receipt for week 1 is a different story. The computer will not move that quantity, since it does represent real resource commitments. Instead, it will notice that those 300 units are not really needed in week 1, but instead are needed in week 3. The system will then generate an exception message to move the scheduled receipt to week 3.

At that point it is up to the planner whether to actually move the order. If, for example, the workers in the supplier operation have already started on the order and it would be highly disruptive to destroy the equipment setup for the order, they may decide to go ahead and make it as originally planned. If not too disruptive, however, it may be better to move it as they potentially could use those resources for another critical production order. To paraphrase the late Oliver Wight, who was one of the great pioneers in the development of MRP systems: "Whenever you get something you don't need, it is almost always at the expense of something you do need."

Other Sources of Demand

Service parts.   Even if an item is generally considered as a dependent demand item, sometimes it can also experience demand from independent sources. As an example, look at a bicycle tire. Certainly the major demand for bicycle tires is to make bicycles, but it is also possible to buy just a tire as a replacement for an older bicycle. Many items that typically have dependent demand also have independent or **service demand.** Such demand should be recognized and accommodated in the MRP record. Let's take our item B from the example.

Item: B On-hand: 35 Lot size: 50						Lead time: 1				
Week	1	2	3	4	5	6	7	8	9	10
Gross requirement	10	10	10	20		40		40		
Scheduled receipts										
Projected available 35	25	15	5	35	35	45	45	5	5	5
Net requirements	0	0	0	15	0	5	0	0	0	0
Planned order release			50		50					

Now let us assume that there is an independent service demand of 5 units per week from service customers. The record would now look like:

Item: B On-hand: 35 Lot size: 50						Lead time: 1				
Week	1	2	3	4	5	6	7	8	9	10
Gross requirement	15	15	15	25	5	45	5	45	5	5
Scheduled receipts										
Projected available 35	20	5	40	15	10	15	10	15	10	5
Net requirements	0	0	10	0	0	35	0	35	0	0
Planned order release		50			50		50			

There is not only an additional planned order needed, but the timing has changed. Note also that since item B is a parent of two components, *the gross requirements for those components will also change.*

Safety stock. Unfortunately, there are often uncertainties in any operation, many of which cannot be completely controlled. Sometimes inventory records are inaccurate, sometimes a problem occurs with the quality of a certain part, sometimes the timing of delivery is not precise, and so forth. In some cases there is even uncertainty if the lead time for replenishment materials extends beyond a reasonable planning horizon. Many companies will elect to deal with these issues by the use of safety stock, "just in case" something goes wrong. The MRP system can be used to generate planned orders with safety stock in mind. As an example, let's take the item B record from above, with the service requirements. Now let's include a safety stock requirement of 10 units:

Item: B On-hand: 35 Lot size: 50 Lead time: 1 Safety stock:10										
Week	1	2	3	4	5	6	7	8	9	10
Gross requirement	15	15	15	25	5	45	5	45	5	5
Scheduled receipts										
Projected available 35	20	55	40	15	10	15	10	15	10	55
Net requirements	0	5	0	0	0	35	0	35	0	5
Planned order release	50			50		50		50		

The changes are again obvious. In week 2 the record before the safety stock requirement shows the inventory dropping to five units, which would violate the safety stock level. The system therefore moves the planned order a week earlier to keep the projected available to 10 units or higher. It also causes an additional order to be generated in week 9 to prevent the week 10 inventory from falling below safety stock. The decision to use safety stock should be weighed carefully. To again paraphrase Oliver Wight, "Safety stocks pollute priorities." What he meant by that is that when workers might see the order come to make 50 of the item B in week 1, and they know there is enough in inventory to meet demand in week 2, they may become skeptical about the validity of the system and the numbers it is generating. It also obviously will increase inventory expense. It is often recommended that with a good system and good quality controls in place that safety stock be used primarily at the highest levels in the bills of materials, often only at the MPS level. It is at that level where the largest uncontrollable variable exists: customer demand. Anything at the lower levels should, therefore, be calculated and managerially controlled.

Quality yield. Some processes are just not able to produce 100% quality for an entire batch. When a yield problem is known, the system can once again be used to accommodate the situation. Let us again return to our example. Suppose the process used to make component D has a yield of 90%, meaning that historically on average only 90% of the parts made on the process have an acceptable level of quality. Let's look at the original record and the new record with the yield built in:

Original Record:

Item: D   On-hand: 20   Lot size: 300   Lead time: 2

Week		1	2	3	4	5	6	7	8	9	10
Gross requirement				250		250					
Scheduled receipts											
Projected available	20	20	20	70	70	120	120	120	120	120	120
Net requirements		0	0	230	0	180	0	0	0	0	0
Planned order release		300		300							

New Record:

Item: D   On-hand: 20   Lot size: 300   Lead time: 2   Yield 90%

Week		1	2	3	4	5	6	7	8	9	10
Gross requirement				250		250					
Scheduled receipts											
Projected available	20	20	20	70	70	120	120	120	120	120	120
Net requirements		0	0	230	0	180	0	0	0	0	0
Planned order release		333		333							

Notice the system accommodates the poor yield by planning to start 333 units. Then with a 90% yield we would expect 300 to emerge at an acceptable level. *The rest of the numbers in the record, it should be noted, are based on the 300 good units.*

Engineering design changes. The fact that MRP is a "forward-looking" scheduling approach makes it ideal for dealing with design changes in the product. Using the projected available balance figure, we can easily see when the inventory will be very low, or even equal to zero, allowing us to time a design change with a minimal impact on making existing inventory obsolete. To allow the system to plan the new inventory requirement, then, all that need be done is to build the new part number into the BOM with an effective date and allow the system to plan its need.

Pegging. From time to time there are unforeseen problems with a lower-level item in the bill of materials. For example, in our case what happens if the supplier for part C informs us that the order for 300 units in week 1 will be a week late? How will that affect our production and, more importantly, our customer orders? To obtain that information, we use a concept called **pegging,** which essentially allows the system to work its way back up the bill of materials and determine which parent assemblies or even which customer orders will be impacted by the late purchase order. In this way customers can be notified or contingency plans activated long before the late order becomes a potential crisis. Replanning based on using pegging data is often called **bottom-up re-planning.**

Firm planned orders.   Changes in customer orders tend to be frequent in many operations, and since the change usually occurs in the top level of the bill of materials, any change will generally generate numerous changes in all the lower levels. Such a condition is sometimes referred to as "system ner-vousness," because a little change at the top causes all the records to "shud-der" in response. This condition makes planning a relatively stable environment very difficult. To prevent this from being too disruptive, the con-cept of the firm planned order is sometimes used. The **firm planned order** is used by the planner to tell the system that the planned order is to be fixed, thereby taking it out of control of the computer. If the system detects that the order should be moved or changed in quantity, it will not be allowed to do so automatically. Instead, the system will generate an exception message to the planner that it would like to move the order, but now it is in the discretion of the planner whether it is wise to do so or not. Another way of looking at the concept is to consider that the computer will treat the firm planned order much as if it were a scheduled receipt, even though it still appears in the planned order release row and does not yet represent committed resources of the company.

Allocation.   In some cases there is a need to "save" some inventory aside for a special use. As an example, suppose a service technician calls the planner and says they need to replenish their stock of a component that is used for ser-vice as well as production. Certainly this demand could be included as a ser-vice order, but if it is a "one-time" situation, it could be handled by allocation. This essentially means putting the components aside and saving them, making them unavailable for production. There are two ways to handle this. One is called a "**hard allocation**." where the parts are physically removed from stor-age, and the inventory records are changed to reflect the withdrawal. The parts are then saved in another location until the technician can claim them. The other method is "**soft allocation**." In this method a field on the MRP record is filled in to show the part usage. If, for example, there are 100 parts in inventory and the technician needs 20, the field for allocation will be filled in with the 20 parts. The 100 parts will still show in inventory, but the planning record will be computed on the basis of having 80 units instead of 100.

Soft allocation is generally preferred, in that the real situation is shown in the record for all to see. With hard allocation, people will sometimes know the components really exist, and can get confused as to what really is available for other uses.

Low-level coding.   Sometimes an item appears on the bill of materials multi-ple times, such as in our early example when item C appears twice. In some cases, however, the item will appear at a different level in the bill of materials.

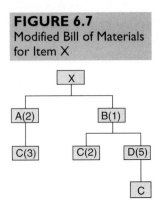

FIGURE 6.7
Modified Bill of Materials for Item X

In our earlier case, both times item C appeared it was on level 2 of the bill. Suppose, however, that item D also needed an item C for production, as shown in Figure 6.7.

In this case item C would appear on both level 2 and level 3. Since MRP tends to make its calculation level by level, it would tend to compute need for C at level 2 and then need to again calculate when it got to level 3. To prevent that problem, items appearing multiple times on a bill of materials will generally be assigned the lowest level code on which they appear. In that way all the item Cs will be calculated together, on level 3.

Planning horizon.   One major issue that must be addressed is the planning horizon, or how far into the future to develop the MRP plans. The answer generally lies with an understanding of the cumulative lead time of the product in question, as was discussed in the chapter on master scheduling. Using our product X (the original one in Figure 6.6) as an example, let's look at the cumulative lead times as we work our way down the bill of materials. There are three "paths" from top to bottom. One is X to A to C. The second is from X to B to C, and the third is from X to B to D. Adding the lead time for each path, we see the X-A-C path is 7 weeks (2 + 3 + 2), the X-B-C path is 5 weeks, and the X-B-D path is also 5 weeks. The longest cumulative lead time is 7 weeks, meaning that is the minimal time horizon we need to plan for the future component procurement.

As discussed in the chapter on master scheduling, failure to plan far enough ahead will lead to a lot of problems. Suppose, for example, we add a customer order for product X in week 6. That implies the order release for product X will need to be made 2 weeks earlier in week 4. The gross requirement for A will then be in week 4, and with a 3-week lead time a planned order release would need to be made in week 1. The gross requirement for C would then come in week 1, and since it has a 2-week lead time we are already late—and we didn't even know it!

6.5   POTENTIAL MRP CHALLENGES

In spite of the attractive logic of MRP systems, sometimes their effectiveness is hindered by a variety of implementation issues. Some of the most significant potential challenges to implementation include the following.

Data accuracy.   As can be easily seen from the examples developed in this chapter, MRP is *extremely* data dependent. It uses several databases, including:

- Inventory count and location
- Item master records
- Purchasing records
- Bill of materials
- Master schedules

To the extent that any of these databases have inaccurate data or poor timing of data input, the planning system will reflect the poor data with poor planning numbers.

User knowledge.   Education and training of users is very important. People who do not understand what the system does or do not understand how to use the planning numbers effectively have little chance to make it work effectively.

Overloaded MPS.   Most of the planning numbers start from the master schedule. It is of critical importance, therefore, that the master schedule be effectively developed and maintained. Techniques for doing so are elaborated in the chapter on master scheduling. One of the most common problems that adversely impacts using MRP effectively is to overload the MPS. From time to time in almost any facility certain unexpected problems (equipment breakdowns, absenteeism, late supplier deliveries, etc.) can cause a failure to meet all planned production in the master schedule. When this occurs, many well-meaning managers will merely push the past-due schedule into the current time period without any regard to the impact on both capacity and material usage. Such practices will eventually lead to unworkable and unrealistic schedules and ultimately turn people into skeptics with respect to the MRP planning numbers.

Top management commitment.   Proper operation of an MRP system requires a substantial level of discipline in the organization, and in some cases a drastic change in the "corporate culture" and priority of performance measures within the organization. This is very difficult to accomplish in most organizations without the active leadership of a strong top manager. The top manager must understand what the system will do for and to the organization, and they must take an active, committed role to make the organizational modifications necessary to support the use of such a system effectively.

Capacity insensitivity.   The basic MRP explosion generates planned order releases with the underlying assumption that those orders will have adequate capacity of the right type to be produced or purchased. For that reason modern systems must utilize capacity planning in conjunction with MRP. Some of this is accomplished with the development of the sales and operation plan, but that plan is typically at too high a level for detailed production orders. Two other levels of capacity are generally used. The first, often called "rough-cut," is generated from MPS data, while detailed capacity plans are generated from the MRP planned order releases.

The "push" nature of MRP.   MRP represents a "push" system, meaning that orders are released according to the plan and "pushed" to the appropriate work area. The assumption is that if the plan is correct, the specific material in the designated quantity will be needed. In spite of the possible care taken in developing the plan, the reality is that often orders are pushed to a work center before they are really needed, and sometimes not needed at all. This is because of the volatile nature of many operation environments. Some problems that can occur to cause this include:

- Changes in customer orders, including timing and quantity
- Work center problems, such as machine breakdown
- Poor work standards, implying the actual work on existing work in the work center may take longer than planned
- Supplier delivery problems in which a component needed for production is not available

As one might expect, the opposite conditions could also be true, in which the order may be late in being released to the work center. This is quite common when a condition causes the operation to expedite an order for some reason, often related to customer requirements.

6.6   ENTERPRISE RESOURCE PLANNING (ERP)

Since the output from MRP basically represents the major activity of the production facility, these numbers can in fact be used as the basis for planning most of the firm's overall activity, including marketing, finance, engineering, and human resource needs. That has led to the development of very comprehensive and sophisticated systems over the last several years. First came the generation of "closed loop" MRP, which later evolved into what was called MRP II (sometimes called manufacturing resource planning). MRP II dealt with the issue of capacity insensitivity of the basic MRP calculations by allowing capacity and resource calculations to modify the MRP plans. Lately those systems have continued to evolve into what is typically called "ERP," which stands for enterprise resource planning

The basic premise behind ERP is that the production plans of the company derive from or in turn drive the decisions of virtually every other part of the company. In other words, the implication is that no functional area in a company can or should operate in isolation. Virtually all functions in the company are (or should be) linked together in the overall pursuit of maximizing service to the customer and achieving the financial and other strategic goals of the company. Given this fairly obvious premise, the "heart" of the planning system (MRP) can be used as the basis for developing highly integrated software that can literally be used to run the entire business. Not only are these systems integrated, but they generally use a common database, making the key data used to make company decisions available to all key functions equally. Given the growth in power, flexibility, functionality, and ease of use of modern computer systems, this evolution in software linkage and integration was a logical "next step" in planning and control.

As these systems developed and became more integrated and "seamless" in their approach to supplying functional information, the name **enterprise resource planning (ERP)** was given to them. This name attempted to reflect that they had expanded in their use well beyond production planning and control and in fact could be used to manage the entire enterprise in a functionally integrated manner. Some examples include:

- Sales and Marketing, for example, provide input into future sales and can use the system for both order promising and order tracking. Distribution is also included.
- Engineering can make plans for product and process changes based on production schedules and marketing plans as well as the availability of key people with key skills.
- Finance and Accounting can project cash flows and the need for investments or loans and can also track production and other costs in a more timely and effective manner. ERP also includes accounting systems such as payables and receivables.
- Human Resources can project the need for people, including timing, skill levels, and quantity. They can also use the information to determine training requirements and schedules.
- Top management can have ready access to all the information needed to make key operating and strategic decisions.
- Suppliers and Distributors can become an integral part of the planning system, making the concept of "supply chain management" more of a reality than just a conceptual point of view.
- Operations, of course, can make effective plans for scheduling of work and for effective utilization of capacity and other resources. Ready access to all relevant planning information makes this possible.

In spite of the obvious advantages such an integrated system can bring, the successful implementation can potentially be even more challenging than for that of a less integrated system. The integration implies the need for effective and efficient flows of information, meaning the business processes that generate and support those information flows must also be effective and efficient. The people involved with those processes must be knowledgeable and effective in their use of the system, and must also be constantly vigilant to ensure the data generated is maintained in both an accurate and timely manner. An integrated system is like a complex piece of machinery: each part of it must work well and all parts must work together or the entire piece of machinery will fail to meet the expectations for which it was designed. These concepts imply that most organizations will need to conduct a detailed process analysis for the entire organization, and most will find that significant work in process improvement or total process reengineering is in order before they can logically proceed with any ERP implementation.

A modern ERP system brings great power and value to those companies that implement them successfully. Unfortunately, with the integrative nature of the systems making the successful implementation potentially very difficult, many companies have failed to achieve a truly successful system implementation, and it is usually not because they haven't tried hard. It takes a skillful and knowledgeable group of people to successfully build (implement) such a complex system, and also takes a similar level of skill and knowledge to manage and maintain it on an ongoing basis.

Given the nature of ERP (involving the entire organization and its functions), further discussion of ERP is beyond the scope of this book. In addition, much of the implementation challenges involve individuals other than operations personnel. With this in mind, one note of caution must be made when considering ERP. Since ERP requires a large and often expensive software package, many think that ERP is primarily an Information Technology issue. While Information Technology plays a vital role, the decision to implement ERP must be considered an enterprise-wide decision, for virtually all parts of the enterprise will be impacted.

6.7 BUSINESS ENVIRONMENT ISSUES

While the concepts of MRP can work in virtually any environment, the data requirements and formality of the system make it impractical for some environments. Among the most obvious is the service environment, where the "bill of materials" (if such a thing exists for many services) is so dependent on customer requirements that in the most extreme cases a company may find itself designing a new bill of materials for each customer. That is a condition in which it would obviously be inappropriate to run such a formal and complex system. The same can often be said for many make-to-order (MTO) and engineer-to-order (ETO) environments because of the very large variety of end items and final product designs.

The make-to-stock (MTS) environment is clearly a good example of a well-defined structure that would lend itself well to an MRP setting. If, however, there is a relative degree of stability in demand and design of the final product, then there may be simpler methods available that will reduce both the complexity and cost of the system (see Chapter 9). The assemble-to-order (ATO) environment, however, is virtually the perfect environment for an MRP system to work well. In addition, any environment where there are environmental complexities tend to reinforce the value of MRP. Such complexities include complexities of design (lots of engineering changes or new products), complexity of demand (high variability in demand, for example), or high complexity in other environmental issues (product quality, supplier delivery, equipment availability, etc.). In general, an MRP system is a "forward-looking" system that allows planning as opposed to reaction. The more the environment is characterized by instability, the more MRP can provide serious benefits over other systems and can often make the costs of implementing and running such a formal, structured system worthwhile.

Modern ERP systems, since they represent analysis and resource planning for virtually all aspects of the business, represent another opportunity to help the business. Specifically, their "forward-looking" nature allows managers to input data to evaluate the impacts of various scenarios on the business as a whole. This is sometimes called "what if" analysis, and can prove to be very insightful and valuable in making intelligent business decisions.

KEY TERMS

Bill of Materials	Process Routing	Planned Order Release
Net Requirements	Lead Time	Purchasing Time
Independent Demand	Dependent Demand	Processing Time
Move Time	Setup Time	Product Structure
Wait Time	Queue Time	Scheduled Receipt
Indented Bill of Materials	Parent–Component	Batch Processing
Item Master	Relationship	Safety Stock
Regeneration	MRP Explosion	Bottom-up Replanning
Exception Messages	Net Change	Soft Allocation
Engineering Change	Service Demand	MRP II
Firm Planned Order	Pegging	
Low-Level Coding	Hard Allocation	
Enterprise Resource	Planning Horizon	
Planning (ERP)	Gross Requirements	

SUMMARY

This chapter develops a primary methodology for planning dependent demand inventory—material requirement planning (MRP). Even though many firms have struggled to successfully implement MRP (primarily because of the significant need for data accuracy and knowledge as to how to use the system), it remains a highly logical and potentially valuable approach. The many successful implementations have demonstrated the value for the firms willing to develop the environment necessary to support the highly integrated nature of a comprehensive MRP system. As computers have become more powerful and practical, the power of the information generated by MRP can be expanded to be used as a basis for running the entire enterprise, thereby evolving into today's modern enterprise resource planning (ERP) systems.

REFERENCES

Chase, R. B., and N. J. Aquilano, *Production and Operations Management.* Homewood, IL: Irwin, 1985.

Fogarty, D. W., J. H. Blackstone, Jr., and T. R. Hoffmann, *Production and Inventory Management.* Cincinnati, OH: South-Western, 1991.

Plossl, G., *Orlicky's Material Requirements Planning.* New York: McGraw-Hill, 1994.

Vollmann, T. E., W. L. Berry, and D. C. Whybark, *Manufacturing Planning and Control Systems.* New York: Irwin McGraw-Hill, 1997.

DISCUSSION QUESTIONS AND PROBLEMS

1. What do you think should happen if you were asked to allocate some inventory for R&D, but by doing so you would drop below safety stock levels?
2. Product Y is made from one component P, three components Q, and two components R. P is made from two part S, Q is made from one S, and R is made from two part S and three part T. Other data includes:

Part	Lead Time	Lot Size	On-hand	Scheduled Receipts	Safety stock
Y	1	lot-for-lot	30	none	5
P	2	40	15	none	none
Q	2	100	8	none	8
R	3	120	30	none	none
S	2	500	20	500, week 1	20
T	2	600	370	none	50

   a. Complete the MRP explosion for product Y. Identify any problems and discuss possible solutions
   b. The supplier for part S informs you that the scheduled receipt for that part will be 1 week late. What problems does is cause and what possible alternatives are open to you?
3. Product "X" has the product structure given below. In addition, relevant details for each component are given.
   a. Complete the master schedule and create MRP records for each of the components.
   b. Suppose the supplier for the 600 part "C" scheduled for week 1 notifies you that an equipment problem will prevent them from shipping the parts until week 3. What are the implications? Describe ALL possible options open to you in this case.

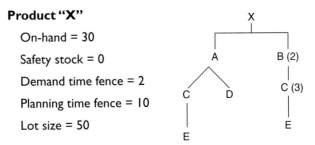

Product "X"

On-hand = 30

Safety stock = 0

Demand time fence = 2

Planning time fence = 10

Lot size = 50

Master Schedule for X:

Week	1	2	3	4	5	6	7	8	9	10
Forecast	20	25	20	30	20	20	25	25	25	25
Customer orders	26	21	13	8	3	1	0	0	5	0
Projected available										
Avail. to promise										
MPS		50		50		50		50		50

Component Information:

Component	A	B	C	D	E
Lot size	Lot-for-Lot	150	600	70	1000
On-hand	20	30	110	55	0
Lead time	1	2	3	1	2
Safety stock	None	None	100	20	None
Scheduled receipts	None	150, Wk 2	600, Wk 1	None	1000, Wk 1
Service requirements	None	20/week	None	None	40/week

4. Product A is made from two components, B and C. It takes one B and three Cs to make a single product A. Component B is made from two part Ds. Component C is made from one part D and 2 part Cs. Use this information together with the data below to answer the following questions:

Part	Lead Time	Lot Size	On-Hand	Scheduled Rcpts.
B	1	Lot-for-Lot	10	none
C	2	200	100	none
D	1	300	120	none
E	2	500	0	500, week 1

Part E also has a safety stock quantity of 100 units.
a. Make MRP records for B, C, D, and E. Production quantities and production start dates for A are: 20 in week 2, 50 in week 4, 30 in week 6, 40 in week 7, 50 in week 9, and 40 in week 11.
b. Suppose the quality manager told you the 120 part Ds on hand were damaged in a sprinkler accident and not available for production. What actions should you take?
c. The purchasing manager has just informed you that the supplier for part E was only able to ship 480 of the 500 you are scheduled to receive in week 1. What potential problems would this mean and how would you deal with it?

5. Use the attached MRP record blanks to complete the records for components B, C, D, and E, to answer the three questions. Item A is the finished product, made from one B and two Cs. Item B is made from three Ds and one E. Item C is made from one D and two Es.

The following is the MPS quantities for Item A (MPS quantities, not customer demand):

Period	1	2	3	4	5	6	7	8	9	10	11	12
MPS			20	30		50		40	30		50	

Other data needed:

Item	B	C	D	E
Lot size	Lot-for-lot	150	250	400
Lead time	1	2	1	2
On-hand10	10	50	10	320
Scheduled receipts	None	None	250, Wk 1	None
Safety stock	None	None	20	None

a. Is there anything of special note that is a concern? What and why?
b. The R&D Department wants to take the 10 units of D that are on-hand immediately and also wants 20 more in week 1. What would you tell them and why?
c. The master scheduler asks you if they can move the MPS of 20 in week 3 to week 2. From the data on the MRP records, what would you tell them and why?
d. R&D has a new design they want to implement for part C, and they are asking you when they should plan to do that. What do you tell them and why?

6. a. Product A is made from three Bs and two Cs. Subassembly B is made from two Es and one D. Subassembly C is made from one E and two Ds. Given this information and that below, fill in the MRP explosions for each of B, C, D, and E on the attached worksheet (lot sizes are minimums).

Component	Lot size	Lead time	Scheduled recpt.	On-hand	Safety stk.
B	Lot-for-lot	1	none	15	none
C	80	2	none	30	none
D	200	1	200, week 2	10	none
E	250	2	none	180	75

Product A has the following MPS values:

10 in week 3
20 in week 5
10 in week 6
30 in week 8
20 in week 10

b. The inventory specialist has just informed you that 140 of component E in inventory have a defect and must be scrapped. What actions do you need to take?

7. The figure below shows the bill of material (BOM) for the Acme PolyBob. Complete the MRP records on the next page. All the information you need is shown in the BOM and on the MRP records.

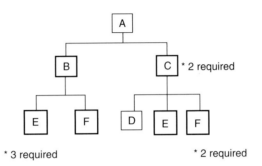

* 3 required   * 2 required

B   Lead time = 1 week   Minimum order quantity = 1

Week	1	2	3	4	5	6
Gross requirements		250	300	300	300	200
Scheduled receipts						
Proj. On-hand 0						
Net requirements						
Planned receipts						
Planned order releases						

C   Lead time = 3 weeks   Minimum order quantity = 500

Week	1	2	3	4	5	6
Gross requirements						
Scheduled receipts		500	600			
Proj. on-hand 0						
Net requirements						
Planned receipts						
Planned order releases						

E   Lead time = 4 weeks   Minimum order quantity = 5000

Week	1	2	3	4	5	6
Gross requirements						
Scheduled receipts						
Proj. on-hand 5,750						
Net requirements						
Planned receipts						
Planned order releases						

quired to produce the products, work center 200 uses 45% of the hours, and work center 300 uses 35% of the hours.

Using the total hours for each product, we can calculate the total hours required to meet the master schedule:

Week	1	2	3	4	5
Total hours	148.845*	148.845	129.975	129.975	156.63

$$*[10(1.557) + 25(5.331)] = 148.845$$

Now by simply multiplying the total hours by the historical percentages we can obtain a rough estimate of the capacity requirements for each of the three work centers:

Week	1	2	3	4	5
WC 100	29.77	29.77	25.0	25.0	31.33
WC 200	66.98	66.98	58.49	58.49	70.48
WC 300	52.1	52.1	45.49	45.49	54.82

Using this information, we can now get a rough idea of the capacity requirements for each work center in order to meet the master schedule. At this point, clearly there are decisions that must be made. Either the capacity must be planned in order to meet the projected build schedule as defined by the master schedule or the master schedule must be modified in cases where capacity cannot be changed or where it is determined that it is too expensive or difficult to change it.

The reason that this method is so "rough" should be obvious—there are no accommodations made for existing inventory of component parts, nor is there any offset for lead times of those components.

Capacity Bills. The next type of capacity planning approach is more complex, yet gives better and more specific information. To obtain this information, the capacity bills utilize two additional pieces of information from the database of the products in question. The first is the bill of material, and the second is the routing information. Bills of material have already been introduced and discussed. The routing, as the name implies, describes the "route" that the product must take in order to be produced. The information presented on the routing file can vary somewhat from business to business, but generally the file will show at a minimum:

- The operations that must be completed in the order of completion.
- The work centers that should be used to perform the various operations.
- Standard time for each operation, including setup time for the equipment and run time per piece.

In addition, the file may indicate any tooling used for an operation and alternate work centers for an operation, if there are any. Figure 7.3 shows a sample routing.

FIGURE 7.3   Sample Routing

Part Number: 6768240
Outer half of bearing 676824
Drawing No.: 676824-150

Operation number	Work center	Setup time (hours)	Run Time (hours/piece)	Operation description
10	3A	1.1	0.17	Cut outer from tube
20	4A	0.7	0.20	Grind raceway
30	7A	0.5	0.11	Grind face
40	11A	0.4	0.22	Mill face slot
50	2A	0.6	0.08	Grind surface
60	Stockroom			Move to inventory

To illustrate the use of a capacity bill, let us take a simple bill of material and routing for two example products, X and Y:

Bill of Material

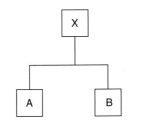 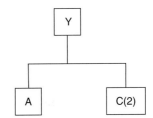

Routing Information

Product/part	Lot size	Work center	Operation	Setup hours	SU hrs per unit	Run time per unit	Total hrs per unit
X	30	100	1 of 1	0.5	0.017	0.5 hrs	0.517
Y	20	100	1 of 1	0.5	0.025	1.1	1.125
A	100	200	1 of 1	2	0.02	0.7	0.72
B	50	300	1 of 1	1	0.02	.03	0.32
C	40	200	1 of 2	1	0.025	0.8	0.825
C	40	300	2 of 2	0.7	0.018	0.9	0.918

Using this information, we can now get a good idea of the actual standard hours each product will use at each work center, rather than just using a historical average percentage, which may have been used for the first method:

WORK CENTER	PRODUCT X TOTAL TIME/UNIT	PRODUCT Y TOTAL TIME/UNIT
100	0.517	1.125
200	0.72	2.37
300	0.32	1.836
TOTAL	1.557	5.331

Some of the numbers on this chart are self-explanatory, but others may need some additional explanation. The 2.37 hours that product Y takes in work center 200, for example. Product Y is made from one part A and two parts C. Notice in the chart that each part A takes 0.72 hours in work center 200 and each part C takes 0.825 hours in work center 200. Since we need two part Cs to make a Y, we will use 2(0.825) or 1.65 hours. Add the 1.65 hours to the 0.72 hours and you get 2.37 hours. For work center 300, item A has zero time since it does not use work center 300 for processing. Item C does, however, use 0.918 hours per unit. Since 2 C units are required, work center 300 processing time to make a Y is 2 times 0.918 or 1.836 hours.

With this more specific information based on standards and the bill of materials, we can get more accurate capacity requirements for each work center to accomplish the master schedule given. The master schedule data is, once again:

Week	1	2	3	4	5
X	10	10	15	15	15
Y	25	25	20	20	25

Multiplying the standard times from the capacity bills times the master schedule quantity then develops the chart below:

Week	1	2	3	4	5
WC 100	33.295	33.295	30.255	30.255	35.88
WC 200	66.45	66.45	58.2	58.2	70.05
WC 300	49.1	49.1	41.52	41.52	50.7

Resource Profiles.   The next rough-cut method is more detailed by adding the dimension of lead time to the calculation. We will again continue our example to illustrate the development of resource profiles. To do so we will assume, for convenience sake, that each operation in the routing takes 1 week to accomplish. That implies that for the products due at the end of week 5 (and therefore assembled during week 5), the components to assemble those products must have been built in week 4. The one exception is the fact that there are two operations to perform on component C. Since the lead time is 1 week for each operation, the first of those operations (assume that is operation 2) has to be completed in week 3 so that the second of the operations (operation 1) is done in week 4. The following chart shows the hours per unit for each work center to make one product of X and one Y for week 5, shown in the week when the work will be done:

	WC	WEEK 3	WEEK 4	WEEK 5
Product X	100	0	0	0.517
	200	0	0.72	0
	300	0	0.32	0

Product Y	100	0	0	1.125
	200	0	2.37	0
	300	1.836	0	0

Using this information, we can now create the capacity requirements chart once again, only this time multiplying the MPS quantity for each week offset by the lead times as shown in the chart above:

Week	Past Due	1	2	3	4	5
WC 100	0	33.295	33.295	30.255	30.255	35.88
WC 200	66.45	66.45	58.2	58.2	70.05	0
WC 300	95	39.92	41.5	50.7	4.8	0

At first glance one would be concerned about the past due hours. Since this is rough-cut capacity, however, we do not include work in progress. If the scheduling has been done correctly all along and production orders released appropriately, we should expect that the orders represented by the past due hours have not only been released but are most likely finished and ready for assembly of the final products in week 1.

There are no specific "rules" for determining which rough-cut method should be used for various operational environments, but in general the decision should be made based on the level of detail needed and the amount of information available. The overall factor approach clearly yields less detailed information, but has the advantage of needing little information, often implying it can be done quickly and easily. Resource profiles, on the other hand, often represent the opposite situation. As computer spreadsheet models have become readily available, however, the more detailed and complex models have become much easier to develop, and they do provide significantly more information.

7.3   CAPACITY REQUIREMENTS PLANNING (CRP)

CRP inputs production requirements not from the master schedule, *but instead directly from MRP.* MRP, of course, already takes into account the bill of materials, the routing (to some extent), and the lead time offsets. In addition, it also accounts for work in progress and offsets for existing inventory, as well as other demands such as service inventories and anticipated scrap. As a result, it is the most detailed of all the capacity planning techniques.

In addition to the planned order releases from MRP, detailed capacity planning requires information from other sources. Specifically, information is needed from:

- *The open order file.* These are jobs that have been released for production and are in process. They appear on the MRP files as a scheduled receipt. The reason detailed capacity planning needs the open order information in addition to the scheduled receipt information on MRP is that the MRP file does not indicate what operations on the open order have been completed. The open order file will generally contain information as to how far along the order is toward completion or, from a capacity perspective, what specific capacity is still required to complete the rest of the order.

- *The routing file.* Containing information about the route the work is to take through the facility work centers, including the operations that are to be performed.
- *The work center file.* Generally contains information on the various elements of lead time associated with the type of equipment in the center. These time elements can include:
  - *Move time* – the time it usually takes to move material from one work center to another.
  - *Wait time* – the time material has to wait to be moved after it has had an operation completed.
  - *Queue time* – the time material has to wait in front of an operation before it can be processed by that operation. In many operations queue time tends to be the largest element of total lead time.

Production lead time is generally defined to be the total of move time, wait time, queue time, setup time, and run time for the given lot size of the material produced.

The "downside" of using detailed CRP is that while most of the rough-cut methods can be set up on a spreadsheet using only standard information with the master schedule, CRP requires MRP to be run. In fact, most modern systems include a detailed CRP module that is linked directly into the MRP run. CRP tends to be too complex and requires too much data from other files to be run on a "stand-alone" spreadsheet application.

A major issue clouding the effective use of detailed CRP is that MRP is constantly changing as material is produced, received, or used in production. For this reason the associated CRP is constantly changing, making it more difficult to manage effectively.

An additional potential problem with CRP is that it is based on time standards (also true of more detailed "rough-cut" methods), which are somewhat subjective in their development and can change substantially over time due to learning curves and process changes. Even if one can manage all the data generated by CRP, in many operations the accuracy of much of the data is somewhat suspect. This implies that a good business practice to develop is the regular review of work standards, followed by updating of work standard files as required.

Even though detailed CRP is difficult to manage due to the changing nature of information that is always somewhat suspect in the first place, it can still be useful to have as an input to management decisions, especially if the manager understands the way the information is developed and the most appropriate approaches to deal with the information.

7.4   INPUT/OUTPUT CONTROL (I/O)

The key word in the description of this method is *"control."* This means it is not a planning tool, but instead a method developed to *control capacity in the operation once the orders for production requirements have already been released.* Even the level of the tool is different, in that it is usually done (in operations where it is done) at the work center level. The real intent is to monitor and control the total hours of work at any work center by attempting to control the workflow into and out of the center. Another important value of using this method is to identify possible sources of problems in maintaining proper flow of activity in the operation.

To use the analogy established earlier with the load on a work center being like liquid stored in a tank, the major purpose of input/output control is to control the amount of liquid (load) by controlling both the amount of liquid entering the tank (input) and the amount flowing out (output) (see Figure 7.4).

As an example, look at a simple I/O report for a work center in Figure 7.5.

It is obvious that the overall plan for this work center was to reduce the size of the queue of work to do, in that over the 5 weeks shown there is a planned input of 110 hours with a planned output of 125 hours. Specifically, the plan was to reduce the size of the queue at the work center to 20 hours by the end of the 5 weeks.

FIGURE 7.4   Liquid Tank Analogy of Input/Output Control

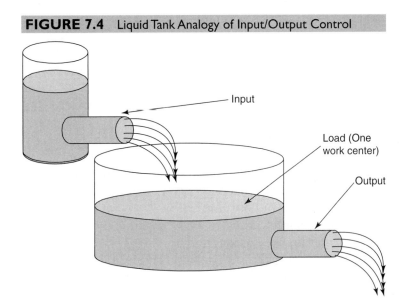

FIGURE 7.5   Sample I/O Report

Week	1	2	3	4	5
Planned input	25	20	30	15	20	
Actual input	22	27	24	23	27	
Cumulative deviation	−3	+4	−2	+6	+13	
Planned output	25	25	25	25	25	
Actual output	21	26	23	25	22	
Cumulative deviation	−4	−3	−5	−5	−8	
Actual backlog (load)	35	36	37	38	36	41

In an actual production environment little ends up going exactly as planned. In this case more work entered the work center (material moved to the center for processing converted to standard hours of production) than was expected—13 hours of work, to be exact. The actual result was an increase of 6 hours of backlog in the operation, from 35 hours to 41 hours. This gives the manager of the work center a good idea of how well the work center is doing with respect to the plan for the work center, and even an idea of the potential source of the problems. In this case, for example, there are two issues worth investigating. First is why more work entered than expected and second is why the workers lost 8 hours of work output over the course of the 5 weeks.

7.5   CAPACITY MEASURES

There are several common measures used to manage capacity. This section defines some of the most common. As you use these measures, it is quite important to realize that there should always be some skepticism with respect to the accuracy of the measure, especially since most of them use time standards in some way. As mentioned earlier, time standards have some aspects of subjectivity in their development (specifically, the use of a performance rating and the application of an allowance for unavoidable delays). More seriously, however, is how the time standards can change over time. As an example, one actual case was discovered when a company (call them Company A) discovered that they were no longer able to be competitive in their market on the basis of price. Some investigation allowed them to discover that the reason was that the assembly workers, who were being paid on a piece-rate basis based on a time standard, were easily making 300% of standard on a regular basis! It seems that the standards had not been reviewed for over 7 years, and the learning curve had been constantly at work. What that meant to Company A was that their assembly workers were making three times the wage of the competition, and that the assembly operation cost Company A three times as much in labor, making them noncompetitive. Of course, you can imagine the problem they faced negotiating with the workers by suggesting that the production output should remain the same while the wage should be one-third of what it was!

- *Utilization.*   In general, utilization shows the maximum hours we can expect to use the work center. Many things can affect the hours the equipment can be used, including machine problems, absentee workers, material problems, and other types of delays. Therefore, utilization is defined as:

$$\text{Utilization} = (\text{Hours worked})/(\text{available hours}) \times 100\%$$

Or, from a product perspective:

$$\text{Utilization} - (\text{Actual Output})/(\text{Design Capacity}) \times 100\%$$

- *Efficiency.*   Efficiency essentially measures the actual output of a defined area as compared to the standard rate of production based on the same number of hours. The standard rate of production is, of course, based on the time standards. Given the above discussion, it should be easy to see how many operations can obtain an efficiency well in excess of 100%.

$$\text{Efficiency} = (\text{standard hours produced})/(\text{hours worked}) \times 100\%$$

Or, from a product perspective:

$$\text{Efficiency} = (\text{actual production rate})/(\text{standard production rate}) \times 100\%$$

- *Rated Capacity.*   Defined as the product of available time, efficiency, and utilization.

$$\text{Rated Capacity} = (\text{available time}) \times (\text{efficiency}) \times (\text{utilization})$$

- *Demonstrated Capacity.*   As implied by the name, demonstrated capacity is the actual capacity output as shown by the production records.

7.6   GENERAL APPROACH TO CAPACITY MANAGEMENT

As indicated on Figure 7.1, capacity management is a critical activity in managing an operation. The best production plans and schedules in the world are of virtually no use without the right amount of the right capacity with which to execute those plans.

The key to capacity management is, therefore, to be constantly comparing the capacity available with the capacity required to meet the needs of the customers as defined by the MPS and the MRP output. If a mismatch exists, the prudent manager will analyze the options and make the most cost-effective decision possible to address the mismatch. Much as in the discussion in the chapter on Sales and Operations Planning (S&OP), the manager can elect to change the amount and/or timing of the capacity, can change the load, or both. Given that the time frames are much shorter when dealing with the MPS as compared to the S&OP, many of the options dealing with load are not available. Much of the load in the short term represents firm customer orders as opposed to the forecasts found in the S&OP. Since many of these customers have already been promised delivery, it becomes difficult to alter those delivery promises.

The major issue then focuses on using relatively short-term solutions to manage the amount and type of capacity available to process the load. As with the S&OP, there are several options available, including:

- Overtime
- Subcontracting
- Hiring/firing workers
- Temporary workers
- Shift workers from one work center to another (assumes workforce flexibility)
- Use alternative routings for the work (in some cases, even if the alternative routing is not as cost-effective). In fact, many operations discover that if they have one operation that is more efficient than the alternatives, all jobs will be selected to use this more efficient operation, thereby overloading it. It must be recognized that using a less efficient operation may be highly preferable to missing a customer order due date merely to make it in a more efficient manner.

The "good news" with this discussion is, however, that if a good job was done with forecasting and using that forecast for effective sales and operations planning, the correct resources should largely be in place. More specifically, the entire process of capacity planning as detailed in this chapter should really be little more than "fine tuning" of the required capacity. If this is not the case, it is the S&OP and forecasting approaches that should first be examined, rather than the more detailed capacity planning approaches discussed in this chapter.

KEY TERMS

Capacity
Rough-Cut Capacity Planning
Resource Profiles
Input/Output Control

Rated Capacity
Load
Capacity Bills
Capacity Requirements Planning (CRP)

Utilization
Capacity Planning
Routing
Efficiency
Demonstrated Capacity

SUMMARY

This chapter discusses the importance of capacity, for without adequate capacity of the correct type there will be little chance of implementing the best of production plans. Several approaches are discussed, from the roughest of the rough-cut methods to the most detailed, CRP. In addition, the control of capacity while the plan is being executed is discussed. Finally, some of the more common measures of capacity are discussed.

REFERENCES

Fogarty, D. W., J. H. Blackstone, Jr., and T. R. Hoffmann, *Production and Inventory Management.* Cincinnati, OH: South-Western, 1991.

Schonsleben, P., *Integral Logistics Management.* Boca Raton, FL: St. Lucie Press, 2004.

Vollmann, T. E., W. L. Berry, and D. C. Whybark, *Manufacturing Planning and Control Systems.* New York: Irwin McGraw-Hill, 1997.

DISCUSSION QUESTIONS AND PROBLEMS

1. There are two products being produced by a firm with the following bills of material:

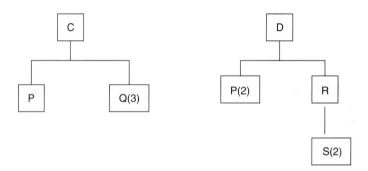

Routing Information (all times in hours)

Product/part	Lot Size	Work Center	Operation	Setup hours	Run Time Per Unit
C	20	100	1 of 1	0.6	0.8
D	40	100	1 of 1	0.8	1.2
P	100	200	1 of 1	1	0.4
Q	70	300	1 of 1	2	0.7
R	50	200	1 of 2	1.6	0.5
R	50	300	2 of 2	0.8	1.3
S	100	200	1 of 2	1.2	0.6
S	100	300	2 of 2	0.5	0.9

With this information, set up the capacity bills and determine the capacity needed per work center to run the following master schedule:

Week	1	2	3
Product C	50	40	45
Product D	15	20	18

2. Describe how the following conditions have potentially been caused by poor capacity planning
   a. Expediting
   b. Premium shipping cost from suppliers
   c. Poor equipment utilization
   d. Poor worker efficiency
   e. Excessive inventory
   f. Cash flow problems
3. The following input/output report was prepared for a work center with a beginning backlog of 10 hours:

Week	1	2	3	4	5	6
Planned input (hrs.)	60	60	60	60	60	60
Actual input (hrs.)	65	67	61	58	57	55
Cumulative deviation						
Planned output (hrs.)	60	60	60	60	60	60
Actual output (hrs.)	62	64	63	58	55	56
Cumulative deviation						
Actual backlog						

   a. Complete the input/output report for the center.
   b. What recommendations would you make to the manager of this work center? Why?
4. The following capacity bills are given for Items S and R:

Work Center	S	R
10	0.14 hours	0.07 hours
20	0.82 hours	0.71 hours
30	1.16 hours	0.88 hours

   a. In week 1 there is an MPS of 60 Ss and 70 Rs. Week 2 MPS quantities are 50 Ss and 90 Rs. What are the capacity requirements for each work center for week 1 and week 2?
   b. If each work center has a stated capacity of 120 standard hours available per week, what actions need to be taken (if any)?
5. Given the following bills of material and routing information, develop capacity bills for each of the products P and Q:

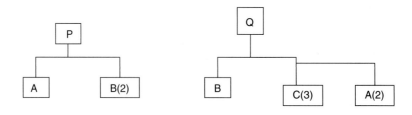

Item	Work center	Lot size	Operation	Setup (hrs)	Run (hrs per unit)
P	10	30	1 of 1	1.2	0.43
Q	10	50	1 of 1	0.6	0.57
A	20	60	1 of 2	0.8	0.18
A	30	60	2 of 2	0.9	0.33
B	20	80	1 of 1	1.3	0.19
C	20	50	1 of 2	2.1	0.22
C	30	50	2 of 2	0.8	0.09

6. a. Fill in the missing data on the following input/output report. Then answer the questions concerning the report. The work center has a beginning backlog of 25 hours. All values in the report are in hours:

Week	1	2	3	4	5	6
Planned input (hrs.)	80	80	80	70	70	70
Actual input (hrs.)	88	83	85	80	73	75
Cumulative deviation						
Planned output (hrs.)	82	82	81	70	70	70
Actual output (hrs.)	80	79	83	74	71	72
Cumulative deviation						
Actual backlog						

   b. Interpret the report. What do you think the plan was? What is happening?
7. Items P and Q have capacity bills as follows:

Work Center	P	Q
10	0.31 hours	0.09 hours
15	0.55 hours	0.82 hours
20	1.23 hours	0.47 hours

   a. In week 1 there is an MPS quantity of 90 Ps and 75 Qs. In week 2 the MPS quantity calls for 78 Ps and 103 Qs. What are the capacity requirements for each of the work centers for weeks 1 and 2?
   b. Each work center has a standard stated capacity of 120 hours per week. If the facility uses infinite capacity planning techniques, what should they do, if anything (be specific)?
8. The following input/output report was prepared for a work center with a beginning backlog of 23 hours:

Week	1	2	3	4	5	6
Planned input (hrs.)	50	50	50	55	55	55
Actual input (hrs.)	57	53	51	56	53	59
Cumulative deviation						
Planned output (hrs.)	60	55	55	55	55	55
Actual output (hrs.)	53	51	54	56	52	58
Cumulative deviation						
Actual backlog						

a. Complete the input/output report for the center.
b. Explain what the center was probably trying to accomplish, based on the planning numbers.

9. Birchmark Industries makes two items for the furniture industry: end panels and shelves. Routing and standard time data for the two items are shown below.

Item	Lot size	Operation	Machine center	Setup time (hr.)	Run time per unit (hr.)
End panels	60	1 of 3	Saw	0.7 hours	0.1 hours
		2 of 3	Planer	0.25	0.15
		3 of 3	Router	0.0	0.075
Shelves	100	1 of 3	Saw	0.1	0.06
		2 of 3	Planer	0.25	0.03
		3 of 3	Router	0.5	0.06

Assume that the three operations above are the only ones needed to complete each item. Write out the capacity bill for each item. What is the standard time per unit?

10. Describe the environment where detailed capacity planning may become difficult if not impossible to use effectively. Would rough-cut capacity planning be more effective in such an environment? Why or why not?

CHAPTER 8

Production Activity Control

Chapter Outline

Introduction—**Production Activity Control** (PAC), as the name implies, is concerned with controlling the actual activity of making a product or delivering a service. This implies the planning has been done and the actual order to produce the product or deliver the service has been executed. We already dealt with one aspect of PAC (controlling capacity) when the Input/Output Control approach was discussed in the chapter on capacity management. While Input/Output Control primarily dealt with controlling the capacity (load) at a work center, PAC deals with controlling the *priority* of the jobs at that work center.

As in the case of master scheduling (where every business and type of business has one) so too does every business have some methodology for establishing the execution of the order. The primary difference, of course, is that master scheduling is a *PLANNING* activity, while PAC is an *EXECUTION CONTROL* activity. A simple example may help clarify. In their personal life every person has a basic plan of what they want to accomplish in a given day, week, month, and so on. Once the day or week has started, however, the plans for that day and week need to be executed. As events occur and unanticipated things happen to us, we may frequently find the need to reprioritize what we are working on. The control of the priority and the execution of the task is an ongoing need for most of us on a regular basis. That need also exists in any business operation, only because of the size and scope of business needs the information, systems, and actions required to monitor, prioritize, and control the actions tend to be much more formal and structured. It is those activities, methods, and systems used to perform that control that is typically called production activity control or PAC. PAC is sometimes referred to as **shop floor control,** although that title has an implication that it is applying primarily to a manufacturing setting. Since most of the principles of PAC also apply to service operations as well as manufacturing, the name PAC is used to imply the more generic applications.

8.1   GENERAL PAC INFORMATION AND DATA

Two of the major inputs to a PAC system are the source of orders that need to be processes and the information by which to control and process the orders. These major inputs to the system include:

- Newly released orders (often from MRP).
- Existing order status.
- Routing information (as discussed in the capacity system). Routing describe the process steps, in sequence, that must be done to complete the job.
- Lead time information (from the item master).
- Status of resources (quantity of resources available, equipment problems, maintenance schedules, etc.).

It should be obvious that resources are also required to execute any production schedule. Another critical input into the PAC system must be the number, type, and condition of those resources. Major resources used include:

- People—How many people with what skills are available? Also necessary is the amount of time they are available on a day-to-day basis.
- Tooling—Any fixtures or equipment the operation must use for setup or operation of the machinery or production process.
- Machine or equipment capacity and any scheduled downtime.
- Materials—what components and/or other material are needed to complete the order.

Any good PAC system will also produce useful managerial information in addition to using information. Some of the information that a PAC system may generate includes:

- Status and location of orders.
- Status of critical resources.
- Performance to standards (time and/or cost standards).
- Scrap/rework reporting.
- Notification of any problems (e.g., equipment or tooling breakage).

Some production systems, of course, have much simpler systems or no real formal systems at all. Process industries, such as some chemical processing, and companies with highly repetitive assembly lines producing a high-volume standard product, have little in the way of detailed PAC. Most of their responsibility is to launch the production requirements into the system from a master schedule and then process and monitor the quantity as it is produced. In systems that have smaller quantities of discrete jobs, however, the inputs to the system are processed and the resulting output is often in the form of a **dispatch list.** The dispatch list supplies, as the name implies, the list of jobs to be performed at a given work center in the order in which the jobs should be done. In many cases, the list also provides a great deal of additional useful information, including:

- Time estimates, including scheduled run date, setup time, and run time. This should include an estimate of the capacity available.
- Processing information, such as which equipment to use and the specific operation to run.
- Lot sizes.
- Where (which work center) the job will move after processing.
- Jobs expected to be moved to the work center in some specified time period.

That list of future jobs allows the workers to plan more detail in the job sequence to, for example, minimize the setup required by moving jobs with similar setups back to back in the processing approach.

In almost every case there is also a need to report back to the PAC system as to what has happened:

- What has been produced (part number and quantity).
- Problems, such as quality problems or part shortages.
- Workforce data, often used to define efficiency and utilization.
- Equipment status.

The Gantt Chart.   The *Gantt chart* is a simple visual aid to not only schedule work according to the priority, but to quickly assess the status of all jobs in order to both communicate that status quickly and to reprioritize as necessary. The use for PAC is very similar to the application for Gantt charts used in project management. It visually shows the work to be done, an expectation of the time required, the start and end times, and usually the job status. It is often done by work center or even by a specific piece of equipment. A simple example is given in Figure 8.1.

In the case shown in Figure 8.1, there are three jobs (part numbers) with multiple tasks to be performed on the given work center. In some cases (Part A, operation 2 and Part B, operation 1) jobs are scheduled to be run in parallel

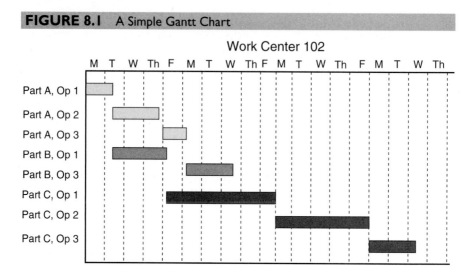

FIGURE 8.1   A Simple Gantt Chart

because they are for different operations (and therefore probably using different equipment). On the other hand, the operations for part C cannot be run in parallel since they are to be performed on the same part. In this case, it appears that operation 1 must be completed on all parts C before the next operation can begin.

As time progresses, the current date can be noted on the chart together with the graphical representation of the status of each job. This is what can be used to establish specific status reports as well as a pictorial method to reschedule.

As the diagram shows, job status is clearly indicated. In this case, operation 1 for part C is ahead of schedule while operation 3 on part B is behind. Part A

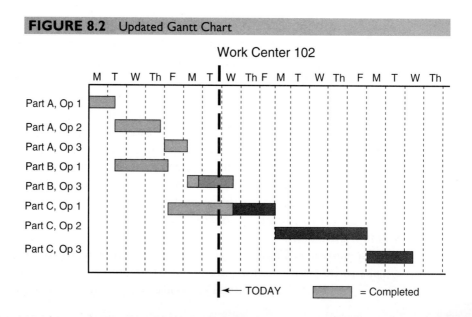

FIGURE 8.2   Updated Gantt Chart

has been completed. The manager of this operation can now investigate the possible problem with the part B job and either reschedule or correct the problem if possible. Clearly this chart needs to be updated frequently if it is to be useful, not only with job status but also the addition of new jobs as they arrive and the removal of completed work.

8.2   PRIORITIZING WORK

There are several approaches used to prioritize work at a work center. These rules work for both service operations as readily as they do in manufacturing. While many more complex rules have been developed for specific applications (multiple machines, for example), coverage of those rules are beyond the intended scope of the chapter. The simple rules include:

- *Due date* (also called earliest due date).   As the name implies, this rule selects the job with the earliest due date to be done first. In case of ties, another secondary rule (from the list below) can be used to break the tie. This rule is often used in operations using MRP for planning, as the due date is inherent with MRP planning and is naturally generated from the system.

- *Shortest processing time (SPT).*   Again the name itself is quite descriptive. Jobs are prioritized according to the estimated processing time it takes to do them, with the shortest processing time first. An advantage of this approach is that a lot of jobs are completed quickly. Unfortunately, there is nothing in the rule that captures when the order is needed by the customer. Often this rule will tend to leave the large jobs at the end, and will therefore frequently make them late. That is not a good condition in environments where the large jobs often represent a large and valuable customer.

- *Total slack.*   For all remaining operations on the job, the total processing time remaining is computed. Then the total time until the job is due is calculated. Subtracting total processing time from total time until due yields slack. Slack is really buffer time, or time that can pass without danger of making the job late. The rule is to select jobs with the least total slack to be done first, since they are in the greatest danger of being late if held up.

- *Slack per operation.*   A variant of total slack, the total slack for this rule is divided by the number of operations left. The job with the least total slack per operation is scheduled first. This gives more information than the total slack rule, in that it gives the average slack at each operation rather than the total slack for the entire job.

- *First come, first serve.*   Again the name describes the rule. This is the rule that is heavily used by service organizations such as banks and retail stores, often because they have no alternative. The underlying assumption is that the first job is also needed first. In addition, this rule implies a common perception of fairness, given that a job that enters the operation first has first priority.

- **Critical ratio.**   For this rule a ratio without units of measure is calculated. The ratio is time remaining until due divided by the work remaining. Work remaining is the total processing time, while time remaining is the time until the job is due to be done. If the critical ratio is greater than 1, there is slack. If equal to 1, there is no slack and work must proceed without delay. If less than 1, the job is already late. Clearly the job with the lowest critical ratio is scheduled first with this rule. Many people consider this a superior rule since it takes into account both the due date and the slack time.

EXAMPLE 8.1

Suppose a work center has the following six jobs awaiting processing (they are listed in the order in which they arrived at the work station):

Job	Due in	Hours of work remaining
A	3 hours	4
B	9 hours	2
C	4 hours	1
D	15 hours	5
E	11 hours	3.5
F	19 hours	4

We need to examine the "best" schedule for the work we have at the work center. Note that regardless of what we decide, it is highly likely there will be a problem. Job A, for example, is due in only 3 hours while there is still 4 hours of work remaining. We can also note that there is 19.5 hours of total work and the job with the latest due time is due at time 19, meaning that at least one other job will be late. In any case, we need to look at the job sequence according to the various "rules" to determine the best order:

Due date.   Establishing the priority is easy. We merely look at when the jobs are due and the one due first has the top priority. We also look at the implications to order "lateness," assuming we start from time "0":

Job	Due in	Work remaining	Start time	Completion time	Late?
A	3 hours	4 hours	0	4	Yes, 1 hour
C	4 hours	1 hour	4	5	Yes, 1 hour
B	9 hours	2 hours	5	7	No
E	11 hours	3.5 hours	7	10.5	No
D	15 hours	5 hours	10.5	15.5	Yes, 0.5 hours
F	19 hours	4 hours	15.5	19.5	Yes, 0.5 hours

Shortest Processing Time.   Note that when we apply this rule we have a "tie" between two jobs, A and F. We will then use a secondary rule, in this case due date, to break the tie:

Job	Due in	Work remaining	Start time	Completion time	Late?
C	4 hours	1 hour	0	1	No
B	9 hours	2 hours	1	3	No
E	11 hours	3.5 hours	3	6.5	No
A	3 hours	4 hours	6.5	10.5	Yes, 7.5 hours
F	19 hours	4 hours	10.5	14.5	No
D	15 hours	5 hours	14.5	19.5	Yes, 4.5 hours

Note the trade-offs developing. In the due date case, we had four of the six jobs late, but none were very late. The total lateness for all four jobs was only 3 hours. In the SPT rule case, however, there were but two jobs late—but they were very late. The combined lateness of the two jobs was 12 hours.

Total Slack.   To determine the priority, we have to figure the slack and then establish the priority from that. Slack in this case is merely the difference between the work remaining and the time until due.

Job	Due in	Work remaining	Slack	Start time	Completion time	Late?
A	3 hours	4 hrs.	1 hr.	0	4	Yes, 1 hour
C	4 hours	1 hr.	3 hrs	4	5	Yes, 1 hour
E	11 hours	3.5 hrs	6.5 hrs.	5	8.5	No
B	9 hours	2 hrs.	7 hrs.	8.5	10.5	Yes, 1.5 hours
D	15 hours	5 hrs.	10 hrs.	10.5	15.5	Yes, 0.5 hours
F	19 hours	4 hrs.	15 hrs.	15.5	19.5	Yes, 0.5 hours

It should be fairly obvious in this case that this method is probably not the best for this set of jobs. While each late job is not very late, all of them except for one have some degree of lateness.

Critical Ratio.   The last rule to illustrate is the critical ratio. Recall that the ratio is calculated by taking the time remaining until due and dividing it by the work remaining. Jobs with the smallest critical ratio are taken first.

Job	Due in	Work remaining	Ratio	Start time	Completion time	Late?
A	3 hours	4 hrs.	0.75	0	4	Yes, 1 hour
D	15 hours	5 hrs.	3	4	9	No
E	11 hours	3.5	3.14	9	12.5	Yes, 1.5 hours
C	4 hours	1 hr.	4	12.5	13.5	Yes, 9.5 hours
B	9 hours	2 hrs.	4.5	13.5	15.5	Yes, 6.5 hours
F	19 hours	4 hrs.	4.75	15.5	19.5	Yes, 0.5 hours

Even though this method might have a great deal of appeal because it incorporates most of the information about the jobs, it clearly is not the best approach for this particular set of jobs. All but one is late, and two are quite late. One must recognize that because of the kind of results shown in this example that there is often no one "best" approach.

Scheduling in MRP and "Pull" Production Environments

The scheduling rules described above are generally applicable in production environments where integrated production control systems are not used, such as is often the case in smaller job shop environments. Where integrated approaches are used (e.g., MRP or Kanban pull systems) the systems themselves provide inherent scheduling priorities:

- MRP systems. As the master schedule is exploded through the MRP logic, the due date for the master schedule item and the lead time offsets used in the MRP logic will generate due dates for all subassemblies and components. These due dates are then used to establish the priority for production. The MRP approach, therefore, uses due date priority scheduling as part of the basic logic of the system.

- Kanban "pull" systems (described in detail in Chapter 9). Pull systems are basically reactive systems, generating information about demand from use of the material. Production signals merely come from the need to replace material that has been used and "pulled" from the in-process inventory. In this sense, the system basically is a first come, first serve priority system. The primary modification comes from the condition where multiple pull requirements may be presented to the work center at virtually the same time. In other words, it may not be clear which requirement was generated first. In addition, it is often important to assess material needs beyond just recognizing a pull signal that came to the center first. The modification of priority comes from information about the rate of production or need for the material as it is being used in subsequent work centers. The rule here is that when pull signals arrive for multiple parts at virtually the same time, in general it is better to first process the material that is being used more rapidly in subsequent work centers.

8.3   SCHEDULING

Assuming that an MRP or Pull system is not being used (as discussed in the previous section), an estimation of when the job will reach certain work centers, and when the work should be completed at the work center, can be developed. There are two basic approaches to establishing these time estimates. The first, called backward scheduling, starts the calculation from the time the job is due (or has been promised), and uses lead time information to work backward to determine when the job should reach and be completed by each work center. The second, called forward scheduling, is essentially the opposite. This method starts when the job is to be released into the production process. Again using lead time estimations, the method calculated when the job should reach and be completed by each work center, ending up with an estimation of final completion of the work. This final completion time represents the most logical promise time for the customer. Because backward scheduling starts with the customer-expected due date, it is often the preferred method, and is in fact the method used by MRP.

EXAMPLE 8.2

The following information is available for a particular job. It is now the start of day 214, and there is but one shift in the operation with seven productive hours. For illustrative purposes, we assume that productive capacities will be available when called for. The job calls for a quantity of 100 to be built:

Operation	Total lead time for 100, including setup, run, queue, and move time
A	21 hours
B	14 hours
C	35 hours
D	7 hours
E	10.5 hours
F	3.5 hours

If we were to use forward scheduling, we would launch the job into production as soon as possible. In this case, assume we can launch the job into production immediately (day 214). That would imply the following:

Operation	Completed
A	End of day 216 (3 shifts)
B	End of day 218
C	End of day 223
D	End of day 224
E	Half through day 226
F	End of day 227

Using this approach, we can assume that the earliest the job can be completed is the end of day 227, which probably implies we can deliver on day 228. This of course assumes no problems that will impact the queue time. Note that the simplified assumptions of total time assumes queue time is built in. Queue time is, of course, typically the largest and most variable of all the elements of lead time.

Now we examine the use of backward scheduling. Suppose the job has been promised to the customer on day 240, using (perhaps) a standard quoted lead time commonly used by many sales functions. We then assume that the job must be completed on day 239 at the latest in order to prevent late delivery. Backward scheduling works backward from that day 239 date:

Operation	Must complete by	Must start by:
F	End of day 239	Mid-day 239
E	Mid-day 239	Start of day 238
D	End of day 237	Start of day 237
C	End of day 236	Start of day 232
B	End of day 231	Start of day 230
A	End of day 229	Start of day 227

Note that backward scheduling provides the latest possible start date at the beginning of day 227. There is, of course, nothing to prevent starting the job before day 227, but to do so implies an increase in the amount of inventory. Many operations will elect to do so, given the variability and unpredictability in determining lead times, especially when queue times are involved.

8.4   LOADING

The total time estimate to complete all the jobs at a given work center is often called the work center load, as was indicated in the discussion about input/output control (Chapter 7). Load is often measured in time units, such as hours of work. Before discussing the methods by which loading can be done, it will be helpful to understand two fundamentally different approaches to manage a load.

Infinite Loading

In this approach, jobs are loaded into a work center according to when they need to be done with respect to customer need regardless of what the load is compared to capacity. In some respect, the jobs are loaded under the assumption the work center has almost infinite capacity (clearly not really the case). A load may look much like the diagram in Figure 8.3.

The major issue with infinite loading is how to manage the load. In the case above, for example, there is little chance to do the extra week 2 load early in week 1. The manager will probably have to do something to increase the capacity temporarily in week 2, such as scheduling overtime. The overload in weeks 4 and 5 may, however, be done in week 3 since there is clearly slack capacity in that week. That is, of course, assuming that the jobs are available to be worked on early. If not, the manager may again be faced with finding capacity-expanding alternatives.

Finite Loading

As the name implies, this approach implies you have a known, measurable, finite capacity for the work center. There is as much loaded into the work center as possible for a given time period, then the work is moved on to the next time period since there appears to be no more capacity in the given period. This approach has gained a great deal of use in the last few years, as numerous finite

FIGURE 8.3 "Infinite" Load Example

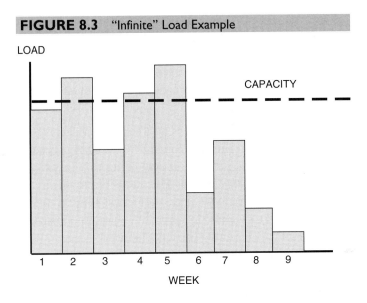

scheduling software packages have been introduced. The graphical representation is in Figure 8.4.

While this finite loading approach clearly has advantages in smoothing the load and in decreasing extra expenses from overtime and other expediting activities, there is also a clear disadvantage. Specifically, when the load is shifted to a later time period in cases when the capacity is reached, customer due dates may be adversely affected. In other words, while it may be better for the stability of the facility, it may be highly disruptive to customer service. In spite of that it is frequently used, especially in operations where adding short-term capacity is very expensive or impossible.

FIGURE 8.4 Finite Load Example

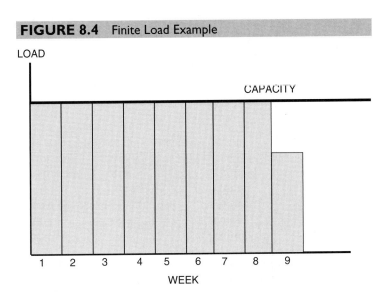

There are also some assumptions that must be understood before using this system. An inherent assumption with loading is that the capacity is known and accurate and the processing time for jobs is also known and accurate. Unfortunately, both those measures tend to be based on job standards that are not only somewhat subjective when developed but also change over time due to learning curves.

There are basically two methods used to load a work center:

- **Vertical loading.** In this approach a work center is selected and jobs are loaded into the center job by job according to a priority rule such as those described earlier in the chapter. The focus is the work center, with the job loaded work center by work center, one job loaded at a time

- **Horizontal loading.** In this approach the highest priority job is loaded work center by work center into all the work centers that will be required. Then the next job is loaded work center by work center, and so forth. This method is the one most commonly used by the finite scheduling systems mentioned above. The focus here is the job, with a job selected and loaded work center by work center.

EXAMPLE 8.2   LOADING EXAMPLE

A work center (Center X) has the following jobs. They are listed in the order in which they arrived at the work center. The work center uses due date with first come, first serve to break "ties" as its approach to loading. The current day is the start of day 137, and there are 7 productive hours (420 minutes) in a day:

Job	Quantity	Due day	Setup time	Standard per piece
A	130	136	10 minutes	1.5 minutes
B	100	137	30 minutes	1.8 minutes
C	50	137	10 minutes	0.6 minutes
D	200	138	25 minutes	0.8 minutes
E	120	138	15 minutes	1.1 minutes
F	100	138	20 minutes	1.3 minutes

First, assume that we will use vertical loading and assume infinite capacity. The first chore is to determine the time it should take to complete each job at standard:

Job	Time standard × quantity	Setup time	Total time
A	$(130) \times (1.5) = 195$ min.	10 min.	205 min.
B	180 min.	30 min.	210 min.
C	30 min.	10 min.	40 min.
D	160 min.	25 min.	185 min.
E	132 min.	15 min.	147 min.
F	130 min.	20 min.	150 min.

To use infinite loading, you would load the work center according to due date. That means that jobs A (already late), B, and C would be loaded into day

137 and D, E, and F would be loaded into day 138. Doing that would require 455 minutes in day 137 and 482 minutes in day 138. Since both days have more minutes required (at standard) than what is available (420 minutes), the work center would probably need to schedule overtime to accomplish the work (assuming relatively accurate standards).

By contrast, if finite loading is used, you would only try to complete jobs A and B in day 137. Since they require 415 minutes, the best you should expect to do is start the 10-minute setup for job C before the end of the day. Day 138 could then finish job C (the 35 minutes remaining, and then complete jobs D and E. They should finish job E at the 367-minute mark, allowing 53 minutes to set up and start running job F. They should be able to complete approximately 25 of the 100 items (53 min. − 20 min. setup = 33 min. run time; 33 min/1.3 min per item = 25.4 items). The implication here is clear—both jobs C and F will likely be late.

This example illustrates the trade-offs implicit with the two loading approaches. In general, it could be said that infinite loading tends to assume flexibility in capacity and places due date higher in importance with respect to adding extra capacity (and potentially cost). Finite loading, by contrast, assumes the facility either cannot or chooses not to assume flexibility in capacity and the accompanying costs, where the consequence is potentially poor performance in customer service.

There are, of course, other scheduling techniques that have been developed in recent years. JIT has its own unique approach, as does scheduling by using the Theory of Constraints. The approaches inherent with those concepts will be discussed separately in the specific chapters dealing with those subjects.

8.5   CORRECTIVE ACTIONS

It should be quite clear that most of the approaches discussed in this chapter have a basic assumption that process times and other elements of lead time are known and essentially accurate. Practically speaking, however, we know that is seldom the case. There are subjective elements in developing standard times, the "learning curve" effects will be constantly altering the true processing time, and all types of conditions on the production floor will disrupt or affect the true time to accomplish many of the tasks.

As a result, it is highly likely that corrective actions will be needed on a fairly regular basis. Some of the more common corrective actions include:

- *Subcontracting or purchasing components.* This involves buying required parts instead of making them, or contracting with an outside organization to make the parts instead of using inside production facilities.
- *Lot splitting.* Involves taking only the minimal amount of parts and "pushing" them to completion. This will allow shipping a minimal amount to the

customer while leaving part of the order behind to be completed at a later date.

- *Operation overlapping.* This implies moving part of the order to the subsequent operation before the entire order has been processed by a given operation. Generally, this method will allow faster completion of the order.
- *Operation splitting.* This implies assigning more resources (people and equipment) to the order so that processing can proceed in parallel and therefore be completed more quickly.
- *Alternative routings.* This implies moving the job to operations not normally used for the production, primarily used when the primary production resources are not available or are already engaged with other work.
- *Order cancellation.* Clearly this is often the last resort, but may be used when the cost to complete the order using these "special" actions may exceed the expected profit from the order. Certainly customer goodwill and the long-term reputation impacts must be considered before using this approach, however.

KEY TERMS

Production Activity Control (PAC)	Forward Scheduling	Shop Floor Control
Dispatch List	Gantt Chart	Infinite Loading
Finite Loading	Vertical Loading	Horizontal Loading
	Backward Scheduling	

SUMMARY

The best plans in the world are of little value unless they are properly executed. This chapter examines several of the more common scheduling rules for jobs once they are released into the operation. As conditions change, it is important to control both the priority of work in the facility as well as to control the capacity being used by the work. This chapter identifies many of the more common issues and approaches that are used to increase the probability of effective execution of work in the operation.

REFERENCES

Chase, R. B., and N. J. Aquilano, *Production and Operations Management.* New York: Irwin, 1995.

Fogarty, D. W., J. H. Blackstone, Jr., and T. R. Hoffmann, *Production and Inventory Management.* Cincinnati, OH: South-Western, 1991.

Melnyk, S., and P. Carter, *Production Activity Control.* New York: Irwin, 1987.

Schonsleben, P., *Integral Logistics Management.* Boca Raton, FL: St. Lucie Press, 2004.

DISCUSSION QUESTIONS AND PROBLEMS

1. Discuss the impact that job standards may have on the major activities of PAC. Given that job standards are seldom exact and impacted by learning, what are the implications for the major PAC activities?

2. Ben's Bike Shop has the following repair jobs awaiting Ben when he arrives in the morning for his typical 10-hour work day. All the bike repair jobs listed below were promised to their owners to be ready at certain times today. Determine the priorities for scheduling the jobs using due time; first come, first serve; shortest processing time; total slack; and critical ratio rules. The jobs are listed in the order in which the owners brought the bikes into the shop:

Repair job	Time until due (hrs.)	Estimated repair time
A	2	2.5
B	3	0.5
C	5	1.5
D	5	2
E	6	0.5
F	7	1
G	9	1
H	10	1.5

   a. If his customers are willing to have their job slightly late without getting upset, which rule should he use and why?

   b. If his customers are likely to get upset if the job is not ready exactly when promised, what rule should he use and why?

   c. With the information in this chapter, what changes/approaches would you recommend that Ben should adopt in the future when it comes to both promising job completion and scheduling jobs?

3. A new job has just arrived at a production facility. It is currently the start of day 143, and we assume 8 hours of productive capacity available per day. The job calls for the production of 200 units. The following lists the operations required and the appropriate time standards:

Operation	Setup time	Run time, per unit
A	1.2 hours	3.5 minutes
B	0.5 hours	1.7 minutes
C	2.5 hours	4.4 minutes
D	3 hours	7.1 minutes
E	1.5 hours	2.3 minutes
F	1 hour	3.1 minutes

   a. If the operation uses forward scheduling and launches the job into production immediately, when should we expect it to be done, assuming the right capacity is available when called for?

   b. The customer has requested a delivery date of day 170. If we use backward scheduling from that day, when is the latest the job should be started, again assuming the right capacity is available when called for?

4. An operation manager was heard saying, "I don't have to make a decision to use forward or backward scheduling, since I use MRP. The MRP system makes that decision for me." Discuss—do you agree or disagree, and why?

5. The following jobs are waiting for processing at a work center. There are 7 hours in each productive day. It is currently the start of day 211. The due days are all when the jobs are due by the end of the day they are due, and the jobs are listed in the order they arrived at the work center. The work center uses a due date priority system, with first come, first serve to break "ties."

Job	Quantity	Due day	Setup time	Standard time per piece
A	120	211	30 minutes	2.1 minutes
B	200	212	40 minutes	1.7 minutes
C	100	212	20 minutes	1.2 minutes
D	250	213	35 minutes	1.5 minutes
E	150	214	50 minutes	2.3 minutes
F	200	214	65 minutes	3.2 minutes
G	150	214	30 minutes	1.9 minutes

a. Use vertical loading to load the jobs, assuming infinite capacity. What possible problems/issues do you see and how would you resolve them?

b. Now load the jobs assuming finite capacity. Again, what problems do you see and how would you resolve them?

CHAPTER 9

Lean Production and JIT

Chapter Outline

Introduction—The Just-in-Time (JIT) movement started in Japan (primarily Toyota Motor Company) in the mid-1970s as a response to the worldwide oil crisis earlier in that decade. Since Japan has virtually no natural resources other than their people, they had to import virtually everything else. With the energy crisis making everything less plentiful and more costly, they could little afford to waste much of anything if they were to be competitive in the world marketplace.

As manufacturers in the rest of the world became aware of the incredible improvements in product quality, cost reductions, and significantly better delivery that the new approach was bringing to the successful implementers, there was a great deal of interest and activity generated to discover the methodologies used. Initial efforts in understanding led to several misconceptions about JIT, such as the assertions that it:

- would only work for repetitive, highly standard products;
- would not be appropriate for service operations;
- was only effective because of very close ties and geographic proximity of key suppliers; and
- would only work if given great support from government agencies.

Since that time, fortunately, operations professionals have been able to understand the basic principles inherent with JIT to the point where they have been generalized to be applicable in modified forms to virtually any operation—large or small, manufacturing or service.

The rush to implement during those early years was met with numerous failures, however, as companies tried to make changes without really understanding the implications or the proper approach for their unique conditions. Fortunately, those early "false starts" did not deter the development and improvement of the concepts. Today they have evolved into what is often called **"lean production."** The basic concepts are virtually the same as the original concepts developed by Toyota, but the current approach is to not only understand the concepts in a more generic form, but also to add approaches that improve the understanding of what is to be done as well as the system implications of the changes to be made. An example of this is the use of **value stream mapping.** In this approach, all activities, inventories, and information flows are carefully "mapped" and analyzed. The approach is similar to the heavily used process mapping, but adds a careful analysis of inventory (size, functions, and costs) and information flows, both into and out of various process operations.

It should be noted that a complete discussion of lean production is outside the scope of this book, since proper implementation impacts virtually all aspects of the organization. For our purposes, we will concentrate on areas of lean production that primarily impact the planning and control of operations.

9.1   FUNDAMENTAL CONCEPTS

The focus on waste reduction of the original approach to JIT went well beyond the energy shortages that served as a catalyst for its development. It focused on waste of movement, waste of time, waste due to excessive inventory, and waste resulting from poor quality. The only way an operation could effectively focus on all these forms of waste was to redesign the process used for production and, as a consequence, often the design of the products themselves. In general, it was recognized that the source of much waste (especially the most visible source of waste, excess inventory) was a result of or a response to uncertainties in the system, including the following:

- Market conditions. As discussed in the forecasting chapter, real market demand represents some degree of uncertainty until an actual customer order is placed. Even then, for some companies the customer orders are frequently altered by the customer in quantity, timing, product specifications, or all three.

- Quality problems. If a manager is uncertain as to the quality of a product produced by an operation, they will frequently order more "just in case" some are unusable. For example, if someone needs 100 good items from a process but they know that traditionally the process only produces 90% good outputs, they will likely order 110 or more just in case the poor-quality trend continues.

- Design changes. If the design of a component changes and is not properly implemented, it is highly likely that some of the old design will remain.
- Mistakes. As long as humans are part of the system, there is always the possibility that mistakes will be made. Extra inventory is often called for just in case a mistake is made.
- Inaccurate databases. When a person is uncertain of what they really have in inventory because of historically poor data, the typical response is to order more "just in case."
- Equipment problems (e.g., downtime, setup time, or poor quality). If there is a good chance that a piece of equipment will fail to operate with good quality or at all, extra inventory will serve as a buffer.
- Workforce problems (e.g., training and lack of flexibility). This implies that if there is a possible lack of a properly qualified worker to produce an item just when it is needed, there will be a need for buffer material.
- Supplier problems (e.g., quality or delivery problems). Extra supplier raw material is often kept just in case the supplier is late with their delivery or delivers poor quality or the wrong quantity.

There was another good reason that inventory became a fairly major focal point, other than the obvious potential for wasting capital. Companies were becoming more competitive across several dimensions during the time when lean production methods were evolving, and one of those critical dimensions is delivery speed (time). A well-known relationship, known as Little's law, relates inventory and time in the following way:

$$I = RT$$

Where R is production rate, T is throughput time, and I is inventory. Since there is little that most firms can do to appreciably alter production rates for most products, the law shows the direct relationship between inventory and throughput time in the system. Specifically, if the "R" (production rate) is essentially constant for some operation, then there is a direct relationship between inventory and throughput. The message: significant reduction in inventory could represent significant improvements in throughput time, which is directly related to delivery speed.

It was also recognized (as was discussed in Chapter 5) that inventory in any organization tends to exist as a symptom of the way the business is being run. Where this concept really became visible during the move to JIT is that in the early stages of JIT companies would often focus on the reduction of inventory as the first course of action, almost as if the inventory itself was the problem. It became very clear quite rapidly to most of these companies that reduction of the inventory would only create an entirely new set of problems, and these would often be more costly than the inventory itself was. Some of the common problems caused by inadequate levels of inventory for a given set of process characteristics include:

- Expediting activities and costs increase.
- Premium freight shipments from suppliers increase.
- Split production lots causing excessive setups.
- Poor efficiency and utilization measures caused by shortages.
- And, of course, the obvious problem of stockout conditions.

If we take each of the uncertainties and problems mentioned in the first list in the chapter, we can see how the JIT approach was an all-encompassing systematic effort to alter the basic production processes and even the "culture" of the production areas. Specifically, what was done in each area included:

- *Market conditions.*   The biggest improvement here was in the reduction of lead times through setup reductions, lot size reduction, layout changes, mixed-model scheduling, and rapid information processing (at least partially through Kanban). Significantly shorter lead time means we can start production much closer to the customer delivery time. As discussed in the forecasting chapter, this shorter required forecasting horizon allows for greater forecasting accuracy and less waste. Also the increased flexibility in the system allowed more effective and faster responses to any change in market conditions.

- *Quality problems.*   Many people recognize the close relationship between JIT and Total Quality Management (TQM). One of the major purposes of the TQM movement is to minimize quality problems in the production and design system by focusing on analyzing and improving processes. In addition, a major goal of TQM is minimizing waste in all forms, but especially related to quality. These approaches are not only compatible with JIT concepts, but are a major focus of a JIT implementation.

- *Design changes.*   Part of the TQM effort focused on quality of design. In addition, many products were designed in such a way that any options or special features could be added at the latest possible time in the production process, allowing for more stability in the early portion of the production flow.

- *Mistakes.*   Process designs, as well as product designs, were purposely designed to be as mistake-proof as possible. A good example is the "poke-ayoke," meaning "mistake proofing." Color-coded connections are an example of this approach.

- ***Inaccurate databases.***   Not only were data accuracy problems "cleaned up," but when a system allows for producing with less, there is naturally less to keep track of and often the less you have to track, the easier it is to keep data accurate. In addition, some of the "rules" allowed for ease of obtaining information. For example, the rule that for any given part there be a standard container with a standard number of parts. These standard containers are usually not allowed to be stored with only a partial quantity. In such cases, it is not necessary to count parts—merely count containers and multiply by the standard quantity per container.

- ***Equipment problems.***   The approach here is quite simple to explain: a comprehensive preventive maintenance program that is followed without exception.

- ***Workforce problems.***   There are a number of methods used here, including training, employee involvement, and flexibility of workforce skills.

- ***Supplier problems.***   The development of supplier partnerships with single sources of supply allow for close ties and better relationships. Communication channels are strengthened, and this allows the supplier to both understand the needs of the customer more completely and also to feel more commitment to make sure shortages are rare. All this was done with lower cost of making purchase orders because of the better communication channels (in fact, many companies use electronic data interchange [EDI] or Internet connections to make communication costs almost negligible). Since the supply linkages are more certain, total inventory can be reduced and the supplier can be more intimately involved with the design of the product, making for better, higher quality designs at lower costs.

In general, then, the processes and systems were changed in order to

- Reduce or eliminate disruptions.
- Make the system flexible.
- Reduce setup and lead times.
- Minimize inventory needs.

Several concepts were used to attack the problems, each of which fell under one or more of three categories. Each contributed something, but together they made for a dramatically new system of production. The three categories:

1. Direct reduction of waste.
2. Reduction in process uncertainties that cause waste, usually as a buffer.
3. Finding more effective methods to cope with process uncertainties that cannot be eliminated.

Examples of some of the programs that were used (together with a summary of how they moved the facilities toward JIT) included:

- Stable, uniform loads—eased some of the uncertainty of market demands.
- Market-paced production rates—minimize inventory, reduce lead time, increase customer service (eased uncertainty).
- Total quality management—reduce waste of poor quality, reduce need for buffer inventory "just in case" the quality was bad on some product (eased uncertainty).
- Integrated supplier networks—increase certainty of supply, decrease cost of purchase orders, reduction of inventory, increased quality and value through better designs (reduced waste and eased uncertainty).
- Participative management—more motivated workforce, employee involvement, more flexibility (increased ability to cope with uncertainties that remain).
- Simple, interactive communications—rapid communication of needs and issues at very low cost (increased ability to cope with uncertainties that remain).
- Increased emphasis on preventive maintenance—better assurance of equipment availability; better, more consistent quality of production (eased uncertainty, reduced waste).
- Setup reduction programs—Allows for smaller lot sizes, reduced inventory, shorter lead times, and higher quality with less radical setups (reduced waste with eased uncertainty).
- Cellular layouts—allows for better communication, lower in-process inventory, reduced setup times, lower handling costs, shorter lead times (increased ability to cope with uncertainties that remain and reduced waste).
- Integrated product designs—allows for reduced design costs, better quality, shorter time-to-market lead times, reduced product costs (reduced waste and eased uncertainty).
- Focused facilities—similar to the benefits for cellular layouts.
- Line and flow balancing—reduction in overall lead times and inventory levels (reduced waste and eased uncertainty).
- Increased worker training—flexibility of workers, better quality, improved worker morale (reduced waste and eased uncertainty).

All these system changes not only affected production, but also necessitated a dramatic change in the methods by which the processes were managed. With so much inventory and buffer removed as a result of the changes, operations could no longer be treated separately. For whatever reason inventory existed previously, it ultimately served to decouple operations and allowed them to be managed almost as separate entities. No longer was that the case. Managers were forced to manage using a total system perspective, and since the goals and approaches were different, so too were the methods and measures used. An example may help explain the impact:

Suppose we have a simple operation with three work centers (A, B, and C), as illustrated in Figure 9.1.

The triangles in the diagram represent inventory. Take one of the work centers, say center B, and ask some questions, such as what happens if work center B has an equipment breakdown? The answer, *in the short run,* is that only work center B is affected. Since there is space for inventory between A and B, then center A can continue to work and have a place to put inventory. Since inventory exists between work center B and C, the center C can continue to work as long as the inventory lasts. Most importantly, the customer can continue to be served. The same result occurs regardless of the reason for any disruption in B—including worker absenteeism, poor-quality products being produced, and so forth. The managerial focus can be exclusively on center B to eliminate the problem, and the cost to the facility is essentially that of whatever it costs to fix the problem at B.

This illustrates a very important point with respect to inventory that was briefly mentioned above. *Inventory in any system, regardless of the reason it exists in the system, will automatically serve as a decoupling agent, allowing for focused attention on only one part of the system at a time.* As also indicated above, this only works in the short run, or more specifically, until the inventory between the work centers runs out.

Now examine the same facility, but look at it after a successful JIT program has been put into place. While significant reduction in inventory levels is not the only focus on JIT, it is not only a fairly important goal but certainly a byproduct of all the JIT activities described earlier. If we assume the program has been in place for a while, we can also assume that the inventory levels are very low, giving us a revised picture of the facility, illustrated in Figure 9.2.

In this situation the inventory has been reduced to the point where any significant amount may show up only in the customer facility (we assume the

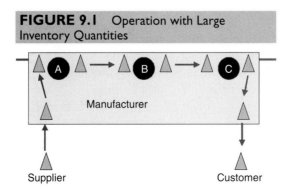

FIGURE 9.1   Operation with Large Inventory Quantities

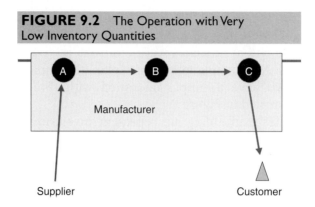

FIGURE 9.2   The Operation with Very Low Inventory Quantities

supplier partnering has been successful, allowing both the reduction of raw material in our facility as well as the comparable finished goods in the supplier facility). In this condition, we can once again ask the same basic question: what happens in the short run if the equipment at center B breaks down? The answer this time is that everything stops, *including shipments to the customer.* Center A has to stop because there is no spot for them to put inventory nor is there any demand for it (assuming a pull system is in place). Center C has to stop because there is no inventory on which they can work. In the absence of decoupling inventory, the manager of the facility *must manage the facility as a tightly linked system.*

The potential impact of that managerial change in focus can be profound indeed. A simple example can illustrate. Suppose the facility has the capability of producing 1,000 units per day (shift) of whatever it is making. Now assume the market demand for some time period is only 800 per day. What do they do with the 20% excess capacity? Clearly they could either send the workers home or allow them to stay but be idle. Typically, however, that is not the approach of JIT systems. With respect to the use of capacity, it is often said that *idle equipment is expected, but idle people are not.* That statement then begs the question as to what they should do. The answer is that there are lots of productive activities that are not direct production—working on quality programs, training, performing maintenance on equipment, and setup reductions are but a few.

The managerial problem with using workers for those activities? These are typically direct labor employees, and the measures used for those employees (labor efficiency and utilization being common ones) will not correctly reflect the nonproduction productive work, since those measures essentially capture only the impact of direct production. In addition, these employees will need direction, training, and motivation to accomplish those new activities. Clearly the managerial challenges for managing and measuring the performance of those workers will need close examination and will probably need significant changes from those of a typical non-JIT system.

A TRUE ANECDOTAL EXAMPLE OF NONSYSTEM THINKING

In the early 1980s a researcher in the United States was trying to learn more about JIT. One way he tried to learn was to identify companies that were reported to have implemented JIT. When he went to one such company, he was told to talk to the purchasing manager, since JIT was a "purchasing system." This was typical of many company interpretations at that time. Rather than focusing on their own operation, managers who did not really understand JIT instead assumed it was the reduction of inventory by having suppliers deliver small quantities of material "just in time" for its use. The researcher talked to the purchasing manager of the company and also to the general manager of one of the major suppliers over the space of several days. A summary follows:

> *RESEARCHER:*   "What do you think of the JIT program?"
>
> *PURCHASING MANAGER:*   "It's great—our raw material inventory has dropped by quite a bit."
>
> *SUPPLIER:*   "It's fine—as part of the program they are reducing the number of suppliers. For those of us that 'survive' it means a lot more business."
>
> *RESEARCHER TO SUPPLIER:*   "JIT is supposed to reduce inventory throughout the entire system. Is your inventory dropping?"
>
> *SUPPLIER:*   "Are you kidding? It's going higher than ever. I'm leasing two new warehouses just to store it all!"
>
> *RESEARCHER:*   "I guess I can understand it going up with more business to your customer. Is the inventory going up at the same proportion as the increase in business?"
>
> *SUPPLIER:*   "No, the inventory is going up a lot more than the business increase."
>
> *RESEARCHER:*   "Why is that?"
>
> *SUPPLIER:*   "Because the customer is just as 'messed up' with their scheduling as before. They often don't know what they need until the last minute, and now that they don't have inventory they expect us to get it to them, and fast. We don't have time to make it, so we had better have it in finished goods. They just change their minds on what they need too often and with too little notice."
>
> *RESEARCHER TO PURCHASING MANAGER:*   "Are you aware your supplier is keeping a lot more inventory for you than they ever did before?"
>
> *PURCHASING MANAGER:*   "Yes, I know they had to do that."
>
> *RESEARCHER:*   "Doesn't that bother you? Doesn't that cost a lot more by having to pay for all that inventory storage?"
>
> *PURCHASING MANAGER:*   "It doesn't bother me at all. We have long-term contracts with the suppliers that lock in the price. We don't have to absorb that cost, the supplier does. I guess they figure it's worth it to keep our business."

> RESEARCHER TO SUPPLIER: "Your customer says you are absorbing all the cost of keeping that extra inventory. Is that right?"
>
> SUPPLIER: "No, they are absorbing the cost."
>
> RESEARCHER: "I don't understand. They say you have the price locked in and cannot pass along the cost of the inventory."
>
> SUPPLIER: "That's correct, but another part of that contract says we can pass along to them any cost we incur as a result of a change in product design. They're always changing designs on the products we make for them. Do you think the only cost we're passing along as design change cost are just the costs associated with the design changes?"

This true story clearly illustrates how to be effective, a manager in a lean production program must understand the overall system and the system effects. In this case, for example, the cost of the extra inventory that was necessary because the program was not correctly implemented would be passed on to the final customer, and does not represent the overall goal of JIT—to reduce overall waste in the system.

This story also helps illustrate how as managers learned more about how to implement JIT and realized the system approaches and impacts, they continued to improve and evolve the system. Some people believe that the modern approach to purchasing and logistics often called "supply chain management," had as its roots the evolution and continuous refinement of the principles of JIT purchasing. In the supply chain approach, the purchasing manager in the illustrative story would never allow themselves to be so neglectful of the impact that his policies could have on the suppliers in particular and on the total chain of material in the system in general. We will revisit the concept of supply chain with more detail in Chapter 11.

9.2   SOME IMPACTS ON CAPACITY

Some additional comments on capacity management in lean production are appropriate. Earlier it was mentioned that a manager in a lean production system must view capacity in a more flexible manner. That discussion was made in the context of workers having capacity available beyond that needed directly for production. There are other issues that will also cause the JIT manager to manage capacity differently than in a normal system.

Going back to the discussion on inventory (Chapter 5), it was stated that one way to view inventory was as stored capacity. In a lean production system where inventory is reduced, the producer tends to have to manage capacity requirements more in "real time" since they don't have the luxury of having stored capacity in the form of inventory. In most production environments the customer demand for any period has some degree of uncertainty, even with all the improvements made to reduce the uncertainty (described earlier). Since there is little inventory to respond to those uncertain demands, it is important that there is buffer inventory available to produce product for that demand (as opposed to providing from inventory).

The good news is that with all those efforts made to reduce uncertainty, increase flexibility, and reduce lead times, the amount of buffer capacity does not have to be excessive. It does, however, need to be carefully planned and should be recognized as one of the costs of having an effective JIT program.

9.3   THE PULL SYSTEM

MRP is often called a "push" system, meaning that the material needs are calculated ahead of time (planned order releases) and, assuming there are no significant changes to the plans, "pushed" out to the production system in the form of a production order. The "trigger" for the entire plan is the projection of the final product need, as represented by the master production schedule (MPS). Part of the difficulty with MRP is that many times the plans are not effective because of problems or changes, including:

- Changes in customer requirements, both in timing and quantity.
- Supplier delivery problems, including timing, quantity, and quality.
- Inaccurate databases that can make the plans invalid, depending on the nature of the inaccurate data.
- Production problems, including:
  - Absenteeism in the workforce
  - Productivity and/or efficiency problems
  - Machine downtime
  - Quality problems
  - Poor communication

These problems generally promote an environment that, despite the best-made plans, can allow for ineffective execution and a growth in the very inventory levels they were meant to reduce. It also should be noted that this list is essentially the same list of problems that represented a major attack from a JIT implementation.

The pull system was developed as an alternative to classical "push" MRP. The underlying concept is to not preplan and generate schedules, but instead to react to the final customer order or "downstream" operation needs and produce only what is needed to satisfy demand and then only when it is needed. Essentially, this system is much the same as the basic reorder point system used for independent inventory. If that is the case, why can it now work when it did not work effectively for so many years before MRP? MRP was primarily designed as a more effective alternative to reorder points because they did not work well.

The major reason reorder points do not normally work well in a dependent inventory environment is a significant violation of the assumption of relatively constant demand that allows a reorder point to work well in some independent inventory environments. A simple example may help to illustrate the problem.

> Suppose the product of interest is a specific model of bicycle. The bicycles are made in batches, which is a typical mode of production for an assemble-to-order environment. The batch size, for our example, is 200 bicycles of the model of interest.
>
> Now we look at an item of dependent inventory that is but one level lower on the bill of materials—the bicycle seat. Suppose it has a lot size of 300, a 2-week lead time, and, since we are examining the use of a reorder point, a reorder point of 80.
>
> ***Example 1.*** In this case suppose we have an inventory of 290 of the seats. A new batch of bicycles has just been ordered, requiring us to use 200 of the seats in a very short time. We are left, therefore, with 90 seats—10 above the reorder point. We do not reorder since the reorder point has not been reached. The 90 will stay in inventory until the next order for the bicycles is generated, which may be a significant amount of time. When that order does come to build another 200 bicycles, we can only build 90 because that is the only inventory we have. We need to immediately order another lot of 300, but it will be 2 weeks before they are available.
>
> ***Example 2.*** Now let us assume we have less inventory—enough less so that by building the lot of 200 bicycles we will hit the seat reorder point. Suppose, for example, we have 270 seats. The order for 200 bicycles comes in, we use 200 seats, and the seat reorder point is reached. That will cause us to immediately reorder. Two weeks later the 300 seats arrive, which are added to the 70 left in stock. We now have 370 seats, which will stay in inventory (costing a lot of money) until the next time we build the model of bicycles, which may be a very long time.

As the example illustrates, the lot sizing problem with dependent inventory often leaves us with either a crisis shortage or a replenishment of stock well before it is actually needed. What this example shows, however, is that the critical conditions causing the problem is the large lot sizes and the long lead times, both of which are major "targets" of lean production waste reduction.

First, we look again at the standard EOQ model, which helps determine the most economical lot size. It is, of course, the basic trade-off of inventory holding cost and order cost, as described in most introductory courses in operations management (see Figure 9.3).

A fundamental assumption of this model is that the two major costs involved are known and relatively fixed. While that is essentially true with holding cost, it is not true with order cost. If the order cost is equipment setup, then a major JIT effort is to reduce this setup cost. If it is a purchased item, the major effort is to work with suppliers to reduce the cost and time of purchase order and delivery. With these efforts, the order cost curve is driven downward and to the left, as in Figure 9.4.

FIGURE 9.3   The Basic EOQ Model

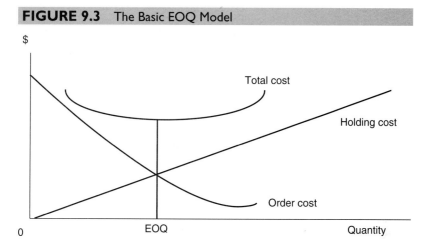

When these actions are taken, a new total cost curve based on the new order cost curve is generated, resulting in a significantly smaller EOQ, as Figure 9.5 illustrates.

This change in order cost and total cost will imply the economic order quantities and the reorder points are very small, meaning that we will be ordering frequently, but in very small batches. Since the actions are also taken at the final product level, there will be, in our bicycle example, frequent lots of very small quantities of bicycles built requiring small lots of seats frequently reordered.

The Bicycle Example Revisited

If we are to reexamine the scenario with the bicycles and bicycle seats, we can now see the impact of the order cost changes that have been made. The lot size for the bicycles is very small, as is the lot size for the seats. Lead time to replenish the seats, also a "target" for lean production improvement, has

FIGURE 9.4   Reduction of Order Cost in EOQ

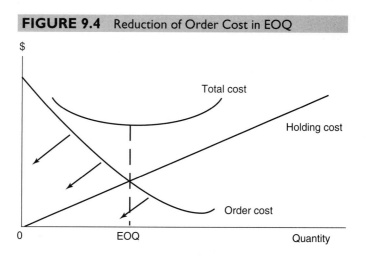

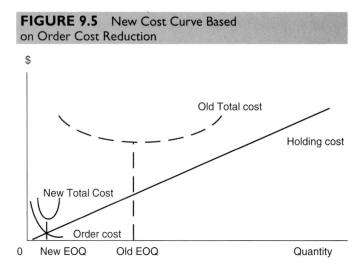

FIGURE 9.5 New Cost Curve Based on Order Cost Reduction

shrunken as well. Suppose the bicycle lot size is now 7 and the seat lot size is 10. The reorder point for the seats is now zero. If we build one lot size of bicycles (7), we will have not reached the seat reorder point, and it appears as if we do not have enough seats to make another lot of bicycles. With such a small seat lot size, however, we can easily afford to keep two, three, or even more lots on hand (the number being dependent on the new replenishment lead time). We can therefore build the next lot of bicycles with the second lot of seats while the first lot of seats is being replenished.

The "Down Side" of the Change

While the average inventory is clearly lower in the small lot size scenario, there is a cost involved beyond the one-time cost to reduce the order cost and the lead time. Given that the overall customer demand has not diminished, we will need to order batches to be built much more frequently since each batch is smaller in size. Each time the inventory of a given batch gets close to the reorder point, we risk a stockout if the demand during the replenishment lead time exceeds expectations. Figure 9.6 illustrates the condition.

9.4   KANBAN

With shortened lead times a constant goal in JIT, a system is needed to generate the reorder point signal without having to rely on a formal, structured system that could take time to react. Instead the developers of the JIT concept utilized a simple card system called "Kanban," which roughly translated from Japanese means "card" or "ticket."

The system works very simply. The Kanban signal (often merely a piece of cardboard) identifies the material to which it is attached. The information on the Kanban will often include:

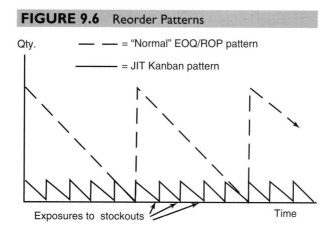

FIGURE 9.6   Reorder Patterns

- Component part number and identification
- Storage location
- Container size (if the material is stored in a container)
- Work center (or supplier) of origin

How It Works

The following sets of diagrams illustrate the use of what is often called a two-card Kanban system. The two types of cards are a production card (authorizing production of whatever part number is identified on the card in the quantity specified) and a withdrawal card (authorizing the movement of the identified material).

At the start of the process there is no movement, since all the cards are "attached" to full containers. It is only when a card is unattached that activity is allowed. In this way the number of cards will clearly limit the inventory authorized to be at any location.

At some point a downstream process needs some of the parts produced by work center 2 (in their "Finished Production" stock). They take a container of

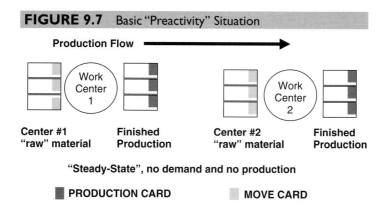

FIGURE 9.7   Basic "Preactivity" Situation

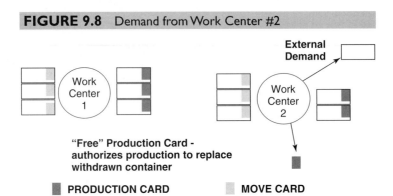

FIGURE 9.8 Demand from Work Center #2

the material, leaving the work center 2 production card with the center. This illustrates two additional rules of the system—all material movement is in full containers (recall the container lot size is supposed to be very small) and Kanban cards are linked to a work center, not to the material itself. This initial movement is illustrated in Figure 9.8.

The "unattached" production card is the signal to start the work center 2 production to replace the container that was taken. Of course, to do that work they need raw material, which is in the containers in front of the work center with the "move" cards attached. When that material is used to replace the Work Center 2 finished material, the raw material container is now empty and the associated move card is "unattached," as shown in Figure 9.9.

The unattached move card authorized movement—specifically movement of material to replace the material that was used. That material is found in the "finished goods" section of work center 1. The operator (or material handler) will now move the material and place the move card on the container as proof of the authorization to move the material. Before doing so, however, they must remove the production card that had first authorized its production. That represents another critical rule for Kanban: Every container with material

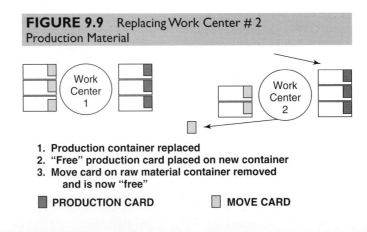

FIGURE 9.9 Replacing Work Center # 2 Production Material

1. Production container replaced
2. "Free" production card placed on new container
3. Move card on raw material container removed and is now "free"

■ PRODUCTION CARD   □ MOVE CARD

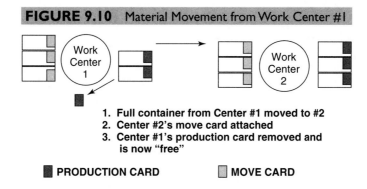

FIGURE 9.10   Material Movement from Work Center #1

1. **Full container from Center #1 moved to #2**
2. **Center #2's move card attached**
3. **Center #1's production card removed and is now "free"**

■ PRODUCTION CARD   ☐ MOVE CARD

must have one, but only one, card attached. Therefore, when the move card was attached the production card must be removed. This is illustrated in Figure 9.10.

Now, of course, there is an unattached production card for work center 1, allowing it to now produce, using some of the raw material for work center 1 and freeing a move card for that material, as shown in Figure 9.11.

This process continues upstream even to the suppliers, who can also receive the Kanban move cards as a signal for their next shipment to the facility.

Notice there are *no published production schedules* with this system. Production and movement of material is only authorized as purely a reaction to the utilization of material for production downstream. The production of the final product may in fact be the customer taking material, but in some facilities there is a final assembly schedule for customer orders. In those facilities that may be the only formal schedule used.

Also note that the cards only circulate within and between work centers, as shown in Figure 9.12.

Kanban Rules

Note that even though there are no formal schedules in a Kanban system, there is a fairly important set of rules. Those recommended rules are:

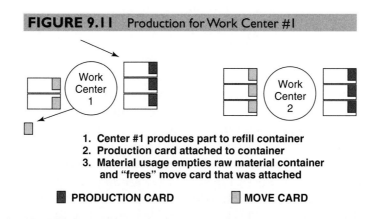

FIGURE 9.11   Production for Work Center #1

1. **Center #1 produces part to refill container**
2. **Production card attached to container**
3. **Material usage empties raw material container and "frees" move card that was attached**

■ PRODUCTION CARD   ☐ MOVE CARD

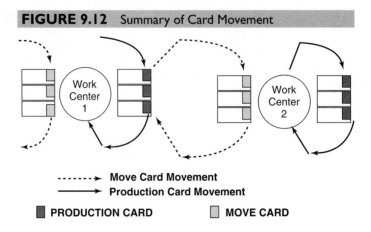

FIGURE 9.12   Summary of Card Movement

- - - - ▶   **Move Card Movement**
————▶   **Production Card Movement**

█ **PRODUCTION CARD**   ▢ **MOVE CARD**

- Every container with parts shall have one, but only one, Kanban.
- There will be no partial containers stored. Every container will be filled, empty, or in the process of being filled or emptied. This rule makes inventory accounting easy. You don't need to count parts—only containers and then multiply by the container quantity.
- There will be no production or movement without an authorization in the form of an unattached Kanban card.
- Kanban cards "belong" to the work center.

Number of Kanban Cards

There is a relatively simple formula that one can use to determine the suggested number of cards in the system. The formula is:

$$y = \frac{DT(1 + x)}{C}$$

Where: y = the number of Kanbans
D = the demand per unit of time
T = lead time to replace container
x = a safety factor (expressed as a decimal; e.g., 0.20 represents a 20% safety factor)
C = the container size (quantity of parts it will hold)

While this formula is useful, what many people prefer to use in practice is to start the process with enough material (containers and Kanbans) in the system to feel comfortable. What "comfortable" means is that there is enough material in the system to buffer against most normal uncertainties. While that is often a good way to start while people become used to the system and comfortable with how it works, the key is *to never allow the feeling of comfort to remain too long.* Specifically, the managers need to start the systematic reduction of the inventory to expose problems and fix them as they are exposed. (See the section later in this chapter on using Kanban for process improvement.)

Kanban Card Alternatives

Since the development and successful implementation of Kanban systems in many facilities, many alternatives have been designed and implemented. Some of the alternative methods include:

- Single card systems. The single card is the production card, with the empty container serving as the move signal.
- Color coding of containers—each color designating one item.
- Designated storage spaces, which limit the amount being stored and also visibly indicating when more is needed.
- Computer systems, often with bar codes on the container serving as the signal generator.

AN EXAMPLE OF A SINGLE "SIGNAL" SYSTEM:

Company "A" has a manufacturing cell that produces 10 different assemblies. They have developed a very simple visual Kanban-type system that allows them to easily satisfy demand and also cope with the fact that their setup reduction program has not yet allowed them to economically produce one container at a time, let alone one assembly. What they have done is to put ten shelves beside the cell. Each shelf represents a part number for one of the 10 assemblies they produce. The parts are produced in dedicated containers that each hold a defined number of the assemblies. As the containers are used up, the empty containers are placed on the shelf for their particular part number. These empty containers will line up until they reach a line painted on the shelf. When the row of containers reaches that line, it is a signal that the economical lot size for that part has been reached. The cell operators, when done with a given production run, merely have to look at the shelves to determine which assembly has reached an appropriate lot size and can represent the next setup and production run.

FIGURE 9.13   Visual Reorder Point

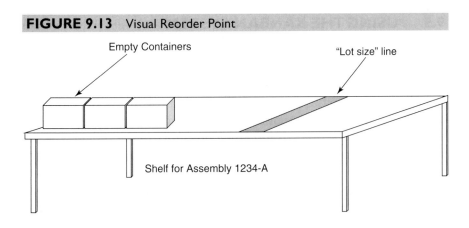

Empty Containers

"Lot size" line

Shelf for Assembly 1234-A

issue of linkages between business environment and appropriate planning and control system design more completely. The intent of this chapter is merely to explain the fundamental concepts of the Theory of Constraints itself.

10.1   FUNDAMENTAL PRINCIPLES OF THE THEORY OF CONSTRAINTS

The fundamental concept behind the Theory of Constraints (as it impacts planning and control) is that every operation producing a product or service is primarily a series of linked processes. Each process has a specific capacity to produce the given defined output for the operation, and that in virtually every case there is one process that limits or constrains the throughput from the entire operation. Consider the diagram in Figure 10.1.

The analogy often used is, as the diagram illustrates, that production flowing through operational processes is like liquid flowing through a pipeline. Each process has a certain defined capacity, illustrated in the analogy by the diameter of the associated pipe. In the diagram shown, process "E" has the largest capacity to process production, while operation "C" has the least amount of capacity. Since operation "C" is the constraint on the entire process, it will limit the amount of output from the process, regardless of the capacity of the remaining processes. Improving any of the other operations (increasing the size of the pipe in that section) will not improve the total amount of liquid coming out of the system of pipes.

A **constraint,** in its most general form, is anything that limits the firm from meeting its goal. For most firms, that goal is to make money, which manifests itself by increasing throughput—as measured by sales, not just production.

As a numerical example, consider the operation producing product A in Figure 10.2. It should be clear from this simple example that the total operation is constrained by process 3 at 4 per hour. No matter how much efficiency you have in the other processes and how many process improvements are made in processes 1, 2, and 4, you will never be able to exceed the overall operational output of 4 per hour unless you address the constraints of process 3. Increased efficiency and utilization in processes 1 and 2 will, in fact, only in-

FIGURE 10.1   The Linked Process Pipe Analogy

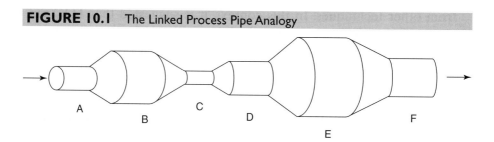

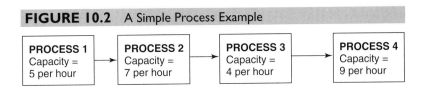

FIGURE 10.2   A Simple Process Example

PROCESS 1	PROCESS 2	PROCESS 3	PROCESS 4
Capacity = 5 per hour	Capacity = 7 per hour	Capacity = 4 per hour	Capacity = 9 per hour

crease inventory—not sales. That issue is one of the key points of TOC—the major measure for any operation should be on the throughput of the organization, or, in other words, the contribution to sales. Any other measures of process efficiency, utilization, or other commonly used operational measures have little relevance to the overall effectiveness of the entire system.

This approach has implications far beyond how the process is viewed. Even accounting systems are impacted. For example, many accounting systems allocate overhead costs to products based on direct labor hours of production. Such systems may give the impression that producing more product will help to "pay" for the overhead costs. Unfortunately, if the extra product produced is not linked to actual sales, the result is only more costly inventory and an overall negative impact on the business. TOC principles make the point that only sales should be counted as operational throughput. Another accounting implication is the labor cost itself. Most traditional accounting systems view direct labor as a variable cost. TOC principles, on the other hand, contend that in the short run all operational costs except direct material are largely fixed and should, therefore, be "lumped" together into an overall operational expense. One of the key points made by this example is that *products do not really have a profit—companies do.* This point helps to view the operation more as a system rather than as a set of largely independent functions. Such a view is a critical part of managing by TOC principles.

10.2   UNDERSTANDING AND MANAGING THE CONSTRAINTS

There are several fundamental guidelines developed for understanding the TOC principles and how to manage a constraining process. Some of the more noteworthy guidelines include:

- *A system optimal performance is NOT the sum of local optima.*   Any system that is performing as well as possible usually implies that not more than one part of the system is performing at an optimal level. If all parts of the system are performing optimally, the system as a whole will probably not be performing optimally. In other words, it is virtually impossible to obtain a perfect system balance. Even if the system was designed to be perfectly balanced, normal variations in performance will inevitably cause some degree of imbalance.

- *Systems are like chains.*   Each system will have a "weakest link" (a constraint) that will limit the performance of the whole system.

- *Knowing what to change requires a complete understanding of the system and the system goal.*   Often in TOC, the system goal is to make money through sales, not production. Production completed without a sale (making and storing inventory) does not contribute to the goal of the company until it does become a sale. This is one of the major reasons that Goldratt gave the title "The Goal" to his first book on TOC, where he essentially introduced the concepts to the world.

- *Most undesirable system effects are caused by a few core problems.*   This is a common theme in many other systems. For example, the well known cause-and-effect ("fishbone") diagram from Total Quality Management (TQM) makes the same point. Overall, solving a symptom of a problem will often do little good. If the core problem remains, the symptom (or another one associated with it) will likely reappear very soon. True long-term relief from the undesirable effect will occur only if the core problem is identified and corrected.

- *Core problems are almost never obvious.*   They tend to show themselves as a series of undesirable effects, most of which are really symptoms of the underlying problems.

- *Eliminating the undesirable effects provides a false sense of security.*   Working on "problems" (often really symptoms) without finding the root cause tends to provide short-lived improvements. On the other hand, eliminating a core problem generally eliminates all of the undesirable effects associated with it.

- *System constraints can be either physical constraints or policy constraints.*   Policy constraints are generally more difficult to find and eliminate, but the elimination of a policy constraint generally provides a more pronounced system improvement. The differences between those two types of constraints are discussed more fully later in the chapter.

- *Ideas are not solutions.*   Generating ideas can be beneficial, but only if there is follow-through to develop the idea into a solution and then implement it completely.

- *The focus should be on balancing flow through the shop.*   The key is throughput that end up as sales, not on throughput that may end up as inventory. As discussed earlier, some accounting systems promote high production rates even if the sales are lower. The systems recognize that adding value to the product will "pay" for the overhead, in that the system allocates overhead to the product as value is added. These systems essentially fool managers into thinking they are helping the company, when in fact they may be doing nothing more than adding extra expense in the form of inventory.

- *Utilization of a nonbottleneck is determined by constraints in the system.*   Nonbottleneck operations do not restrict system output. Those resources should, therefore, be managed in such a way as to provide maximum support for constraint resources. Efficiency and utilization for these resources are not deemed that important for the good of the entire system, only their support for the system.

- *Utilization of an operation is not the same as activation.*   In the TOC concept, an operation is considered activated only when it is providing benefit for the entire system to give more output. The operation may be utilized, or producing material not needed until some time in the future, but that does not necessarily help the entire system.

- *An hour lost at a constraint operation is an hour lost to throughput for the entire process.*   For example, in Figure 10.2, if a quarter hour is lost to just process 3, then the entire operation will be able to produce only three units that hour, regardless of how well the other processes can perform. It is for this reason that the major focus of managing and scheduling an operation is on the constraint.

- *An hour lost at a nonconstraint is a mirage, in the fact that it will not impact total throughput.*   It represents instead excess capacity. For example, in Figure 10.2 if there is a loss of time to produce one unit at process 2 it will mean that process 2 can only produce 6 units per hour, but the overall operation will still only have a throughput of 4 per hour, based on the capability of process 3.

- *Transfer batches do not have to be the same size as process batches, and often should not be.*   Process batches for constraints should be of a size that maximize the effective utilization of the process (minimize downtime). Process batches at nonconstraints are not so critical. Transfer batches (the amount of material moved, may often be smaller to maximize throughput and minimize process inventories.

- *A schedule should be determined by using all the operational constraints.*   In many operations schedules are set sequentially. TOC argues that all constraint areas should be considered at the same time when making a schedule. The theory also argues that lead times are a result of the schedule and should not be determined before the scheduling process.

10.3   IMPROVING THE PROCESS USING TOC PRINCIPLES

If a TOC approach is deemed appropriate to help improve a business system, there is a five-step process that is recommended to help improve the performance of the business. Those five steps are summarized below:

1. *Identify the constraint.*   This implies the need to examine the entire process to determine which process limits the throughput. The concept

does not limit this process examination to merely the operational processes. For example, returning again to Figure 10.2, suppose the sales department was only selling the product output at the rate of 3 per hour. In that case, the sales department would be considered the constraint and not process 3. It must be kept in mind that a constraint limits throughput with respect to overall business sales, not merely inventory production.

2. ***Exploit the constraint.***   Find methods to maximize the utilization of the constraint toward productive throughput. For example, in many operations all processes are shut down during lunchtime or during breaks. If a process is a constraint, the operation should consider rotating lunch periods so that the constraint is never allowed to be idle. Suppose, for example, an operation has a certain process that represents a clear and large constraint. Suppose also that they currently have 7 productive hours for an 8-hour shift (30 minutes for lunch and two 15-minute breaks). Assuming they have multiple workers that can operate the process (or can train more), they could stagger lunch times and break times for just that one process, allowing it to operate the full 8 hours. In such a case the business would add an entire productive hour of output per shift with the addition of no more resources of any kind.

3. ***Subordinate everything to the constraint.***   Effective utilization of the constraint is the most important issue. Everything else is secondary.

4. ***Elevate the constraint.***   Essentially this means to find ways to increase the available hours of the constraint, including adding more of it.

5. ***Once the constraint is a constraint no longer, find the new one and repeat the steps.***   As the constraint effective utilization increases, it may cease to be a constraint as another process becomes one. In that case the emphasis shifts to the new process constraint. It is also possible (even likely in many businesses) that a sales-related change in the product mix will cause a different process to become the constraint.

Notes on the five steps:

1. The first two steps are really a method to loosely link measures (including throughput and utilization) to the logistics of the system.

2. The third step, as we will discover in the section on scheduling with TOC, is really accomplished by

   • Releasing material at the gateway (first processing) center at a rate that will keep the constraint busy.

   • Prioritization of nonconstraint tasks based almost exclusively on constraint needs.

3. The concept of *exploit* really implies getting the most from existing constraint resources. TOC suggests that exploiting should be maximized prior to spending additional money to acquire more of the constraint resource.

4. The fifth step is really a warning to continually check to ensure the constraint has not shifted. Effective exploitation of existing constraints and a shift in product mix are examples of events that can cause the constraint to shift.

After understanding these five steps, it may be helpful to consider that not all facilities operating in all types of business environments may find the approach to TOC easy to implement. For example, if an operation has a highly volatile product mix due to constantly shifting customer orders for a large variety of products, they may discover that the constraint will also be volatile. At one time the mix of process requirements may point to one constraint, while at another time the mix may create an entirely different constraint. If the constraint shifting occurs frequently, then there could be far too little opportunity to apply the TOC approaches on one constraint before it shifts to another point in the process.

10.4   IMPACT ON OPERATION STRATEGY

Knowledge of the Theory of Constraints can impact the operations strategy of the business in several ways. Some of the impacts on strategy can include:

- For a given type and mix of products, management can elect to consciously decide where the constraint should be located and then proceed to develop the operational strategy around that selected constraint.
- Marketing and Sales can be tightly tied to the constraint. Specifically, an analysis can be made to determine the mix of products to sell to maximize profits, and also it is possible to sell more of products that do not use the constraint (implying that excess capacity is available to make more of those products).
- Engineering and other process improvement activities can and should be focused on making the constraint process more efficient and effective.
- The company should consider if and how the nonconstraint processes may be used to supplement or be used to make the constraint resources more effective.
- If the company has a choice as to where the constraint is located in the process, they may elect to have the constraint early in the process. In that way the size of the required buffer needed to guard the constraint against "starvation" of material will be minimized. This will become clearer when the method for determining buffer size is explained later in the chapter.
- If, on the other hand, there are processes early in the overall process that have poor quality yield, the constraint should be placed later in the overall process. Some processes, especially certain chemical processes, have poor yield by their very nature. The idea is to have those processes placed prior

to the constraint. If they were placed after the constraint, then the implication is that some product that has already been through the constraint will not be scrapped or need rework using the constraint. Since the idea behind TOC is to have all items going through the constraint be turned into sales, clearly it is not a good idea to have constraint time being wasted by being used for a product that will later be rejected.

- There are other considerations that may also impact the strategic issue. They include the response time needed for customers and the amount of capital investment necessary for various combinations of resources.

10.5   GENERAL TYPES OF CONSTRAINT CAUSES

The sources of constraints can be classified in several ways. The most common ways are policy constraints, capacity constraints, and marketing constraints:

POLICY:

- Pricing policies that may affect demand.
- Incorrect focus on sales commissions (selling the wrong product).
- Production measures inhibiting good production performance.
- Personnel policies that promote conflict between people or production areas.

CAPACITY:

- Investment policies, including methods of justification, planning horizon, and fund availability.
- Human resource policies.
- Governmental regulations.
- Traditional measurement systems.
- Product development process.

MARKETING CONSTRAINTS:

- Product "niche" policies.
- Distribution systems.
- Perceived capacity versus demand.

10.6   LOGISTICS AND THE THEORY OF CONSTRAINTS

Logistics, of course, deals with the physical movement of material through the production process. The Theory of Constraints has specific issues dealing with logistics, as well as some methods to deal with making logistical movement effective. In general, TOC highlights two essential characteristics of any logistics system:

- Most systems are made up of a series of dependent events, or a series of specific steps that must be followed in a correct order to complete a job. This implies that any lateness at an early station in the process will potentially impact negatively later stations in the process.
- Most activities have statistical fluctuations inherent in their operation. This implies that activity times are not deterministic and deviations about the mean will exist. The TOC approach suggests that it is these statistical fluctuations that make traditional assembly line balancing approaches impractical.

There are often three reasons given for a loss of throughput, and again these reasons are focused on the constraint in the system. The three reasons are given here, together with the typical approach suggested for minimizing or eliminating the potential loss of throughput:

1. *The constraint is "broken."*   There are many reasons a constraint could be nonoperational. The reason is not as important as the fact that when the constraint is down it cannot be used to produce. Since no excess capacity exists on a constraint, the loss of capacity will directly result in a loss of throughput for the entire business. One major solution to this potential problem is a good program of preventive maintenance. Such a program needs to be scheduled and managed carefully, for even preventive maintenance represents a use of capacity for the constraint. In general, this situation is compatible with a basic principle of maintenance—the higher the cost of an unscheduled breakdown of a process, the more critical the following of a well-designed preventive maintenance program. This is the same basic issue we found with a lean production system. Without much inventory in the system, processes tend to be tightly linked, and the loss of any operation will quickly bring the entire system down. Maintenance becomes important for TOC for roughly the same reason as for lean production systems—the potential high cost of a drop in throughput for the entire system.

2. *The constraint is starved.*   In this condition, there is no inventory from the preceding processes available for work by the constraint. The constraint is capable of production, but cannot produce without material to work on. The solution to this problem is using a buffer in front of the constraint. The buffer is inventory released early into the system, but is really a "time" buffer, for reasons explained in the scheduling section below.

3. *The constraint is blocked.*   In this condition, the constraint is available and there is material available on which to work, but there is no physical space in which to place the completed units. The solution to this potential problem is to have a space buffer available after the constraint in the process in which to place production completed by the constraint operation.

10.7 SCHEDULING AND THE THEORY OF CONSTRAINTS

The scheduling system developed for the Theory of Constraints has its own specific approach, although fairly closely related to a pull system inherent with lean production. It is often described as ***drum–buffer–rope:***

- ***Drum.*** The drum of the system refers to the "drumbeat" or pace of production. Essentially, it represents the master schedule for the operation, which is focused around the pace of throughput *as defined by the constraint.* Put in other terms, the drum can simply be considered as the work schedule of the organization's constraint. In order for the organization to take full advantage of this knowledge, it must be assumed that all nonconstraint functions understand this "drumbeat" schedule and provide total support.

- ***Buffer.*** Since it is so important that the constraint never be "starved" for needed inventory, a "time" buffer is often established in front of the constraint. It is called a time buffer because it represents the amount of time that material is released into the system prior to the minimal normal throughput time to reach the constraint. The idea is to protect the system from normal variations and thereby protect the constraint from disruptions or material starvation. Even though the buffer manifests itself as inventory released into the system ahead of the minimal processing time, the product mix of this material can be very different based on the schedule. Since it is not based on specific inventory of specific products or components, it is generally called a time buffer. This is a key difference in the conceptual use of a time buffer instead of an inventory buffer—the time buffers tend to be largely immune to variations in product mix. As an example, suppose variations in processing and the probability of some disruptions in operations upstream from the constraint could mean that material could be "held up" for as much as 4 hours. The implication, then, would be that based on the processing schedule at the constraint the material for constraint processing would be released into the first operation 4 hours earlier than the normal expected throughput to the constraint would dictate.

- ***Rope.*** The analogy is that the rope "pulls" production to the constraint for necessary processing. While this may imply a Kanban-type pull system, it can be done by a well-coordinated release of material into the system at the right time.

As can be seen, even the scheduling system has its primary focus on effective management of the organization's constraint to throughput and sales.

10.8 MULTIPLE TIME BUFFERS

Time buffers are used to make sure the constraint is not "starved," but other time buffers are also necessary. An example may help to illustrate:

Suppose you have a product made from three components. Component 1 is processed from raw material and then assembled with component 2 after it is processed from raw material. The subassembly is then assembled with component 3 after it is processed from raw material. The final product is then shipped to the customer. The constraint in the system is located in the middle of the processing for component 1. Figure 10.3 illustrates this.

Once component 1 has been processed on the constraint, its value to the system has risen significantly because constraint time has been invested. Nothing should, therefore, impede the progress of component 1. The problem could arise, however, that component 1 will arrive at the Assembly 1 area before component 2 because of some problem with component 2. Since we would never want constraint-invested material to wait for nonconstrained material, we should stage a time buffer of material for component 2 before the Assembly 1 area. This is done by releasing it earlier—the amount earlier depending on the time buffer based on the time estimate needed to overcome any unanticipated shock in the system. In this case the time buffer is called an **assembly time buffer,** as opposed to the time buffer before the constraint, which is usually called a **constraint time buffer.**

The same argument applies to the Assembly 2 area. The subassembly from components 1 and 2 have constraint time invested, so we would not want them waiting for component 3. This calls for another assembly time buffer to be generated at the Assembly 2 area.

Unfortunately, the need for buffers has not been fulfilled. It is possible that the final product with its constraint-invested material could be held up at shipping, since the processes that take place between assembly and shipping have not been part of the protection. This implies an additional time buffer before the shipping area, referred to as a *shipping time buffer.*

In general, then, these buffers have a major purpose in protecting the system. They help ensure good throughput and also help maintain good due date

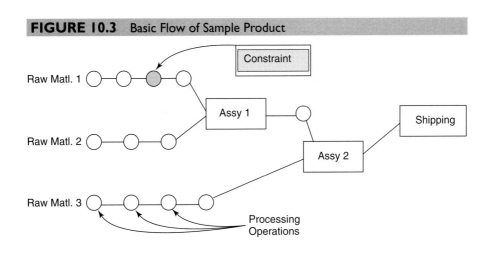

FIGURE 10.3 Basic Flow of Sample Product

FIGURE 10.4 Sample Process with Additional Time Buffers

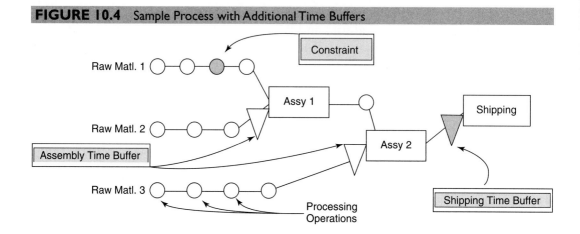

performance. In addition, however, they also can be the source of information for continuous improvement approaches undertaken by the operation. This information can help establish a prioritization for processes being targeted for Total Quality Management process improvement and for lean production approaches. In general, one should always be asking the question, "Where should we target which production technique in order to maximize the overall profitability of the company?"

10.9 CONTROL POINTS AND BATCHES

All this discussion regarding buffers and scheduling may start one to think that the scheduling using TOC approaches are more difficult and complex than standard approaches. That does not need to be the case. Based on the flow of material and the type of operation, there are specifically defined types of control points that may be important for TOC scheduling, measurement and control. A control point is a point in the process where measures are taken and decisions made based on those measures. Typical control points for TOC include:

- *The constraint*—this is clearly the most critical control point, and needs to be scheduled carefully based on sales.
- *The first operation (or the gateway)*—it is quite important to release the right material at the right time into the system so it will reach the constraint. This is, in effect, the "rope" of the drum–buffer–rope system.
- *Diverging points*—these points are where a common part can be processed into one of several different options. They must be managed to ensure that material, especially constraint material, is used in the correct manner for the correct assembly.
- *Converging points*—these are really assembly operations where material from nonconstraint operations is combined with constraint material to produce an assembly or subassembly. It is important to manage these

points to make sure constraint material is not held up from being processed.

- ***The buffers***—these include constraint buffers, assembly buffers, and shipping buffers as described earlier.

TOC also recognizes there can be fundamental differences between **process batches** (the amount of material produced at an operation for a given setup) and **transfer batches** (the amount of material moved from one operation to the next operation). In general, process batches should be fairly large for constraint operations in order to minimize the time lost for setups. Process batches for nonconstraints are largely irrelevant (to a point) since those operations will have excess capacity. Transfer batches, on the other hand, should be fairly small to minimize work-in-process inventory levels.

10.10 MAJOR STEPS IN USING THE DRUM–BUFFER–ROPE METHOD

The following steps are generally given as a summary of how to use the drum–buffer–rope method to plan and control an operation under TOC principles:

1. Identify the constraint in the operation.
2. Examine options and select the preferable method to exploit the constraint.
3. Develop a Gantt schedule (see the section on Gantt chart scheduling in Chapter 8) for the constraint operation.
4. Calculate the appropriate size for the buffers (shipping, assembly, and constraint) based on the time it takes to move material through the operation to those buffer areas.
5. Develop a raw material release schedule to support the constraint schedule and also to support the assembly of other nonconstraint parts, especially with the constraint parts.
6. Determine product ship date. For products not using the constraint, often the ship dates can be based purely on customer request. The major issue here is to not load the nonconstraint areas to the point where they can become a temporary constraint.
7. For work centers that have not been identified as a control point, work can be done as it becomes available.

KEY TERMS

Constraint
Process Batch

Drum–Buffer–Rope
Transfer Batch

Time Buffers

SUMMARY

The Theory of Constraints (TOC) brings a different perspective to visualizing an operation, and therefore brings potentially different approaches to planning and control for that operation. TOC forces a linked system view of the organization, allowing the identification of the total system constraint. Once identified, there are systematic approaches suggested to increase the capacity and output of the constraint, thereby increasing the throughput of the organization as a whole. As this can and should be done while still minimizing the amount of excess inventory and capacity in the system.

REFERENCES

Goldratt, E. M., *It's Not Luck.* Croton-on-Hudson, NY: North River Press, 1994.

Goldratt, E. M., and J. Cox, *The Goal.* Croton-on-Hudson, NY: North River Press, 1994.

Goldratt, E. M., and R. E. Fox, *The Race.* Croton-on-Hudson, NY: North River Press, 1986.

DISCUSSION QUESTIONS

1. Describe the possible special challenges to implementing TOC in a make-to-order environment.
2. Describe the possible implications of a major change in product mix or a major change in design to a TOC-run operation. How would you approach dealing with those implications?
3. Compare and contrast the design of the drum–buffer–rope system and the pull system described in Chapter 9. What are the similarities and differences, and why do they exist?
4. Comment (with supporting reasons) on the following overheard statement, stated by an operations manager: "We don't have any constraints in our company. Our capacity plans show we have plenty of capacity to produce the master schedule for some time to come."
5. Discuss the implication that TOC can bring to a company when they develop their business strategy. How will it possibly impact the approach taken to the sales and operations planning process?
6. Do you believe that TOC will have any impact on other functions in the organization? If so, what might they be? In specific, comment on the possible implications to:
   - Engineering
   - Human Resources
   - Accounting
   - Information Technology
   - Marketing
   - Sales

CHAPTER 11

"Partnering" Functions: Purchasing and Distribution

Chapter Outline

11.1 Purchasing Information Issues
11.2 Purchasing Responsibilities for Material Procurement
11.3 Distribution Requirement Planning

Introduction—There are two boundary functions whose work spans the boundary between organizations and are impacted by the design of the planning and control system of the operation. In the case of purchasing, the boundary is between your own organization and those organizations that supply the goods and services required for you to make your products. Distribution, on the other hand, spans the boundary between your organization and your customers. Clearly both must be included in any treatment of planning and control. Purchasing, for example, must know what they are to procure at what time, and distribution will provide product to customers, meaning information from these sources will become an integral part of the planning system.

This chapter is intended to present merely a basic overview of the concepts of these areas as they relate to planning and control, as area has been the subject of numerous complete books that are far more comprehensive than this book. If the reader wishes to investigate either area in more detail, they are encouraged to investigate one or more of the references listed at the end of the chapter.

It is interesting that these two topics (purchasing and distribution) were often considered to be relatively separate and discrete issues until fairly recently. As computer systems have continued to become more powerful and effective, and as customers have continued to demand ever-increasing responsiveness from suppliers (especially in delivery time), all functions of planning and control, including purchasing and distribution, have been drawn together into what is called **supply chain management.** This concept views all "upstream" and "downstream" activities as part of a complete chain of activities from raw material to final consumable product. Viewing the complete flow of materials as a chain implies rapid and effective communication and information flows up and down the supply chain, and implies that the links to these boundary functions has increased in importance as it relates to the overall planning and control system. There are several advantages to taking a supply chain approach, and they include significant reduction in inventory (both in raw material and finished goods), more rapid response to customer demands, and reduction in both the time and cost to develop new products.

There are several activities that may change as an organization attempts to develop a supply chain approach, including:

- Close partnering with other organizations, implying selection of those partners must consider the potential nature of the partnership relationship, and not merely on who has the lowest price. The specific selection criteria for each supplier must be based on a careful evaluation of the operations strategy for the company and its supply chain, where the selection priorities are consistent with the strategy for the entire chain. Priorities can include issues of:
  - Delivery, both delivery speed and reliability of deliveries.
  - Quality, including both product quality and more intangible issues such as communication and responsiveness of the supplier.
  - Flexibility, including flexibility of design and the flexibility to respond effectively to varying order sizes or delivery times.
  - Cost, including not necessarily just the delivered price but the total component cost including scrap rates, ease of production, holding cost, repair cost, and so forth.
- Development of information systems that can link with other organizations for the proper and complete flow of information and data. These information links include communication of material requisitions and the possible sharing or even integration of production plans and schedules.
- An increase in the direct shipment of items, producing an impact on warehousing and the information contained in distribution systems.

The actual development and further description of supply chains is beyond the scope of this book, since they deal heavily with cross-organizational strategies, information technologies, transportation, supplier selection, and negotiations of relationships. What will be covered here is many of the fundamental principles that are used to plan and control the purchasing and distribution function.

11.1   PURCHASING INFORMATION ISSUES

From the perspective of planning and control, purchasing must consider the requirements for production components, subassemblies, raw materials, and services as well as the need for nonproduction goods and supplies commonly called MRO (maintenance, repair, and operations):

- Information required for production items are typically generated from MRP in cases where MRP is used. The lowest level components on a bill of material usually represents purchased materials. In those environments where a kanban or pure "pull" system is used, the requirements usually come from the depletion of material associated with one of the kanbans, and that material is sometimes supplied from an outside supplier.
- The need for nonproduction goods and supplies (**MRO**) can come from several sources. Some are generated on a "one-time" need, such as the need for a repair service. Others are ordered by reorder point systems, since they represent ongoing demand that is essentially an independent demand pattern. Examples include office supplies (paper, pens, light bulbs, etc.) as well as cleaning supplies (soap, towels, etc.). Maintenance item demand (such as spare parts and replacement parts for equipment) can also be ordered by reorder point systems, but as they can tend to be expensive some companies try to limit the quantity kept in inventory. One way that can be done (for the more expensive items, primarily), is to project the demand, much like a forecast. The typical way this is done is to keep records of when, and under what conditions, these parts may fail or need replacement. These records of "mean time between failures" can be used to procure replacement parts just before the part needs replacement or would have a tendency to fail.

While the examples above represent some of the more common approaches to scheduling and meeting demand for purchased goods and services, there are others. An example of one approach that has become more common in recent years is the use of **vendor-managed inventory.** In this approach, a supplier will keep and manage a stock of inventory in a defined location in the customer's facility. The customer can then take material from the location as they need it and are charged only for the material they actually withdraw. The supplier is responsible for maintaining an adequate supply of material at the location. The parts that are often used for such a system are often standard, in some cases basic commodity parts such as nuts, bolts, screws, and other fasteners.

Other models do exist, and the number and variety seem to be growing as more companies experiment with new approaches to supply chain management. Some companies, for example, have established such close system-to-system linkages that the supplier can tell from the system what the customer needs from that supplier—design, colors, quantities, and timing. They can then sequence their delivery so that the customer receives just what they need just in time for the need—all without a formal purchase request. Clearly this represents an advanced level of supplier linkage and trust, and the information systems must be well developed with accurate and timely information for such an approach to work well.

11.2 PURCHASING RESPONSIBILITIES FOR MATERIAL PROCUREMENT

Once purchasing has received a request for purchase, they often will not place an order for the exact quantity of the request. They will often revise quantities and sometimes timing for the procurement based on several issues, including:

- Quantity discounts. If the supplier offers a quantity discount that exceeds the quantity ordered, there should be a financial analysis done to determine if the order size should be increased beyond what has been requested in order to take advantage of the discounted price. A sample analysis of a quantity discount is given below
- Packaging and shipping units. In many cases suppliers will package or palletize material in standard quantities for ease of shipping, production, or storage. Often the supplier will require that all orders be in multiples of these standard package quantities. Some suppliers will agree to ship material in quantities other than these standard quantities, but will do so only by incurring an increased cost—often passed on to the customer.
- Full truckloads. Most commercial carriers will have different costs for shipment based on whether the shipment represents a full truckload as opposed to a partial truckload. In most cases the less-than-truckload rate is significantly more expensive than that of the full-truckload rate. An analysis needs to be done in these cases to determine if the company is better off financially to incur the extra inventory costs to obtain the full-truckload shipping rate. The analysis should balance the impact of the extra inventory implied from a full-truckload against the extra shipping cost incurred if only the required amount of inventory is shipped.
- Price hedging. Some products are made from material that is subjected to erratic prices on the open market. An example of a commodity that many companies subject to price hedging is a common material used in many products: copper. If the futures markets in these commodity products indicates that the prices are likely to swing higher, it may make sense to buy large quantities while the prices are relatively low. Often the extra inventory holding costs will be more than offset by the lower material costs when the material is purchased at the right time.

EXAMPLE 11.1—QUANTITY DISCOUNTS

A certain product with independent demand has a unit cost of $20. The cost to place an order has been determined to be $32 per order, and the annual inventory holding cost is determined to be 20% of the item cost per year. The average annual demand is 5,000 units. The supplier has recently proposed to the company that if they purchase at least 350 units at a time they will only charge $19.50 a unit. Should the company take advantage of the quantity discount?

Solution: The solution starts out with the assumption that ordering at the cheapest price is feasible. Using that assumption, the EOQ value is computed, using the computation developed in Chapter 5:

$$EOQ = \sqrt{\frac{2DS}{H}}$$

In this case, the D is 5,000, the S is $32, and the H is 20% of $19.50 (recall we are starting with the assumption that we can obtain the cheapest price), which is $3.90.

$$EOQ = \sqrt{\frac{2(5000)(32)}{3.9}} = 286 \text{ units}$$

Clearly, we cannot order the EOQ and get the cheapest price. In that case we find the EOQ at the next cheapest price, which in this case is $20 per unit:

$$EOQ = \sqrt{\frac{2(5000)(32)}{.2(20)}} = 283 \text{ units.}$$

It is clearly feasible to order the EOQ of 283 units and obtain the unit price of $20. What if the order quantity was increased to obtain the price discount? Would the reduced unit price offset the increased cost involved with not obtaining the EOQ? The only way to answer that question is to calculate the total cost for buying the EOQ and comparing it with the total cost of buying the minimum to obtain the price discount. The formula for total cost was given in Chapter 5 as:

$$TC = DC + \frac{Q}{2}H + \frac{D}{Q}S$$

At the EOQ, the total cost would be:

$$TC = 5000(20) + \frac{283}{2}(.2)(20) + \frac{5000}{283}(32) = \$101,131$$

Now at the quantity discount, the total cost would be:

$$TC = 5000(19.50) + \frac{350}{2}(.2)(19.50) + \frac{5000}{350}(32) = \$98,640$$

Clearly, in this case, the reduced price provides a significant financial advantage in spite of the extra inventory that must be held in order to buy 350 at a time instead of the EOQ quantity. The company would, in fact, save approximately $2,491 per year by taking advantage of this quantity discount.

A purchasing department will typically undertake many other key activities. The following provides a brief summary, but the specific approaches and details are beyond the intended scope of this book. Some of the responsibilities include:

- Supplier selection and partnering. As firms move more toward the concepts of a supply chain, and particularly in lean production environments, there is a need to select suppliers very carefully. In order to establish very close relationships to suppliers (necessary if there is to be an ongoing exchange of design and production information, as is implied in good supply chain management) there is often a single source of supply selected for each purchased item. This single source allows a real mutual commitment between the organizations—sometimes referred to as a "co-destiny" relationship. This implies that the suppliers selected must be stable, effective, and cooperative in understanding and working with the requirements of the buying firm. One example of the advantage of such a relationship is the ability to engage in mutual value analysis. In these cases the buying and supplying firm engage in a mutual analysis of the cost and design of the product in question. If the design can be improved and the production costs reduced, both firms gain. The buying firm obtains a better product at a lower price and the supplier can obtain a better margin and a more loyal customer. Note that it is important that both firms gain from the activity. It is this mutual gain that provides the incentive to continue such activity.

- Supplier negotiations. When a supplier is selected, there is typically a fairly intense and sometimes prolonged negotiation necessary, especially if the supplier is intended to become a long-term supplying partner. Issues of cost, information sharing, product quality, delivery, and flexibility are all important considerations.

- Selection of transportation methods and firms. As in the case of suppliers, selection of the firms responsible for transporting goods (particularly to customers) is a very important part of the purchasing function. As is the case with suppliers, the supply chain concepts imply closer linkages with the distribution of goods, and these transportation firms must become an integral part of that activity if the firm is to deliver their goods effectively with the lowest total cost.

11.3   DISTRIBUTION REQUIREMENTS PLANNING

While many of the issues dealing with warehousing, transportation, and distribution of goods are beyond the scope of this book, it is instructive to examine the fundamental principles of distribution requirements planning (DRP), which for many firms represents a major part of the planning and control activity of the firm. DRP uses much the same logic as MRP to allow distribution facilities (such as warehouses and branch sales facilities) to request product from the main production operation. The object is similar to MRP—ensure adequate material to meet customer demand without incurring excessive inventory costs. Specific examples of DRP are covered in the next section of the chapter.

There are often several options available for use to order and replace inventory in warehouses and the distribution system. There is statistical analysis of demand and replenishment patterns, classic reorder point methods (as discussed in Chapter 5), and use of optimizing techniques, also mentioned in Chapter 5. Unfortunately, most of these techniques have one or more of the following issues:

- "Lumpy" demand. This problem, generally associated with lot sizing rules for production or inventory replenishment, can produce either major shortages or excessive inventory, as was pointed out in Chapter 6 when MRP was discussed. Even though much of the demand on warehouse or distribution inventory can be classified as independent, implying a demand that should be smoother than dependent demand, the reality is that a smooth demand condition is seldom the case. Warehouse and distribution inventory is often used to replenish material for retail outlets or another manufacturing facility, and as such orders are often in fairly large lot sizes.

- A lack of integration with strategy and strategic marketing plans. Quantity discounts, advertising campaigns, promotional activities, and development of new customers are examples of marketing activities for many companies. Each of those activities can imply demand levels far different from those that would ordinarily be predicted from statistical analysis of patterns. Those methods tend to only project needs based on past patterns of use.

- Changes in suppliers or supplier contracts. This can impact both the delivery and normal lot sizes of replenishment material.

- Design changes. Clearly, if the design of any of the products changes, the warehouse may be left with a significant amount of inventory that may be obsolete.

The overall problem, in summary, is that most of the statistical and reorder point techniques tend to respond to demand as it occurs rather than anticipating demand. Since it is highly likely that one or more of the conditions noted above will happen regularly, then specific communications and analysis will be required in each instance in order to minimize any adverse impacts.

The alternative that will be discussed here is to use a method that, like MRP, will be more proactive in order to project needs in the future. Like MRP, a more proactive approach can be more effectively used to deal with most of the problems mentioned above.

The alternative is called **distribution requirements planning** (DRP). DRP uses the same basic logic used by MRP, including the gross-to-net calculation of requirements, which ends with a planned order for resupply. DRP can also time phase the requirements by using a **bill of distribution** (BOD), illustrated later in the chapter.

Basic DRP Structure

In physical appearance, DRP is very similar to MRP, and uses essentially the same logic as seen in Figure 11.1.

The following summarizes the elements of the basic DRP format:

- *Time periods.*   As in the case of MRP, time periods, often referred to a time buckets, can be a day, week, month, or any other time period that makes sense in the context of the situation. In addition, it is possible to have a bucketless system. If the time period is longer than a day, a determination should be made as to when during the time period the order is due. The standard convention found in most commercial packages is to have the due date as the first day of the period.
- *Gross requirements*   (abbreviated in the figure as Gross Reqs.). Similarly to the MRP case, gross requirements in DRP is the amount that must be supplied to support demand. There are three typical sources of such demand: actual customer orders, a forecast, and resupply orders from other distribution branches.
- *Scheduled receipts*   (abbreviated in the figure as Scheduled Recp.). This is also very similar to MRP. In this case the open orders for replenishment can come from either a supplier, actual production, or resupply from another warehouse branch. As in the case with MRP, a scheduled receipt represents an actual commitment of the firm's resources, and as such should ideally not be altered without planner intervention. The DRP system will create exceptions messages if the logic shows a suggested change in the schedule receipt, but will generally not make the change without planner action.
- *Planned on-hand.*   Similar to MRP, representing the inventory position for the given period.
- *Planned order receipt*   (abbreviated in the figure as Planned Ord. Recp.). This figure is the quantity that must be received (keeping in mind lot size

FIGURE 11.1   Sample DRF Format

Period	PD	1	2	3	4	5	6	7	8	9
Gross Reqs.										
Scheduled Recp.										
Planned On-hand										
Plan. Ord. Recp.										
Plan. Ord. Rel.										

rules) to prevent the on-hand balance from going negative. Again, as was true with MRP, this is a computer-generated figure that shows no actual commitment of company resources. As such, the logic of the system will alter planned order receipts as situations change, and need no planner intervention. It is only when this planned order is actually released for shipment that it becomes a scheduled receipt and is treated differently.

- ***Planned order release***   (abbreviated in the figure as Planned Ord. Rel.). This value should be the same as the planned order release offset for lead time, in the same way that MRP offsets for lead time.
- ***PD.***   This is merely a convenient abbreviation for "past due."

Key Data Requirements

This section summarizes some of the types of data that must be determined in order to populate the DRP model. The first of these is the ordering policies, of which there are several options:

- Lot-for-lot. As in MRP, this rule merely requests an order that matches the net requirements for the given period.
- Fixed period. Once a period quantity (the number of periods in the future that the order is to cover) is set, the system will forward calculate the quantity that represents the total quantity needed for the number of periods, and that quantity represents the order size.
- Standard lot size plus. In some cases a standard minimum lot size is established for minimizing total cost of shipping. This lot size rule uses that standard lot size, but will add to it any additional quantity needed to cover the net requirement for the period in question.
- Fixed quantity above standard lot size. If the net requirements exceed the standard lot size, this fixed quantity will be added (in multiples) until the net requirements are met. This is often used if there are standard packaging or palletization used to determine shipping quantities.
- Multiples of the standard lot size.
- Economic order quantity (EOQ) models. This approach should be used primarily when the replenishment is continuous and uniform enough to approximate the underlying assumptions of the EOQ model.
- Lot costing models. There are several models that have been developed to minimize costs (similar to the EOQ). A couple of examples include the least unit cost and least total cost models. Specific calculations and examples of these methods are described in Chapter 6.

Some of the other important data items that must be considered include:

- Demand input type. Specifically, it must be decided if only forecasts, only customer orders, or some combination should be used as a demand input. Probably the most common option is to use a forecast, but then have actual customer orders consume the forecast. In this option the system will decrease the forecast quantity in the period in which a customer order is entered.

- Safety stock. As was discussed in earlier chapters (specifically Chapter 5), there are almost always uncertainties in forecast quantities, replenishment quantities and times, and the chance of a customer order changing. To protect the customer service level, safety stock can be used in essentially the same way it can be used in MRP. The trade-offs are also the same—an increase in the safety stock will mean additional protection against the uncertainties mentioned, but will generally result in higher inventory costs.

- Planning time horizon. Much as the planning horizon of the master schedule needs to be at least as long as the cumulative lead time for producing the product, the planning horizon for DRP needs to be at least long enough to equal the lead time for the longest resupply item.

At this point it is necessary to illustrate the calculation logic of DRP with a simple example.

EXAMPLE 11.2—A BASIC DRP CALCULATION

Suppose we have the following gross requirements for a product in a facility:

Period	PD	1	2	3	4	5	6	7	8	9
Gross Reqs.		200	200	250	250	200		400	200	250
Scheduled Recp.										
Planned On-hand										
Plan. Ord. Recp.										
Plan. Ord. Rel.										

In addition, we have a policy to maintain a safety stock of 50 units. The standard order quantity is 500 units. There are currently 300 units on hand. The replenishment lead time is two periods, and there is a schedule receipt due in period 2.

Using this information, we can fill in the DRP chart:

Period	PD	1	2	3	4	5	6	7	8	9
Gross Reqs.		200	200	250	250	200		460	200	250
Scheduled Recp.			500							
Planned On-hand	300	100	400	150	400	200	200	240	540	290
Plan. Ord. Recp.					500			500	500	
Plan. Ord. Rel.			500			500	500			

Some of these calculations need explanation. As with MRP, the planned on-hand for the first few periods is simple. It is basically the planned on-hand from the previous period plus any scheduled receipts less the gross requirements for that period being calculated. When we got to period 4, however, there were only 150 units left from period 3 while the demand in the gross requirement row for period 4 was 250 units. A planned order receipt was generated to cover the demand, and then offset by the two-period lead time to show as a planned order release in period 2. That situation happened again in period 7. The situation in period 8 is somewhat different. There were 240 units left at the end of period 7, which would be enough to cover the gross requirement of 200 units. The problem would be that there would only be 40 units left on hand, which is a violation of the safety stock policy of 50 units. Another planned order release was therefore generated for period 8 to ensure the safety stock policy would be met.

As with MRP, the general output of the DRP is a series of planned order releases, as well as action messages and an exception report. The exception report will show action messages and critical situations. The action messages can include "routine" actions, such as recommending the release of a current planned order release, but can also include expedite, de-expedite, or cancellation messages. These will generally relate to schedule receipts.

The Bill of Distribution

The bill of distribution (BOD) is used to specifically link the branch warehouse with the supplying facility. It is sometimes referred to as an inverted bill of materials, since the BOM "explodes" the parent requirements down to the individual components, while the BOD "implodes" the branch warehouse requirements upward to the parent, or supplying, facility.

The establishment of these relationships are important to ensure total logistic control throughout the supply chain.

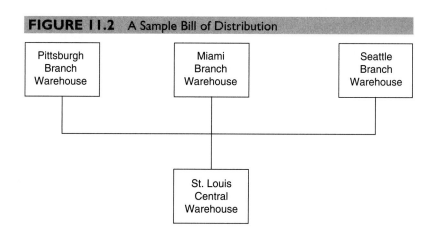

FIGURE 11.2   A Sample Bill of Distribution

Using the BOD for DRP

Once the BOD has been established, we are now ready to use the BOD to "implode" the planned order releases from the branch warehouses in Figure 11.2 to become gross requirements at the St. Louis central warehouse. The following example shows how that is accomplished.

EXAMPLE 11.3—USE THE BOD TO IMPLODE REQUIREMENTS TO THE CENTRAL WAREHOUSE

In this example we use the three branch warehouses in Figure 11.2. First the DRP schedules for the branch warehouses are presented:

Safety stock = 40
Lead time = 2 periods
Order quantity = 300
On-hand = 200

Pittsburgh Warehouse

Period	PD	1	2	3	4	5	6	7	8	9
Gross Reqs.		60	40	90	75	55	60	80	45	50
Scheduled Recp.										
Planned On-hand	200	140	100	310	235	180	120	40	295	245
Plan. Ord. Recp.				300					300	
Plan. Ord. Rel.		300					300			

Safety stock = 60
Lead time = 3 periods
Order quantity = 1,000
On-hand = 800

Miami Warehouse

Period	PD	1	2	3	4	5	6	7	8	9
Gross Reqs.		300	200	350	250	180	220	400	380	300
Scheduled Recp.										
Planned On-hand	800	500	300	950	700	520	300	900	520	220
Plan. Ord. Recp.				1000				1000		
Plan. Ord. Rel.	1000				1000					

Safety stock = 100
Lead time = 2 periods
Order quantity = 700
On-hand = 500

Seattle Warehouse

Period	PD	1	2	3	4	5	6	7	8	9
Gross Reqs.		250	100	380	450	400	150	350	400	300
Scheduled Recp.										
Planned On-hand	500	250	150	470	720	320	170	520	120	520
Plan. Ord. Recp.				700	700			700		700
Plan. Ord. Rel.		700	700			700		700		

Now to establish the total requirements for the St. Louis central supply warehouse the total planned order releases for each of the branch warehouses is totaled, period by period, to become the gross requirements for the St. Louis central warehouse:

Safety stock = 200
Lead time = 2 periods
Order quantity = 3,000
On-hand = 2,500

St. Louis Central Warehouse

Period	PD	1	2	3	4	5	6	7	8	9
Gross Reqs.	1000	1000	700		1000	700	300	700		
Scheduled Recp.										
Planned On-hand	1500	500	2800		1800	1100	800	3100		
Plan. Ord. Recp.			3000					3000		
Plan. Ord. Rel.	3000					3000				

Notes on the example: As can be seen, we have two "expedite" situations, primarily causes by the past-due requirements from the Miami warehouse. It is difficult to know what caused the situation, but the most likely scenarios are an unexpected increase (or addition of) a customer order in the near term periods, a smaller than expected shipment (possible quality problems), or perhaps a data adjustment (an inventory "shrinkage" situation). At any rate, the central warehouse not only needs to expedite the order for 3,000 units due in period 2, but also needs to expedite the shipment to the Miami warehouse.

As can clearly be seen in this example, the "lumpy" inventory demand conditions described in the early part of the chapter can clearly be seen, especially on the central warehouse. It is this type of condition that makes typical reorder points so difficult to use successfully when specific lot size replenishments such as those in the example are used.

DRP in a Lean Production "Pull" Environment

As supply chains are becoming more tightly linked and more and more companies are embracing at least some of the concepts of lean production for their distribution facilities in addition to their production facilities, the obvious question would emerge—How does DRP fit into such an environment—or does it? As in the case with MRP, DRP is inherently a "push" system, and as such may not fit as well with a lean production or "pull" environment. The reality is that many of the same arguments made for using MRP logic in a lean production "pull" environment will apply to the DRP logic:

- Long lead times. As in the case with MRP, there are likely to be certain items that require very long lead times. Such items, if placed on a pure "pull" schedule, would imply a very large inventory, since most pull systems are really a special case of reorder point systems. In such cases it may make more sense to project the needs of these items using the DRP logic.
- Capacity planning. As with production systems, distribution systems require an analysis of capacity requirements if the right amount and type of capacity is to be present with the minimal total cost. DRP can provide such planning, while continuing to use lean production and pull inventory replenishment to minimize inventory cost impacts.
- Design changes. Since pull systems are inherently reactive, they make it difficult to integrate new designs without an adverse impact on obsolete inventory. The DRP logic can provide an indication of when a new design will be available and allow for the planning of using up the old design inventory in order to minimize obsolete inventory problems.
- DRP has the capability to incorporate strategic moves of the firm, including promotions and advertising campaigns. This allows the firm to have more insight into the impact of their actions on the distribution system.

KEY TERMS

Supply Chain Management	MRO	Vendor-Managed
DRP	Bill of Distribution	Inventory

SUMMARY

This chapter provides basic information about the importance and functions of two key "boundary" functions that link planning and control to outside organizations: purchasing and distribution. Each of these areas represent a source of vital information used by the planning and control system, and each must be considered when designing a system. Modern approaches have strengthened and formalized the relationships between organizations in a concept known as supply chain management.

REFERENCES

Heinritz, S., P. Farrell, L. Giunipero, and M. Kolchin, *Purchasing: Principles and applications* (8th ed.). Englewood Cliffs, NJ: Prentice-Hall, 1991.

Leenders, M. R., H. E. Fearon, and W. B. England, *Purchasing and Materials Management* (9th ed.). Homewood, IL: Irwin, 1989.

Ross, D. F., *Distribution: Planning and Control.* New York: Chapman & Hall, 1996.

Schonsleben, P., *Integral Logistics Management.* Boca Raton, FL: St. Lucie Press, 2004.

Vollmann, T. E., W. L. Berry, and D. C. Whybark, *Manufacturing Planning and Control Systems.* New York: Irwin McGraw-Hill, 1997

DISCUSSION QUESTIONS AND PROBLEMS

1. Explain how supplier partnering may be different for a firm that is a lean production firm when compared to one that uses a standard push system such as MRP.
2. For a system that uses MRP or ERP, where would the inputs for the purchasing system come from for production parts? What about MRO material?
3. A product with independent demand has a unit cost of $50. The order cost is $41 per order. The annual inventory holding cost is 15% of the item cost per year. The average annual demand is 75,000 units. The supplier has offered to charge only $49 per item if they order at least 2,000 units at a time. Should they take the price discount or not? Show.
4. Explain how lean production approaches could change distribution approaches and why.
5. A company has a central warehouse in Chicago that supplies the demand of three branch warehouses: one in Baltimore, one in New Orleans, and one in Cleveland. The following tables provide the relevant data:

Warehouse	Safety Stock	Lead Time	Order Quantity	On-hand
Baltimore	50	2 periods	350	250
New Orleans	100	1 period	200	150
Cleveland	80	2 periods	500	200
Chicago	200	2 periods	1500	750

Gross requirements on the branch warehouses:

Period	1	2	3	4	5	6	7	8	9
Baltimore	100	80	150	90	100	85	110	120	100
New Orleans	70	65	75	50	90	80	75	80	55
Cleveland	110	90	65	135	85	70	140	100	60

Use the information to determine DRP records for all four warehouses. What problems do you see? How would you deal with those problems?

6. The Acme Company offers a price discount for ordering Acme Jungflogs:

0 to 50	$22.00
51 to 200	$21.50
200 and above	$21.20

The Ace Company uses the Jungflogs, and has the following inventory data:

Holding cost	23% of item cost per year
Order cost	$19 per order
Annual demand	8,000 units

Calculate the number of Jungflogs that Ace should order at a time to achieve the lowest total cost.

7. The BriteLite Company currently purchases 20,000 lamp bases a year from the Baseless Company. BriteLite recognizes an annual holding cost of 20% and an order cost of $15 per order. Currently they order the EOQ and pay a price of $1.20 per base. The Baseless Company has offered them a price of $1.10 per base if they will order at least 3,000 at a time. Should they take the offer or not?

CHAPTER 12

System Integration and Implementation

Chapter Outline

12.1 General System Design and Selection
12.2 "Push," "Pull," or Somewhere in Between
12.3 General Implementation Approaches

Introduction—While this book has only presented the fundamental concepts of planning and control, it should be obvious to the reader that there are potentially several critical design and implementation issues that must be addressed if the proper system is to be selected given the operation environment. In addition, the proper implementation for the selected approach is another critical activity that must be carefully planned and executed.

This chapter summarizes many of the critical points dealing with both selection and implementation of the planning and control system, both of which must be designed to meet the needs and resource constraints of the individual organization.

12.1 GENERAL SYSTEM DESIGN AND SELECTION

Before any critical system design issues are decided, it is very important that a fairly comprehensive operations strategy be developed. Essentially, the operations strategy is intended to support the overall strategy of the firm, and the operations structure and infrastructure must align with the market drivers for the selected product and market mix if the firm is to position itself in the most favorable competitive stance. This can be accomplished by understanding what the order winners and order qualifiers are, as described in Chapter 1. The design must be made by recognizing the critical nature of being able to at least meet (exceed if possible) the minimal market expectations with respect to order qualifiers, but should be able to perform at a superior level with respect to the order winner(s) in the market. Since it is virtually impossible to be the best in the market with respect to all dimensions of competition, design trade-offs must be made in the context of the clear understanding of these market drivers. The following sections that discuss some design alternatives will, where appropriate, refer to the market drivers that each design alternative will most effectively match.

First, there are certain rather "universal" issues that must be considered for virtually any environment. These are discussed in the context of the earlier chapters of this book:

- *Sales and Operations Planning.*   This is an activity that should be accomplished for virtually every production environment, including service production environments. Recall that the primary purpose of the activity is to plan resources of the firm in support of and in conjunction with the strategy, business plans, and marketing/sales plans. The major design issues here are primarily the length of the planning horizon and the level of detail required for the plan. Once fundamental resource needs and constraints are understood for the markets, products, and market drivers (order winners and qualifiers), then those issues of time and detail should be fairly obvious. In general, the time horizon should be long enough so that the critical resources being planned can be viewed as truly variable. In service industries requiring resources that are easy to obtain, that time horizon may be fairly short, but is usually several months or even years for manufacturing environments. In a similar fashion, the level of detail should at least be able to discriminate between the various types of resources needed, including both labor skills, material, and equipment.

- *Forecasting.*   The issue of whether to forecast or not is based on a fairly simple yet fundamental question; Does the cumulative lead time of the product or service exceed the customer-expected delivery time for the product or service? If the answer to that is "yes" (which is the case for most operations), then production and/or delivery of supplies must begin before demand is known, which implies the need for a forecast. The only issues that remain are the type of forecast used, the time horizon for the forecast, and the level of detail required. If, for example, the need is to forecast capacity requirements, then typically less detail is required when compared to the need to procure a unique and long lead-time component for a particular product. The time horizon is primarily a function of how long in the future to start production, which is clearly related to the cumulative lead time. The level of detail needed and to some extent the time horizon should provide an indication of the type of forecasting model selected. For a more detailed discussion, consult Chapter 2.

- *Master Scheduling.*   Every operation, no matter how large or small, service or manufacturing, has a master schedule. The only issue is how formally or informally it is developed, the structure used, and the time horizon. Small service organizations may have the schedule kept in the mind of the manager and the schedule may only cover a few hours, for example. Chapter 4 has a comprehensive discussion of some of the alternative structures and time horizons for the design of the master schedule.

- *Inventory.*   In the generic sense, every organization, whether service or manufacturing, has inventory. As every organization is made up of a series of processes, the "flow units" having value added by the process activities are really units of inventory. They may be bits of information, pieces of paper, or even people, yet they can still be "managed," planned, and controlled using some of the fundamental principles developed in Chapter 5. Inventory is especially important to consider if the firm has important market drivers related to delivery. Recall that Little's law relates inventory (I) to production rate (R) and throughput time (T) in the relationship $I = RT$. Using the principles developed in this book to control inventory will, therefore, allow the firm to control delivery speed and reliability much more effectively.

- *Capacity.*   Capacity is another aspect of planning and control that is a universal issue across all sizes and types of production environments. No facility can produce the goods and services demanded from them without the right quantity and type of capacity necessary. Excessive capacity can also be a problem, in that the cost structures may be driven out of line. The major issues are, once again, the level of detail and timing of the capacity requirements. Fortunately, if the firm does a good job of planning and implementing sales and operations planning and also uses their master schedule properly, capacity can fairly easily and effectively be planned. Chapter 7 provides more detail as to how to use the output from the master schedule to help plan and manage capacity.

- *Production Activity.*   Also a universal issue across all production environments, as every business needs to provide some type of measurement and control over the production activity as it is taking place. One major issue inherent with the design and selection of the scheduling system to control production activity is the existence and type of detail planning and execution system that is also present. If, for example, an MRP (ERP) system is used to both plan and execute production, then the PAC scheduling will be due-date based. "Pull" systems commonly used for lean production (JIT), on the other hand, will essentially dictate a first come, first serve–based scheduling system. The other types of scheduling prioritization systems may be selected only in production environments where there is essentially no integrated planning/execution system, such as MRP or Kanban, present, although the trend is to integrate all types of PAC systems with the planning systems.

- *Theory of Constraints.*   Every organization processing some input into a defined output will have some constraint (as defined in Chapter 10) for the organization as a whole. The concepts developed in Chapter 10 are largely applicable, even if the operation has very stable processes and pre-dictable demand. The reason is, of course, that normal issues of process variability will confound any attempt to provide perfect production sys-tem balance. Where TOC has some difficulty is if the product mix changes frequently or also cases where the operation primarily operates in a make-to-order environment. It is not that constraints do not exist under these conditions, but primarily that the large mix of production require-ments can cause the constraint to shift from one process to another with a frequency that will frustrate many attempts at applying the approaches outlined in Chapter 10.

12.2   "PUSH," "PULL," OR SOMEWHERE IN BETWEEN?

While the previous section discussed issues that are common across all pro-duction environments, there does have to be some specific analysis and selec-tion done to determine the communication patterns used in an integrated production environment. The two "pure" versions were discussed in some de-tail. Pure "push," represented by MRP, was discussed in detail in Chapter 6. Pure "pull," represented by Kanban, was discussed in detail in Chapter 9.

MRP, however, has as a disadvantage the intense need for timely and accu-rate data collection, as well as computational requirements. Those needs can be both burdensome and costly for a company, and many years of experience have proved that formal MRP systems are neither cheap nor easy to imple-ment, and both the costs and efforts are growing as the systems are becoming more highly integrated, as represented by ERP systems. Once implemented correctly they do, however, provide the capability to effectively plan and exe-cute production in very volatile environments represented by one or more of the following conditions:

- Frequent design changes
- Swings in market demands
- Many products with small or volatile demands

In general, it may be said that the more there is uncertainty and volatility in the environment, the more effective a forward-looking "push" system such as MRP can provide good planning and control. The more the product or ser-vice moves to a mature stage with stable designs, higher and more predictable demands, and increasing cost sensitivity, the more that MRP may represent "overkill" of data, and also can actually prevent good cost control and delivery speed.

Pure "pull" systems, such as Kanban, represent the other end of the pro-duction spectrum. They operate very effectively with low cost efficiency in en-vironments that have very stable designs and demands, and when combined with the other principles of lean production can deliver production very cost effectively with good delivery speed and reliability.

The reality is, however, that few production environments have conditions that put them at one extreme or the other. What makes the issue even more complex is that many production facilities will have a mix of market and product environments that will make it difficult to make the selection of either "pure" system. As a result many firms have developed "hybrid" systems that allow them to take advantage of certain aspects and strengths of both types of systems, depending on the environments. The next several sections briefly describe some of those systems that have been successfully used.

Hybrid System #1—MRP with Lean Principles

As we start to move away from a very volatile environment—one in which MRP handles quite well—we will start to see some "easing" of the volatility. Demand patterns are starting to be more stable and design changes are less frequent or radical. In this system there is still a level of volatility to call for planning and execution by using MRP, but since some stability is evident we may be able to utilize some of the principles of lean production. Setup reductions to reduce lot sizes and inventory investments may start to make sense here, as well as some of the layout changes and supplier relationship building that can bring great benefits in time, cost, and quality. Statistical process control tools can also be used to bring additional quality benefits.

Hybrid System #2—Kanban with MRP Planning

This system uses the MRP logic in a way that allows for planning design changes effectively while providing some of the benefits of a pull system. It tends to be used where there is some improvement in the volatility of demand. The system works by programming the MRP system to look ahead for a set period of time (2 to 3 weeks, for example). The system will then determine total component demand during that time period to calculate the number of Kanban cards required using the Kanban calculation formula provided in Chapter 9. The system will then have two major outputs for that time period—printing the number of Kanban cards as calculated but also generating a standard dispatch list that is the normal output of an MRP system. Both the dispatch list and the printed Kanban cards are issued to the work center. The work center is authorized to produce a part *only* if there is an unattached Kanban card *and* the part number is listed on the dispatch list. Consider the two scenarios where only one of those two is present:

- The item is on the dispatch list, but there is no unattached Kanban card. In this case it is known that the part will be needed (it is on the dispatch list), yet the fact that no unattached Kanban card exists indicates that the part is not yet being used. To produce the part without a "free" Kanban card will only build excess inventory prior to its need—and in some cases this will be at the expense of some other part that is needed.

- The item has an unattached Kanban card, yet is not on the dispatch list. In this case the part is being used, as indicated by the fact that there is an unattached Kanban card. If, however, the part is being subjected to a design change, it should be "phased out" to avoid having obsolete inventory being present. That is why it does not appear on the dispatch list—even though the old design is being used, it should not be replaced. Another situation where this could happen is when there is no future demand for the component beyond what can be met by existing inventory. In this case replacing the used inventory (as indicated by the unattached Kanban) will only produce more inventory that potentially would not be used for a long time, if ever.

Hybrid System #3—Using MRP for Capacity and Long Lead Time Items

This system design tends to be used where the design of the product is relatively stable, but the demand patterns are still too volatile to allow for using pure pull. If they are too volatile, hybrid system #1 should be used, but as they smooth, then this system can be considered. In this system pull production control (such as Kanban) is used, but the MRP system is used to plan for three aspects of production:

- Long lead time items. Some parts, especially purchased parts, can take an excessive amount of time to replace. If the demand is erratic, a pure pull system (which assumes a fairly steady replacement frequency) will likely cause stockout problems. The MRP system can project the need for these items and alert the suppliers for the proper replacement quantity.
- Capacity requirements. As demand and demand mix changes, different levels and different types of capacity may be needed. The MRP system can be used to plan these changes.
- Number of Kanban cards. The demand for a part will impact the number of Kanban cards that should exist in the system, as given by the Kanban formula in Chapter 9. The MRP system can project the demand for each component over a defined time period, allowing for calculating the "right" number of Kanban cards to support the level of demand.

Hybrid System #4—Pull System with MRP "Spike" Control

This system may be considered a special case of hybrid system #3. As the environment moves closer to stable demand patterns, there is still a chance that on occasion extra inventory and/or capacity may be needed. Seasonality, advertising campaigns, and marketing promotions are examples of actions that could produce a "spike" in demand, although they can also be just random events. The MRP system can be used to project such spikes, even though the normal environment is stable enough to allow for pure pull production control under normal situations.

FIGURE 12.1   Positioning
of Hybrid Systems

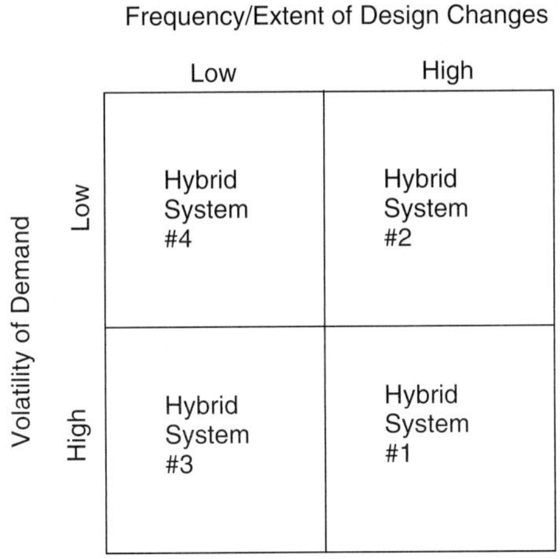

Frequency/Extent of Design Changes

	Low	High
Low	Hybrid System #4	Hybrid System #2
High	Hybrid System #3	Hybrid System #1

(Volatility of Demand — vertical axis label)

Figure 12.1 summarizes the most common use of the hybrid systems described.

Focus on the Point of Customization

In some respects this alternative borrows some approaches from the Theory of Constraints and some from the concepts of the "front office/back office" approach used effectively by service industries for many years. In the front office/back office approach, the front office is designed to understand the needs of and communicate with customers directly, while the back office is designed for effective and efficient production. A good example might be the automobile servicing activity of a major dealer. When the customer brings his or her automobile in for service, they communicate their needs to a customer service representative (the "front office"). Once the customer leaves, however, they may never know who actually worked on their automobile, or when. That "back office" is invisible to the customer.

Borrowing from that system, the production firm can determine the point of customization—the further point into the production system where individual customer product design requirements will have an impact. Once that point is determined, a buffer of inventory, capacity, or a combination can be built to protect the "upstream" portion of the production system from the unknowns of customer design requirements. Essentially this buffer absorbs those variations in design, allowing all processes upstream from that point to be managed for efficiency. To be more specific,

- Downstream from the buffer. These are the processes that are subjected to the variations in design from specific customer requests. These processes need to focus on the customer and customer design requests. Since there is great uncertainty in these requests for most environments, excess capacity for each process is expected, and a forward-looking system such as MRP makes sense. The general focus here is customer service.

- Upstream from the buffer. In these processes the volatility from customer requests in design is protected to some degree by the buffer of capacity or inventory. Their primary goal is to replace product being used from the buffer. As there is stability and predictability in design, pull systems may be very appropriate in order to minimize cost and increase replacement speed. In addition, once the barrier is established, these upstream processes should be improved to allow effective customer service with less and less excess inventory or capacity in the protective buffer.

12.3 GENERAL IMPLEMENTATION APPROACHES

In the last decade or so there have been many advances that have changed the way planning and control systems are designed and used in organizations. Some of the more significant include:

- The growth of service organizations, both in number and in size of the organization.
- The changes in manufacturing that have resulted in far fewer people employed while maintaining the same relative percentage of GNP. This has been primarily caused by productivity gains and automation in operations, but with fewer people the demands on the remaining people are both different and more extensive.
- Increased global competition, allowing for both increased opportunities for new markets and threats from new competition. The result has been a continual, increased need for responsiveness to customers and cost reductions in products and services.
- Continual, rapid increases in the capability of computer hardware and software combined with reduction in the prices for the hardware has allowed for expansion in use.
- New technologies have caused rapid increases in the pace of product and process design changes.
- The Internet has allowed for new forms of communication and information gathering.

With people in organizations needing better, more timely, and more extensive information to deal with the rapid pace of customer demands and competitive changes, planning and control systems have responded. Not only have companies and software suppliers managed to combine some of the best features of MRP and JIT, but even the planning and control systems based on

MRP have become more heavily integrated and more effective. The latest advances have generally become known as ERP (enterprise resource planning) systems.

As mentioned earlier, before any implementation takes place, it is of critical importance that the right system design is made. To do this, a comprehensive business and operations strategy must be completed, addressing such issues as:

- Customer issues
  - Volatility in demand patterns
  - Customer influence on product design (e.g., MTS, ATO, MTO)
  - Delivery lead time expectations
  - Customer communication issues, such as order status
- Product design/engineering issues
  - Bill of material structuring
  - Engineering design change procedures
- Processing requirements
  - Approaches to capacity—flexibility and capacity buffers
  - Details required for production activity control
  - Timing issues for data flows
  - Expected changes to plans—frequency and extent
  - Necessary data outputs—managerial reports, accounting, etc.
  - Managerial policies with respect to inventory management
- System performance expectations

In general, the planning and control system should be selected/designed to meet the needs and expectations of the organization, suppliers, and customers as closely as possible. While the planning and control system should meet the needs, caution should be taken to not select a system that far exceeds the needs. Such a system could prove to be more costly, burdensome, and actually impair effective performance with respect to the expected needs. In any case, a complete cost–benefit analysis should be undertaken to ensure commitment from top managers and other key personnel in the organization.

Major Process Steps in Implementation

The planning and control system is generally selected and/or designed on the basis of how the organization *should* be run, but this is sometimes very different from how the organization is *currently* run. Clearly, most modern planning and control systems are computer based, and as such there is a need for the Information Systems group to work on understanding software, databases, communication needs, and hardware requirements. It is generally a mistake, however, to view the implementation of a major integrated planning and control package such as ERP as an Information Systems project.

While the information system (IS) needs are being analyzed and developed, there are at least two other major areas that can and should be analyzed and altered as necessary to support the planning and control system. For many organizations, in fact, these two areas may need improvements that will far surpass the time, effort, and cost requirements of the IS portion of the project. Those two areas are business processes and database accuracy.

Business Processes

Many companies have developed their business processes over many years of growth. Such processes tend to be developed in response to a crisis or some special situation, and often have never been analyzed or altered after the situation has changed or been eliminated. Processes grown without a good strategic and system perspective often act as "islands" of activity, with communication between those islands often being cumbersome, inefficient, and often highly ineffective.

Once the strategic direction and priorities of the firm have been developed and translated into specific actions and policies, a complete process mapping of major business and operational processes needs to be undertaken, both for specific departments and for the organization as a whole. The process maps should, if done correctly, clearly point out where process improvements or even process reengineering needs to take place. As implied earlier, for many organizations this analysis and subsequent process improvement actions is far from a trivial activity. The concept of value stream mapping mentioned earlier is also now being heavily used by many organizations. While originally developed as part of the approach to lean production, the concepts are universal enough to provide insight for any operation.

It is important to note here that the proper method of software selection for a planning and control system is typically based on the needs of the organization and the processes within that organization. It is generally not good practice to select the planning and control system and then force the organization process to fit the software. This implies that the process analysis and improvement should proceed prior to any software evaluation and selection.

Database accuracy

This area is highly related to the business process improvement activity, since database information usually results from the activity in the specific business processes of the organization. Certainly one should expect that with improvements in the processes that the data resulting from those processes should be more accurate and timely.

Unfortunately, no process can be expected to be perfect at all times, and accurate and timely data is so critical for the effective operation of a highly integrated system that other measures are needed. A formal system of audit and transaction process improvement for each of the databases should be established if not already present. Even if present, it should be analyzed and improved as necessary as part of the overall business process analysis mentioned above. Cycle count programs are an example of such a formal system that have been successfully used for inventory data accuracy.

Virtually all operational databases should be part of this formal analysis and improvement activity. Each one will likely have different methods of audit, process improvement, and control as well as different functional responsibilities, yet they all need to be accurate. Some of the key databases include (but is not necessarily limited to):

- Inventory, including raw material, work-in-process, and finished goods inventory levels and locations.
- Bills of material and routings, including design change procedures.
- Other engineering data, including setup times, maintenance schedules, and tooling and fixture inventory.
- Accounting and cost data, including job standards and product cost information.
- Item masters, including lead times and supplier information.
- Order entry data, including all customer orders and forecasts.
- Supplier databases, including approved suppliers with lead times for replenishment.
- Customer data, including contact information and any order information.
- Production order status data, including location, work completed, work remaining, and any quality reject problems.
- Worker reporting systems, including production times, worker skills, and absenteeism.

Developing the Implementation Project

Clearly, for many organizations the implementation of an integrated system implies methods for conducting business will have to change. New attitudes and expectations will need to be developed for many people in the organization. Fortunately, the implementation of a large-scale production and control system will bring an expectation of change to the minds of most, allowing for more receptivity as associated changes are made. In any case, as part of the business process analysis all associated aspects of the processes should also be evaluated. This includes:

- Job designs. Skills required and allocation of workers to processes.
- Performance evaluation. Performance metrics should be aligned to the priorities established in the operation strategy and the priorities for various customer orders.
- Measurement systems. Measures should reflect the priorities of the organization. They should be clear and comprehensive, yet limited in number to avoid confusion as to which measures are really important.

- Reporting points. There should be a clear establishment of where in the process data is to be collected, who will collect the data, how it will be collected, and how often.
- Timing of data flow. Not only how often will data be collected, but where will it be used and how often.
- Organizational structures. Identification of functional responsibilities, reporting channels, and communication responsibilities.
- Communication channels, both internal and external to suppliers and customers.

There are other critical actions for a successful implementation project. They include (but again, are not limited to):

- *Selection of a project leader and a project team.* For most organizations, the project leader should be close to 100% of his or her time devoted to the project. Certainly in larger organizations both the project leader and the project team should all be 100% devoted to the project. The project leader should not be a top manager, but should be high enough in the organization to have earned respect, and they should also of course be knowledgeable about the organization and its activities. Core project teams should be limited in number (usually about five to seven people) to make the team more manageable. Numerous focused subteams with specific implementation tasks can be formed of noncore members yet reporting to the core team. A steering team consisting of the top organizational managers should also be formed to oversee the project and be ready to break organizational "log jams" as they occur. Functional areas that should be considered for substantial involvement in the project teams include master scheduling, production control, materials management, sales, accounting, purchasing, and engineering.
- *Commitment from management is critical.* Management needs to first demonstrate their commitment through development of a detailed cost–benefit analysis. They then have to provide a vision for the performance of the operation upon completion of the project implementation. It is quite important that the management team develop realistic goals, establish a realistic schedule, and ensure that the proper amount of resources are committed to the plan.
- *Development of a realistically timed project plan.* Such a plan should be able to clearly point out resource needs and the timing of those needs. The organization should try, if at all possible, to make adequate resources available so that the total duration of the plan is no longer than 12 to 18 months. Implementation projects that exceed 18 months tend to lose support as people lose interest and become tired of the extra effort required to implement them.

- ***Development of an education program.*** Virtually all personnel in the organization will need education with respect to the system and how the system and changes in supporting business processes will affect them. Each person will have their role analyzed to determine the type of education, the amount of education, and the correct timing of the education.
- ***Be flexible—expect problems.*** It is almost impossible to anticipate all problems and obstacles to a successful implementation. The project plan must be flexible and the project team must be ready to develop contingency actions as problems arise.
- ***Should an outside consultant be used?*** Even if the project leader and team members are highly knowledgeable, it is sometimes valuable to have an outside consultant assist the team. The largest disadvantage is the cost of such services. In addition, the selection of a consultant is also nontrivial since it is important to have a consultant with experience in the type of project being undertaken. The right outside consultant can often bring the following value to the project:
  - They can often bring different approaches for solving problems based on their experience in other organizations.
  - They are generally perceived as having no "political agenda," making their perspective easier to accept for many in the organization. It is important to note, however, that most consultants will generally have a business agenda—namely, to sell more of their services.
  - They do not have to be as concerned about using the "chain of command" when dealing with issues needing attention.
  - Since they don't work directly in the organization, it is often easier for them to see the "big picture"—keeping the forest in sight without paying too much attention to the trees.
- ***Avoid a premature system cut-over.*** Often when people become knowledgeable about the potential value and features of a new system, they become very anxious to start using it. Patience must be maintained, however. A premature system cut-over often results in a disaster, causing the system to be shut off for reevaluation. In those cases attitudes become soured, and enthusiasm becomes difficult to reestablish in the face of cynicism.

SUMMARY

While most of the book has focused on specific planning and control systems or subsystems, this chapter provides an overview as to how some of those systems can be integrated into the organizational environment. This includes a description as to how "push" systems (such as MRP) and "pull" systems (such as Kanban) can conceivably work together to solve certain situations that appear to need advantages that both systems bring.

The chapter also highlights some of the more important aspects of implementation for planning and control systems. Such implementations are typically large in scope and can imply significant structural and infrastructural changes to the organization, meaning they must be carefully planned and managed.

DISCUSSION QUESTIONS

1. Describe the major information that should be gathered in order to design an effective planning and control system. Describe why this information is important and how it will be used to develop the design.
2. What do you think the approach should be if a planning and control system has been designed and implemented, yet seems to "not work right"? What information should be used to evaluate the problems?
3. Do you believe the Theory of Constraints could be used with any of the hybrid systems described in the chapter? Why or why not?
4. Describe how the approach to planning and control is likely to be different for each of the following operations. Also, how will the approach to implementation differ?
   a. A barber shop
   b. A restaurant
   c. A retail clothing store
   d. A small machine shop
   e. A large assemble-to-order production evnironment
   f. An oil refinery
5. Describe the type of data and information you would gather to try to justify the cost and time required to implement a major planning and control system project.

Index